THE EUROPEAN CONSTITUTION

its origins, negotiation and meaning

The European Constitution

its origins, negotiation and meaning

by

Guy Milton and Jacques Keller-Noëllet

with Agnieszka Bartol-Saurel

The European Constitution
its origins, negotiation and meaning

Published by John Harper Publishing
27 Palace Gates Road
London N22 7BW, United Kingdom.
Telephone: +44 (0) 20 8881 4774
E-mail: jhpublish@aol.com

ISBN 0–9543811–6–5

Typeset in 10/12 pt Palatino

Printed and Bound in Great Britain by the Cromwell Press

Contents

About the authors

Since joining the Council Secretariat ten years ago, **Guy Milton** has served in several posts in the Directorate-General for External Relations, and subsequently as advisor in the office of Javier Solana, Secretary-General of the Council and High Representative for the Common Foreign and Security Policy. More recently he held posts in the secretariats to the Convention and the Intergovernmental Conference which drew up the European Constitution. He continues to work on institutional and general political questions. Before joining the Council Secretariat, he spent several years as a member of the UK diplomatic service.

Jacques Keller-Noëllet is a Deputy Director-General in the Council Secretariat. Before joining the European civil service in the 1970s he spent a short time in the French administration. Since 1981 he held the post of advisor, then director, in the office of successive Secretary-Generals of the Council, with particular responsibility for meetings of the European Councils and for Intergovernmental Conferences. His experience in following the negotiations on the Single European Act, the Maastricht Treaty, the Treaty of Amsterdam, the Nice treaty as well as the Constitution, means that he is well placed to assess the background and process of the negotiations on the Constitution.

Agnieszka Bartol-Saurel, a Polish national, was the only representative from the candidate countries to serve in the Secretariat to the Convention. She was then employed as the first official from one of the new Member States in the Council Secretariat, where she followed the Intergovernmental Conference on the Constitution. She currently works in the Directorate-General for Economic and Social Affairs. Before coming to Brussels, she worked for several years in the Polish Office of the Committee for European Integration and in the College of Europe in Natolin.

Acknowledgments

The idea of writing a book on the Constitution arose before it was even certain that there would be one. That is in itself an expression of the confidence of the authors of the ability of the European Union to overcome what sometimes appear as insuperable difficulties and to deliver a product of quality.

The Convention attracted considerable attention from the media and commentators alike. That is not so surprising. Not only was it an innovative technique, but it was also largely an open one. The public exposure of almost every twist and turn of the negotiations meant that it laid itself open to immediate and detailed scrutiny. Producing a measured assessment of the Convention's work meant stepping back from this process and judging it at least in part in the light of what came after.

Because the Convention was only half the story. The Constitution had to be approved by the Member States' governments in an Intergovernmental Conference before it could be considered as anything more than a draft. So the second part looks at an aspect of the Constitution which is just as important than the first. The book was born of a recognition that the story needed to be told as a whole.

The process of writing about the Constitution has involved re-living parts of our professional lives which were both intellectually challenging and personally satisfying. That is in large measure due to the extraordinary range of talent and experience of colleagues in both the Secretariats to the Convention and the IGC, as well in national delegations and the other institutions. We are grateful to all of them.

Many colleagues, too numerous to mention, have in more direct ways helped us with the writing of this book. Some have challenged us on our judgement, forcing us to rethink; others have suggested useful additions; a few have saved us from major errors. To all of them we are very grateful. Particular thanks must go to John Kerr and Keith Richardson for the time they devoted to reading the entire manuscript and for the suggestions which certainly contributed overall to an improvement of the text. We are also grateful to John Harper for his confidence that we would be able to tell the story of the Constitution in a way which is hopefully accessible to those outside the Brussels 'circuit'.

We owe special thanks to Filomena Antunes and Andrea Laubengeiger for putting in time and effort beyond the call of duty to ensure that the text was in presentable form. Finally many thanks to our immediate colleagues and families for tolerating us when the book threatened to take over our lives completely, and when occasionally we lost sight of the real priorities in life.

Despite our reliance on so much support and input from many friends and colleagues, any errors of fact or judgment remain ours alone.

Guy Milton
Jacques Keller-Noëllet   *Brussels*
Agnieszka Bartol-Saurel   *December 2004*

Foreword

It took the combination of a Convention and an Intergovernmental Conference to produce the Treaty establishing a Constitution for Europe. It also took well over two years of hard work, much tough bargaining, considerable imagination and plenty of ambition. The result, when it enters into force, will be a defining moment for the European Union.

This is the story of the Constitution told by three people working in the Secretariat of the Council who were amongst the most closely involved in the entire process. But the book is not simply written by insiders for insiders. The experience and knowledge acquired as a result of being so directly associated with the drafting of the Constitution has been distilled and presented in a way which makes this book accessible to anyone with an interest in the subject.

The Convention attracted a large amount of attention, and rightly so; it was an innovative approach to treaty revision which delivered a complete rewrite of the texts on which the European Union, as it exists today, is founded. But the extensive literature on the outcome of the Convention has to date not been followed up with an informed account which includes the subsequent Intergovernmental Conference. The Constitution is the product of the two, and it is not possible to assess the Constitution properly without looking at the process in its entirety. This book fills that gap, and does so admirably.

The authors are ready to be critical where justified, but conclude overall that the Constitution is good for the European Union. I share that view. It will for the first time set out clearly in a single text what the European Union is for, what it does and how it does it. It will enable us to do more and to do it better. Above all it will allow us to consolidate the extraordinary achievements of the European Union to date and to build on them for the future so that we can live up to the goal of providing a better, more secure and prosperous Europe for ourselves and for our children.

Javier Solana
Secretary-General of the
Council / High Representative
for the Common Foreign
and Security Policy

Introduction: Signing the Constitution

These days cities which find themselves hosting an international meeting succumb to a temporary but eerie silence. Such are the consequences of security requirements in the era of globalisation. As Rome prepared to receive Europe's leaders for the signing ceremony of the new Constitution on 29 October 2004, the hush descended in anticipation as at the first night at the opera.

The palpable sense of expectation increased as the silence was broken sporadically by the convoys of limousines delivering the twenty-eight principal signatories to the Constitution up to the Campidoglio, the city hall of Rome inspired by Michelangelo. There they would first be directed to the Sala Giulio Cesare where they would listen to speeches by their host, Prime Minister Berlusconi, the Presidents of the European institutions, and by Irish Prime Minister Bertie Ahern, who had so successfully ensured four months earlier that they had something to sign at all. They would then walk to the smaller Sala degli Orazi e Curiazi, to take their place in turn, with their Foreign Ministers, at the transversal table to sign the vast leather-bound tome containing the Constitution.

There were twenty-eight of them because the three candidate countries (Bulgaria, Romania and Turkey), which had been fully involved in the process of negotiating the Constitution from the beginning, were also present and would symbolically sign the Final Act. They were joined by the Prime Minister of Croatia, which had been recognised as a candidate country the same day in June as the Constitution was concluded. The room also had to accommodate the President of the European Parliament, the outgoing and incoming Presidents of the Commission, and last but not least former French President Valéry Giscard d'Estaing, who had presided over the Convention and had proved the driving force behind the Constitution.

So the room was crowded, but the choice of venue was deliberately symbolic. Nearly fifty years earlier the leaders of the six founding Member States had gathered in the same room to sign the Treaty of Rome instituting the European Economic Community. Apart from the obvious historical resonances, no other venue would have so visibly highlighted how much the Union had grown and developed over the previous five decades.

The ceremony was a triumph of flamboyance and grandeur worthy of the backdrop of imperial Rome. The attention to detail was remarkable: in acknowledgement of the Dutch Presidency, the classical lines of the Campidoglio with its sculptures and renaissance paintings were offset by displays of thousands of glossy tulips. The ninety hostesses were dressed by Valentino in uniforms designed especially for the occasion. The whole production was overseen by Franco Zeffirelli. Only the orchestra was missing.

Well not entirely, because as Europe's leaders in turn approached the table to sign the Constitution, they did so against the background of soft music which served to emphasise the solemnity of the occasion. The seating consisted of two double rows of Louis XV style chairs which looked slightly ill at ease with their newly upholstered cloth of almost luminous blue spangled with the golden stars of the European flag. The placing of the two rows of chairs facing each other as if in a choir gave the whole scene a distinctly ecclesiastical atmosphere, enhanced by a huge bronze statue of Pope Innocent X, who with a frozen arm outstretched over the high altar of the signing table, delivered an unwavering blessing over the steady succession of signatories. How different from that same pope's invective against the Treaty of Westphalia which he described in 1648 as 'null and void' and which he said 'filled him with the deepest grief'.

When the six gathered in 1957 to sign the Treaty establishing the European Community, there was at least a common thread of history linking each one of them with Rome, and with each other. Enlargement to twenty-five has since taken the frontier of the Union well beyond even the furthest reaches of Rome at the height of its power. The signing ceremony's slogan in Latin 'Europaeae Rei Publicae Status' was therefore stretching a point, or perhaps making one.

The common thread linking the Member States of today's Union was rather the Constitution which lay on the table in the Sala degli Orazi e Curiazi on that late October morning. It alone contained the values and objectives which brought together such a diverse group of countries to work for a common cause within the unique framework of the European Union. It alone set out the powers, the tools and the institutions to enable the Union to function. It alone provided the guarantee that Europe had turned its back on its bloody past and was committed to peace.

This book is the story of the Constitution. It examines its origins, and in particular the innovative approach of the Convention. It describes the negotiating process; how the very different positions of the Member States on so many issues were in the end bridged successfully. Finally it provides an overall assessment of how the Constitution can contribute to the stability of Europe and improve the lives of its citizens.

1. Historical origins of a Constitution for Europe

The choice of Rome for the signature of the Constitution is charged with symbolism. Most obviously the city had hosted the signing of the treaty establishing the European Economic Community in 1957, forever after known as the 'Treaty of Rome', and so left its mark on the history of European integration. But the resonances go deeper, and far further back than the middle of the twentieth century. For many, Rome remains the very symbol of a universal Europe, a continent unified, albeit initially through the use of force, and a unique and shared European civilisation under the auspices of the *pax romana*. Nostalgia can be misplaced and even abused, but should not be underestimated. It has been the motivation behind many of the initiatives over the centuries to try to create (or perhaps recreate) an integrated continent.

The Constitution signed on 29 October 2004 has a long line of predecessors. Most of them pre-date the founding of the European Community, and many have their origins in a very different Europe from that of today. They almost all share the view that political integration is a tool for achieving lasting peace and stability. Yet they all came to nothing. After such a long history of failure, what changed? Why did the integration of Europe only begin to take shape with the creation of the European Community in the middle of the twentieth century? And why did it then take this entity (in the meantime rebaptised as the European Union) nearly fifty years to produce its own constitution?

The purpose of this chapter is to look back at some of the current Constitution's predecessors, to examine the motives behind them, their objectives and means, and perhaps most importantly to ask why they never left the drawing board. The long history of aborted attempts to integrate Europe, and the various drafts which sought to do so through the instrument of a constitution, offer some pointers as to why the European Union, which has developed into the world's most sophisticated and most integrated multilateral organisation, chose finally to describe itself (and to some extent to organise itself) in constitutional terms.

*   *   *   *   *

The consistent driving force behind the many proposals for European integration over the years has been the desire to eliminate conflict and guarantee permanent peace. Against a background of apparently ceaseless inter-state rivalry, constant struggle for domination, and the failure of the attempt to balance power, Europe has been faced with the challenge of finding a mechanism which would achieve this objective. All of the ideas described in this chapter are attempts by Europeans down the years to respond to this challenge, although the means and geographical scope vary considerably. Some include arrangements for the organisation of trade within Europe, although in most cases these are considered as tools at the service of wider political objectives. An important element in several of the earlier ideas is the need to contain the Ottoman threat: the protection of the very identity of Europe and Christendom. But later history has shown that in the longer term Europe has needed protection from outsiders less than it has needed protection from itself.

The Roman Empire and the Carolingian period have dominated the sense of nostalgia for a past in which security and stability appear unchallenged, and where a single political authority offers the best guarantee of peace. However the idea of Europe as a political entity (*regnum Europae*) dates from the early Holy Roman Empire (which saw itself – as the name suggests – as the inheritor of classical Rome), and this period is therefore the natural starting point for looking at some of the more important proposals for European political integration.

The following brief survey sets out how the approach to European integration has evolved over time. It looks at why none of the proposals succeeded until after the Second World War. It examines briefly the reasons for the success of the European Coal and Steel Community. It also seeks to explain why, despite the very significant developments in European integration over the last fifty years, the various ambitious ideas for drawing up a European constitution during this period never materialised. This then opens the way to a more detailed examination in the second chapter of the reasons why the European Union convened a Convention on its future, and why this Convention opted to draw up a constitution for Europe for the first time in its history.

The integration of Europe: the earliest ideas[1]

The earliest proposals to organise Europe into a single political entity were a direct response to its fragmentation due to a weakening of central authority. The later middle ages were a period of a gradual loss of political leadership. The Holy Roman Emperor and the Pope had served as guarantors of unity and peace in Europe. Yet the Emperor was increasingly incapable of exercising power over his own subjects, and even less able to influence those beyond his control. At the same time, the power of the papacy was in decline as its leadership was increasingly obliged to seek the support of secular powers. More generally, the sense of unity of Christendom, which had been reinforced by the external threat from the Saracens, was beginning to weaken as the empire lost some of its mystique as the principal defender of the collective Christian faith of Europe.

These early proposals therefore contain a mixture of nostalgia for the unitarian political order of the Holy Roman Empire, and an overt attempt to reinvigorate Europe's sense of shared religious identity by identifying a common enemy in Islam. The sense of nostalgia is particularly evident in Dante's *De monarchia*. Written in about 1310, it looks to the return of a golden age of order in which states and their leaders are subordinate to imperial authority. That authority is in turn answerable only to the Pope as the ultimate source of power. For Dante, the sole means of settling disputes between princes is through appeal to the Emperor. In an era when the divine right to rule was unquestioned, the Emperor's decisions would be final, and would lead to order and peace ('the good order of the world depends on the existence of a monarchy or empire'). At the same time, Dante's vision is far from a centralised dictatorship. Not dictatorship because the Emperor remains subject to the spiritual authority of the papacy; he acts in a manner which is just, and exercises his authority without any human ambition because he is predestined by God. Not centralised because Dante anticipates the principle of subsidiarity by recognising that some issues will more appropriately be addressed by individual city states, towns and villages.

In contrast, Dante's contemporary, Pierre Du Bois, stressed the objective of reinforcing Europe's christian identity. In his work *De Recuperatione Terra Sancte* (1306), he explicitly rejects the idea of a universal and single political authority and proposes instead a confederation of sovereign states within a 'Christian Republic'. Disputes between members of this confederation are submitted to a Council responsible for arbitration under the ultimate authority of the Pope, who has the right to impose heavy sanctions. Du Bois' stated objective is to secure peace in Europe, but as the title of his work suggests, this is subordinate to the ultimate purpose of reasserting the primacy of Christendom, in particular through the recovery of the holy places. Indeed the responsibility for convening the Council is placed squarely on the papacy, with the explicit objective of improving the political organisation of Christian Europe with a view to launching a new crusade. For Du Bois this had the added advantage of channelling aggressive tendencies into the liberation of the holy sites rather than into disputes within Christendom itself. Furthermore, placing the ultimate responsibility for the Council in the hands of the papacy added eternal damnation to the list of means of coercion available against recalcitrants, although Du Bois himself recognised that in the shorter term more immediate sanctions were likely to prove more effective.

It was over 150 years before the appearance of further serious ideas. In 1463 King Podiebrad of Bohemia presented to King Louis XI of France proposals for the establishment of a European federation. The title: *Traité d'alliance et confédération entre le Roy Louis XI, Georges Roy de Bohémie, et la Seigneurie de Venise, pour résister au Turc* speaks for itself. Although geographically limited in scope, it is an ambitious project, written in the form of a lengthy and frequently florid treaty text, yet rather modern in its pragmatism. It deliberately excludes for the first time a role for the Pope and the Emperor. It recognises the mutual advantages for the potential signatories of abstaining from conflict amongst themselves (it begins with a commitment between the parties to renounce the use of force), but goes further in proposing that the parties agree to limit their sovereignty through the establishment of shared institutions, including a Court of Justice and a common army, and that these be financed from a shared budget. The whole structure would be overseen by an Assembly composed of representatives of the sovereigns able to take decisions by majority voting. Podiebrad's proposal foreshadows a number of later ideas in that it anticipates the problems caused by the fragmentation of Europe into powerful sovereign nation states. It offers a radical model for the establishment of a confederation, and as such was strongly resisted by the papacy, which rightly saw in it an attempt to limit its own powers. King Louis politely declined to sign up to it.

These three early examples offer an insight into some of main difficulties confronted by those attempting to establish peace in Europe through permanent political arrangements. All of them had to reflect the reality of their time: a Europe fragmented into numerous sovereign states and the inviolable right of sovereign kings or princes to govern (which in the middle ages was still considered a God-given right). They could at best only attempt to regulate relations between states and were therefore by definition based on commitments offered in a spirit of mutual confidence; they were essentially diplomatic solutions to diplomatic problems. Even those earliest proposals which placed the papacy in the position of supreme arbiter recognised that temporal power could only be managed and not controlled; any system, however sophisticated, designed to arbitrate in the case of disputes ultimately depends on the existence of confidence in the system itself. This conundrum still explains today the fragility of any organisation such as the United Nations designed to maintain international order. The extent to which the European Union has been able to surmount this is examined below.

Subsequent ideas for securing peace in Europe can be seen in part as responding to the changing environment on the continent. The Holy Roman Empire had to cope with gradual disintegration from within, as local leaders challenged the authority of the Emperor, and from outside from both France and the Ottoman Empire. The aspiration of a wider unified empire finally came to an end with the abdication of Charles V in 1556, setting the conditions for an intensification of the struggle for power which culminated in the Thirty Years War. Its settlement in the Treaty of Westphalia of 1648 is considered to have laid the foundations of the modern European system of sovereign nation states, a system which was unable to prevent and perhaps even encouraged continuing power struggles, frequently involving recourse to the use of force.

Against this background, a number of ideas for establishing a more stable and peaceful political settlement in Europe were developed during the seventeenth and early eighteenth centuries. In 1623 Emeric Crucé published lengthy and detailed proposals for an open political union, founded on a spirit of tolerance and covering not only Europe but the rest of the known world. Its key feature was a universal Assembly or Senate of states which would have the power to issue binding arbitration in the event of disputes, and which he proposed should be situated in Venice as the geographical centre of the union. However political union was intended to be more than just new institutions. According to Crucé, it should also encompass more practical objectives such as developing shared infrastructure, investing in universal education, and ensuring the free movement of goods and persons. He even proposed the standardisation of weights and measures. Most of these radical ideas were too far in advance of their time to come to anything. The 'Grand Plan' of the Duke of Sully, of which the greatest part was published in 1638, consists of a large number of very concrete proposals for the political organisation of Europe. Since Sully's ideas are scattered across a large number of different texts, it is difficult to piece them together to make a coherent whole. Nevertheless Sully clearly envisaged Europe as a single entity taking the form of a confederation of states, balanced in its membership. It was to be placed under the authority of a Council of Europe which would be composed of six provincial Councils and a Council-General, the composition of which is set out in some detail. Also included are provisions for the settlement of disputes and arrangements covering the external defence of Europe. Like Crucé, Sully proposed that customs tariffs be abolished and a free trade area established. Sully developed his ideas on the basis of his own personal experience as a political advisor at the French Court, and for some commentators this distinguishes them from those of both his predecessors and contemporaries. Not all of his ideas, however, are completely convincing. For example he insisted on the need to make a number of substantial territorial adjustments in order for the confederation to function effectively.

Even grander in scope than the Grand Plan of Sully was the vast 'Panegersia' of the philosopher and theologian Amos Comenius. Born in Moravia (now the Czech Republic) in 1592, Comenius envisages nothing less than a single political federation within Christendom founded on a universal educational system, the reconciliation of the churches and political coordination under the auspices of international institutions. It is nothing if not ambitious, and owes its origins more to philosophical theory than to practical politics.

William Penn, the British dissenter, was inspired by his deeply-held pacifist convictions to draw up detailed practical ideas for the creation of a federation of European nations. Overseeing the proposed European federation would be a General Diet or Assembly which would act principally as a forum for the settlement of disputes through rational debate. However it would also have the power to introduce sanctions (including the payment of damages in the event of recourse to force) against any recalcitrant member. Interestingly, Penn proposed a weighted voting system for decision-making in the Diet.

Perhaps the most well known contribution to the cause of European unity from this period is that of Abbé de Saint Pierre. He published in 1712 a *Projet pour rendre la paix perpétuelle en Europe*, which whilst it clearly draws on many earlier proposals (he explicitly refers to Sully's Grand Plan), differs in that it attempts a serious analysis of the limitations of existing structures for maintaining peace. Saint Pierre looks in particular at the constraints on internal conflict within the nation state and reflects on how these might be applied at the European level. He is sceptical as to whether diplomacy and diplomatic tools are capable of delivering permanent peace, and doubts the value of any system based on a balance of power. He also calls into question the value of mutual commitments to peace in the absence of any overarching authority to enforce them. Yet for all the serious analysis of the problem, Saint Pierre's proposals themselves fail to offer a serious alternative to earlier ideas. His model is that of a political union of individual nation states renouncing war as a means to settle disputes. Peace is guaranteed by a permanent assembly with the power to arbitrate in disputes between members of the union, deciding by majority voting, and if necessary having recourse to sanctions. Borders between member states are fixed irrevocably, and strict limitations placed on the scope for individual member states to enter into agreements between themselves. Furthermore the establishment of free trade is seen as an important tool to help guarantee peace. Whilst Saint Pierre succeeds in identifying the obstacles to permanent peace, his solution falls short of being able to deliver the answer. Like the ideas of his predecessors, his proposed constitution remained a draft.

The development of ideas: enlightenment and revolution

In the eighteenth century increased European self-awareness prompted a burgeoning of ideas about the nature of the political organisation of Europe, in particular amongst French thinkers such as Montesquieu, Voltaire and Rousseau. The religious imperative for peace was replaced by a more utilitarian recognition of the cost of war, and its betrayal of human nature. This heightened self-consciousness was encouraged and spread by the increased interdependence brought about by the beginnings of the industrial revolution. Yet this is in striking contrast to the parallel development of a more robust nationalism, wrapped in new and popular symbols of nationhood. Against this background much of the writing from this period remains strikingly idealistic and utopian; little was on offer by way of practical proposals for guaranteeing peace, and the absence of specific proposals for the organisation of Europe contrasts strongly with developments on the other side of the Atlantic.

For whilst Europeans indulged in philosophical reflection, Americans were getting to grips in very practical ways with how to organise their own society. The difference is striking, but should not perhaps be so surprising.

Although the founding fathers were European in origin and therefore imbued with European ideas (the proposal to create a United States was not so different from many of the ideas circulating within Europe), there were several reasons why the states of America succeeded in uniting within a federal structure. Firstly, America had the advantage of starting with a constitutional clean slate; new ideas were more readily examined and accepted, unencumbered by European historical baggage. Secondly, the motivation to create a single union comprising the thirteen states was precisely to define America in terms which were different from Europe and (as Alexander Hamilton states explicitly in the Federalist papers) to provide America with the political force necessary for it to free itself completely from European influence and act as an independent nation.

The French and American revolutions had a profound effect on the nature of political thought, and so also on the development of ideas on the political organisation of Europe. Until then, relations between sovereign states had been seen exclusively as affairs between individual rulers. Alliances were sealed by kings and princes; the populations were irrelevant and were certainly not consulted. But the effect of revolution meant that the wider population would no longer be willing to accept that decisions fundamental to its well-being were taken with no reference to its own interests. The idea that wars should be launched purely for reasons of princely power or influence became increasingly difficult to justify.

Political revolution also coincided with the beginnings of industrial revolution, and the two were mutually supporting. Increased productivity created immense wealth, and technological progress provided greater mobility and access to information. This in turn led to greater social awareness. So political mobilisation of the masses became an increasingly important factor. As a result, proposals for union in Europe could no longer be the unique preserve of the governing classes. At the same time, technological progress created a new atmosphere of confidence, of a renewed belief that mankind was in control of its own destiny, and that in Europe at any rate destiny had to encompass peace as the cornerstone to civilisation. Wealth creation also led to an enormous increase in trade, helped by the removal of tariffs and other barriers. Free trade was seen as both an instrument and a product of peace, since it constituted a collective response to different interests.

This new range of factors had an impact on thinking on European union. Classical diplomatic models for maintaining peace, even when backed up with innovative dispute settlement systems, were less credible. New ideas were needed. One of these was the draft treaty on 'Perpetual Peace' drawn up by Emmanuel Kant in 1795, and influenced by the proposals of Sully and Abbé de Saint Pierre. Kant saw man's natural state as being that of war rather than peace, and therefore considered that permanent peace could be guaranteed not by treaties (which were temporary responses to specific conflicts), but through the creation of a league of peace designed to render war impossible. Kant's league is not simply a system of arbitration in the event of disputes, but a fully-fledged international legal order to be extended eventually to include all sovereign states. A further innovation in Kant's system is that for the first time the objective of permanent peace is seen as contingent on the existence of republican forms of government.

Perhaps more innovative still were the ideas of the French polymath Saint-Simon, who published in 1814 a draft proposal for a European union entitled *De la réorganisation de la Société européenne*. He adopted a two-pronged approach which does not deny the importance of the nation state as the basis for a union, but nevertheless sees the need for strong supranational institutions as a guarantee against overly dominant national interests. Specifically he proposed a European parliament with its members selected according to 'corporations' or profession. The union would be founded specifically on 'common interests and solid commitments', which for Saint-Simon were essentially economic, and would regulate disputes covering almost any aspect of European life. The parliament would also be charged with overseeing a Europe-wide education policy and with drawing up a moral code. Saint-Simon's emphasis on supranational institutions, as well as the emphasis he places on shared interests, mean that he is regarded by many as one of the closest precursors to the functional approach which led to the founding of the European Coal and Steel Community in the 1950s.

The concept of a federal Europe was taken up in a succession of further proposals put forward during the nineteenth century. The Italian philosopher Carlo Catteneo argued that European civilisation was founded on a variety of national cultures and that this diversity should be protected. He rejected the nostalgic approach to European union, considering instead that federal institutions were the natural and progressive product of an underlying European common set of interests. His compatriot Guiseppe Mazzini, who founded both the 'Young Italy' and its counterpart 'Young Europe' movements, was more an activist than a philosopher. He drew up a charter in 1834 proposing a republican union based on the three principles of liberty, equality and humanity. For Mazzini European union had to be a radical alternative to the status quo, and would therefore result not from intellectual ideas but grass roots activism. He saw the ultimate success of European union as depending on the emergence of a new social order.

Proposals for the creation of a federal Europe were also taken up with eloquence by Victor Hugo, who saw such a move as an inevitable product of realisation of the futility of conflict, and who immediately after the war of 1870 spoke for the first time of a 'united states of Europe'. His contemporary, Pierre-Joseph Proudhon, provided a powerful intellectual justification of the federalist approach in a work entitled *Du Principe Fédératif* published in 1863. The following decade these ideas were given more concrete form in the writings of Johann Caspar Bluntschli, a Swiss lawyer, who attempted to give substance to the concept of a European federal state by drawing on the Swiss national model. Bluntschli is notable in particular for proposing a bicameral institutional framework encompassing a Council of member states and a Senate representing the peoples of Europe.

* * * * * *

As with all the ideas which preceded them, none of the proposals of the nineteenth century were realised. The conditions for the emergence of the political integration of Europe were conceived by the shock of World War I, but it took a further forty years and a second world war for them to be fully realised.

So why did none of the many different ideas and proposals for European integration, originating from many different parts of Europe and over many centuries, ever come to fruition? And what fundamentally changed in the first half of the twentieth century to reverse that situation?

The twentieth century: from ideas to reality[2]

All of the proposals described above have one or more characteristics which do not lend themselves to practical application. Firstly, many of them are rooted in nostalgia; they look to re-establish a golden era in which Europe was considered to be under a single political authority which guaranteed peace and security. For many, that golden era was exemplified by the early years of the Holy Roman Empire. But, setting aside some of less pleasant realities of the period, any attempt to replicate in later times a system which was built on the divine right of kings and a single spiritual authority was unrealistic. Building the future on the basis of nostalgia made little practical sense. The second characteristic has already been referred to above; it is the obvious drawback of trying to construct an integrated and peaceful Europe on the basis of a diplomatic solution. Traditional diplomacy has always had a valuable role to play, but it has also shown it limitations. The extent to which it is useful depends entirely on the confidence which the actors have in it. Much of the time that is not a problem, but once confidence breaks down, the fragility of diplomacy is exposed. Attempts to create a new model for peace in Europe were never going to work using old building blocks. Thirdly, much of the reflection on European union was too idealistic, and even utopian, to be put into practice. Many of the ideas emerging over the centuries were the products of intellectuals and philosophers. Their starting point was frequently the construction of a paradigm, with practical implementation a secondary consideration. Few if any began by asking themselves what realistically was feasible.

But if the ideas rarely lent themselves to practical application, the conditions for their realisation were also often unfavourable. Implementation would have required the support of the political class, yet only a few of the authors attempted seriously to sell their ideas to those who could have delivered them. For the few that did, the gap between vision and political reality was painfully exposed. Europe's rulers (mostly kings and princes) considered that there was greater risk in entering the uncharted waters of political union than in maintaining the status quo. In an age when war was still largely unmechanised, and its consequences considered to be both limited and controllable, this should perhaps not be surprising. In short, the interest in delivering permanent peace was not seen by practitioners as sufficiently strong to justify the sacrifices (most importantly the partial loss of sovereignty) which most of the ideas would have entailed, particularly since in addition there was no guarantee that they would be successful. Furthermore, the growing role of the nation state during the nineteenth century (either through the unification of small principalities or the splitting of larger empires), led to a more aggressive nationalism which was less receptive to ideas of political integration. The shock of the two world wars together brought about a fundamental change of attitude; by the end of the Second World War the conditions were ready for the first steps to be taken on the road to European union.

*   *   *   *   *   *

The First World War totally exposed the fragility of the European system of the balance of power. Traditional diplomatic methods proved incapable of halting the descent into conflict, let alone of addressing its underlying causes. Once hostilities had broken out, the catastrophic effects of modern mechanised warfare became all too apparent. This combination was sufficient to begin to alter the balance of interests. The end of the First World War saw the first serious attempt to establish a permanent organisation with the objective of guaranteeing peace, ironically at the initiative of a non-European power. For Woodrow Wilson, the principal objective of the Paris Peace Conference in 1919 was the establishment of a League of Nations to act as an arbitrator in disputes and with the power to mobilise collective force against aggressors. Lloyd George supported the idea of the League but was sceptical about it ever coming to anything, not least because he doubted whether the US was ready in the long term to give it its full support (the fact that the US subsequently took no part in it after Congress failed to ratify vindicated this view). Clemenceau (for whom the future role of Germany was the priority) was ready to go along with it, but with no great enthusiasm.

The League never lived up to Wilson's high ideals. It suffered from only partial membership: apart from the absence of the US, Germany was only a member of the League from 1926 to 1935 (since the Paris Peace Conference brought together only the victors of World War I Germany had not been present). It was also impeded in its work from a lack of real power to enforce its own decisions; recourse to sanctions in particular proved difficult to apply. It was useful in overseeing and arbitrating in minor disputes, but failed to have any real impact on the major problems of the 1920s and 1930s. From the European perspective, the League had the same drawbacks as the many earlier ideas designed to guarantee peace: it essentially only offered a classical diplomatic solution, albeit in a modern multilateral guise. As such it was only effective to the extent and for as long as its participants collectively wished it to be.

The interwar years also saw a number of proposals for the creation of a

European union. Foremost among these was the initiative of Count Coudenhove-Kalergi for the creation of a 'Paneuropean Union'. First published in 1924, it took the form of a manifesto for Europe which was adopted at a congress in Vienna two years later with the support of a number of leading political thinkers and intellectuals. The manifesto was an impassioned appeal for the establishment of a political and economic union as the sole means to guarantee permanent peace in Europe.

The Paneuropean Union initiative provided inspiration for French statesman Aristide Briand, who had previously served as Prime Minister but who held the post of Foreign Minister from 1925 to 1932. He provided much of the inspiration for the Briand-Kellogg pact for the renunciation of war (an afterthought to the Convention establishing the League of Nations and never incorporated into it), and subsequently set out the outlines of a federal Europe in a speech to the League in 1929. The following year he presented a more detailed set of ideas entitled *Mémorandum sur l'organisation d'un régime d'union fédérale européenne*. The memorandum set out the case for a federal Europe, and outlined a basic set of institutions on which such a union would be built. These included a Conference of member states, a Political Committee, and a Tribunal. The League was invited to take forward preliminary work on the basis of the memorandum but the initial responses from members of the League were at best lukewarm and Briand's initiative never left the drawing board.

One of the more powerful advocates of a federal Europe during the interwar period was Lord Lothian. As Philip Kerr, he had served as private secretary to Lloyd George from 1917 to 1921, covering most notably the Paris Peace Conference. He was instrumental in the establishment in the UK in 1938 of the Federal Union, ironically the first of its kind in Europe. His landmark speech entitled 'Pacifism is not enough nor patriotism either'[3] delivered in 1935 is one of the most intellectually convincing and passionate cases for a federal Europe. Lothian in particular highlights the fundamental weakness of the 'diplomatic' approach, as exemplified in the League of Nations; The League, he says 'is built on the foundation of the complete sovereignty of the signatory and member states. The fact of state sovereignty is its vital flaw... The sovereignty of the national state has been the main cause of the failure of the league and the post-war peace movement, as it was the ultimate cause of the World War and will be the dynamic cause of the next war, unless we can mitigate it in time'. It took only four years for these prophetic words to be fulfilled.

Even at the height of the Second World War the thoughts of some were already turning to the possible shape of post-war Europe. The wartime resistance movements in particular produced several proposals for a future federal Europe. In 1941 Altiero Spinelli, together with a number of fellow prisoners being held on the island of Ventotene, drew up a manifesto which characterised totalitarianism as absolute sovereignty and called explicitly for a Europe based on supranational institutions as the only answer to the excesses of the nation state. In 1944 representatives of a number of resistance movements met in secret in Geneva and published a declaration calling for a federal union. The proposals included the establishment of a European government answerable directly to the people of Europe and not to its nation states, with an army directly under its control. For these resistance fighters, one of the main purposes of such an approach was to 'permit the participation of the German people in European life without their constituting a danger for others'. These proposals provided the basis for the creation of federalist movements which met together after the war in Montreux in 1947 for the first European Federalist Congress.

One of the more intriguing sets of proposals from this period was the product of Ernst Jünger, a German who served with distinction in the First World War. In 1941 he wrote a short work entitled 'The Peace'[4] which was distributed in secret the following year, but only published openly in 1946. Widely seen as offering inspiration to those who took part in the plot to assassinate Hitler in 1944, Jünger considered himself lucky to have escaped with his own life. Jünger's proposals avoid the unrealistic objective of a totally federalist approach, and instead put forward a hybrid model which provides for single European policies in areas such as the economy and trade, but which recognises the importance of maintaining diversity in a wide range of other areas. His two stated principles, unity and diversity, were introduced into the draft Constitution over sixty years later by the Convention on the future of Europe as the proposed motto of the European Union.

Consideration was also being given at the highest political level to the future European order. Winston Churchill crystallised his ideas in a speech delivered in Zurich in 1946 in which he called for the establishment of a 'United States of Europe'. However Churchill's vision was that of a concerned spectator. He saw no direct part in such a union for Britain, which would continue to play a global imperial role and as such would act as a link between Europe, the US and the rest of the world.

The momentum achieved by the European federalist movements was harnessed largely thanks to the efforts of a Polish national, Joseph Retinger, and led directly to the convening of a Congress of Europe which took place in The Hague in May 1948 under the chairmanship of Winston Churchill. Its short concluding document entitled 'Message to Europeans' combined high ideals and practical proposals. In particular it called for the creation of a European Assembly and the adoption of a European Charter of Human Rights together with a Court (with powers of sanction) to oversee its application. The document was to be followed up by a group known as the European Movement, and within one year had led directly to the creation of the Council of Europe, which was to have a separate and quite distinct identity from the European Community.

Historically, external threats such as the Ottoman Empire had provided additional motivation for pursuing European political union. In the immediate post-war period Europe found itself facing a Soviet Union which was both politically incompatible with the liberal democratic values of the new Europe, and a potential military threat. In February 1948, the communists seized power in Prague, and only a few months later Stalin ordered the blockade of Berlin. These events provided the catalyst required to give substance to the Truman doctrine, which guaranteed US support for free peoples in the face of outside pressure, and led directly to its involvement in Europe's defence and security through the North Atlantic Treaty Organisation (NATO), founded in April 1949. One important result of the creation of NATO was that security and defence issues were to remain entirely separate from Europe's political and economic structures for the rest of the twentieth century, with all attempts to bring them together (for example the proposal for a European Defence Community in the 1950s) ending in failure. Even after the collapse of the Soviet Union, it took a further ten years for the European Union to assume even the basic trappings of a security identity.

*　*　*　*　*

The more immediate origins of the European Community are to be found in a declaration delivered by French Foreign Minister Robert Schuman in May 1950. The ideas set out in the declaration, known as the Schuman plan, had been drawn up largely by Jean Monnet, a senior civil servant with a background in business who held a number of influential posts within the French government system. He was convinced of the need to work for full economic and political integration within Europe, yet was pragmatic enough to see that this was most likely to be achieved through an incremental approach. The result was that today's European Union had a rather modest start in life. The main practical proposal of the Schuman plan was that national coal and steel resources should be pooled and placed under the control of a supranational authority. The argument was simple: the capacity to fight wars ultimately depends on access to coal and steel; take these away from national control and you significantly decrease the risk of further conflict. The Schuman plan was accepted and led in 1952 to the treaty founding the European Coal and Steel Community (ECSC).

The failure of the subsequent initiative for a European Defence Community (linked closely to the issue of the role of NATO – see above) led to an increasing emphasis from the supporters of European integration on the economic aspects. The Treaty of Rome signed in 1957 (along with the Euratom treaty) created the European Economic Community, and ensured that the focus of European integration for the next thirty years would be on economic and trade policy.

Why did the Schuman Plan become the successful launchpad for European integration through the creation initially of the ECSC when so many earlier proposals had come to nothing? Firstly, unlike its predecessors, it adopted a functional approach. Economic means were being managed for political ends. The traditional diplomatic approach was therefore neatly sidestepped. Secondly, it adopted an incremental approach. The

Treaty of Rome talked of an 'ever-closer union'. This was to be a dynamic process, based on the recognition that concrete results would be needed before further advances could be made. Yet at the same time the treaty placed no limits on the ultimate scope or aims of European integration. It was therefore possible to satisfy both the ambitious and the cautious at the same time. Thirdly, the original proposal was essentially a French product, rooted in the idea of Franco-German reconciliation: France needed protecting from Germany, and Germany needed protecting from itself. Whilst support from others such as Spaak (former Belgian Prime Minister) and de Gasperi (Italian Prime Minister) was important, similar ideas originating from outside France or Germany would have had less chance of being accepted. Furthermore, not only was the focus on coal and steel practical, it was also highly symbolic, since the main production areas were the Rhineland, Lorraine and Wallonia, all key frontier regions on the borders of France and Germany.

A Community but not yet a Constitution

The ECSC Treaty was just that: a treaty recognised under international law. It was followed by others, the Treaty of Rome and Euratom, the Single Act, the Treaty of Maastricht, and so on, not including the successive treaties of accession which progressively moved the Community of six to a Union of twenty-five. None of these treaties are called 'constitutions', nor are they considered to be 'constitutional' as it is normally understood at the national level, even if some have argued that the inclusion of provisions creating permanent law-making institutions gives them a quasi-constitutional status. The treaties can perhaps be considered to constitute a legal order which, whilst it has its origins in international law, is now a sui generis structure which includes highly sophisticated internal procedures covering an ever larger range of policy areas.

Until the Convention on the future of the European Union, the issue of whether or not the Union should have a constitution was not a serious issue for debate between the Member States. Indeed the only proposals for a constitution had originated in the European Parliament. The first of these was drawn up by the Committee on Institutional Affairs under the chairmanship of Altieri Spinelli in 1984. This was followed in 1990 by the 'Colombo' report, which drew up guidelines for the preparation of a constitution based on the 1984 draft treaty. This report was explicitly endorsed by the Belgian government and the Italian parliament. The idea of drawing up a constitution was taken up more recently in the Oreja/Herman report of 1994 following which the Parliament called for further work on the subject. All these texts have some basic elements in common such as the Union's objectives, its competences, its institutional framework, and in some cases a list of basic rights.

Why was the European Parliament so fascinated with the idea of creating a constitution? Certainly the Parliament had more limited powers than it does today, and much of the work which went into these various drafts should be seen in the context of a still relatively young institution attempting to flex its muscles. On the whole the Member States were distinctly unimpressed. During the 1980s, the Community was preoccupied with absorbing three new Member States, and setting in motion the plan to complete the Internal Market. Rewriting the treaties in constitutional form was seen as an unnecessary distraction.

Similarly, in the 1990s, the Union was developing rapidly as it moved into new policy areas such as the Common Foreign and Security Policy and Justice and Home Affairs, where the incremental approach was proving its worth. Perhaps more importantly, the Union was having to face up to the challenges brought about by the fall of the iron curtain. This led eventually to the decision to bring the central and eastern European countries into the Union, setting in train the lengthy process of modernisation of their administrative systems and the enormous task of bringing their legislation in line with the Union's requirements.

In both decades the Union was focussed on other objectives. In addition the Parliament's proposals for a constitution cut across the incremental approach, tending instead to recall more the grand designs of the past. The result was that there was little interest from most Member States in a constitution.

Yet by the middle of 2003 a complete rewriting of the treaties had taken place. It took the form of a draft treaty establishing a constitution for Europe, and was presented to Heads of State and Government in June of that year. It had been drawn up over a period of fifteen months by a Convention established by the Member States. What had changed in the meantime? Why did the governments decide to call a Convention? And how did the idea of a constitution finally become accepted? These are issues which will be covered in the following chapter.

2. More immediate origins – from Nice to Laeken

In December 2001 the leaders of the European Union gathered at the home of the Belgian Royal family in Laeken on the edge of Brussels for the usual December meeting of the European Council, bringing to a close the six-monthly Belgian Presidency of the Council. The culmination of the meeting was the adoption of a document entitled the 'Laeken Declaration on the future of the European Union'[5]. This declaration established the Convention, set out its composition and working methods, and provided a detailed list of the challenges and possible reforms needed in a renewed Union. Given that the very notion of a Convention had previously and consistently run up against strong objections from a number of Member States (indeed for some it was almost a taboo concept), the fact that the Laeken declaration was adopted at all raises a number of questions. Why had several Member States simply changed their mind? Was there a new situation which made it easier for the concept of a Convention to be accepted? How, if at all, did the language of the Laeken declaration itself help in this process?

These questions are looked at in this chapter under three overall headings. The first takes as its starting point the Amsterdam Treaty of 1997, examines how its shortcomings kept up the momentum for institutional reform, and specifically looks at the initial work undertaken in the Intergovernmental Conference by the Portuguese during the first half of 2000. The second part of the chapter describes the continuation of that work under the French Presidency in the second half of that year, as well as its culmination in the confusion of the Nice European Council in December 2000. The third part explains how the Nice discussions and their widely criticised outcome helped put the idea of a Convention on the agenda. It includes an analysis of how the results of Nice revealed a deeper malaise about the nature of the European Union, and how this was successfully exploited by those who had an interest in a Convention, with the unexpected result that by the end of 2001 all Member States were able to endorse the convening of a Convention to examine the issue of the future of the European Union.

The background to Nice: the Legacy of Amsterdam (1997-1999)[6]

The treaties, which set out the powers and the rules of functioning of the European Union, contain provisions allowing for their own revision. Article 48 of the Treaty on European Union states that any Member State or the Commission may submit proposals to the Council for amending the treaties. This opens the way, if the Council agrees, for the convening by the President of the Council (a post which is held on a six-monthly rotating basis by each Member State in turn) of an Intergovernmental Conference (IGC), which is the only way in which the treaties can be revised. An Intergovernmental Conference brings together the Member States in a classical diplomatic negotiation with a view to (in the words of the treaty) 'determining by common accord the amendments to be made to those Treaties'.

Amending the treaties requires the unanimous agreement of all Member States. It also requires ratification by all Member States in accordance with their own respective internal procedures (normally either through national parliaments or via a referendum) before the new rules can enter into force. With fifteen (and now twenty-five) Member States, this procedure can take more than two years to complete. An Intergovernmental Conference is not therefore something to be entered into lightly.

Despite this, the frequency of IGCs has increased over the years. To some extent this is a consequence of the growing need for the Union to adapt to rapidly changing needs and circumstances. But it also reflects an increasing inability of successive IGCs to deliver the results which are needed to meet the new challenges. So the IGC which led to the Nice Treaty has its origins in the shortcomings of the 1997 Amsterdam IGC, which was unable to reach agreement on all the institutional issues on its agenda. Instead, the most that the Amsterdam meeting was able to do was draw up a protocol acknowledging that the unresolved issues (the so-called 'Amsterdam leftovers') would need to be dealt with in advance of the next round of enlargement, and setting some parameters for the future negotiations. The two leftovers were the issues of the size of the Commission and the voting system in the Council. The protocol already foresaw a smaller Commission, with the larger Member States losing their second Commissioner, provided that these Member States were adequately compensated by a revision of the voting system in the Council. This could either take the form of a reweighting of votes or the introduction of a double majority system (majority of Member States and majority of population).

On procedures, the Amsterdam protocol called for the convening of an IGC at least one year before the membership of the Union reached twenty, and stated that the purpose of the IGC was to 'carry out a comprehensive review of the provisions of the Treaties on the composition and functioning of the institutions'. The text therefore contained two specific issues which the Nice IGC was expected to address, but at the same time offered the possibility, if Member States were both able and willing, of introducing more fundamental changes to the Union's institutions.

The Cologne European Council which brought to a close the German Presidency in June 1999 confirmed the intention of convening an IGC early in 2000, with the objective of completion by the end of that year. This relatively tight timing was foreseen in order to allow for the necessary institutional reforms to be completed (and ratified) in time for enlargement, even though the precise timetable on this was still not clear. In defining a brief for the IGC, Cologne maintained the ambivalence of the Amsterdam protocol by referring to the two specific issues of Commission size and vote weighting in the Council, although it added the issue of the possible extension of the scope of Qualified Majority Voting (QMV) (which had been the subject of a trilateral declaration by Belgium, France and Italy at Amsterdam). However it also left wide open the possibility of more extensive institutional reform. This mandate was confirmed by the Helsinki European Council at the end of the Finnish Presidency in December 1999, although the possibility of the incoming Portuguese Presidency proposing additional issues was also foreseen. Helsinki also called for the IGC to be launched in February 2000, confirmed that it should complete its work within the year, and set out some of the practical and organisational arrangements.

The background to Nice: stocktaking by the Portuguese Presidency (first half of 2000)

Presidencies can in general exercise considerable influence over the functioning of the Council, and similarly can be instrumental in setting the tone, priorities and direction of an IGC. The Portuguese Presidency adopted a highly systematic approach to the IGC from its opening session on 14 February 2000. Its two objectives were: firstly to identify the specific subjects to be covered by the IGC, in particular by clarifying and limiting its mandate on institutional issues which the Amsterdam protocol and subsequent European Council conclusions had left vague; and secondly to analyse the principal difficulties within each issue and to begin to sketch out possible solutions. The analyses of the main issues, in particular that on Council voting methods and the composition of the Commission, remain pertinent, and proved to be a useful quarry during the post-Convention IGC, at which these two issues continued to be the most difficult to resolve.

The analyses of the issues as well as the possible solutions were set out in a report, drawn up by the Portuguese at the end of their Presidency, to the Feira European Council in June 2000[7]. This document was sufficiently well drafted to serve as the main source of guidance for the IGC for the remaining six months of its work. The Feira report confirmed that the scope of the application of Qualified Majority Voting would form part of the IGC's mandate. It also added enhanced cooperation (a provision whereby smaller groups of Member States can deepen cooperation amongst themselves in specific policy areas), on which it suggested that a reassessment of the Amsterdam Treaty provisions was needed. Two subjects were explicitly excluded from the IGC: Security and Defence Policy and the draft Charter of Fundamental Rights, both of which were being covered separately.

On institutional issues, the Feira report made no proposals for change to the overall structure of the Union, nor to the relationships between the different institutions, but treated the functioning of each as a separate issue. Some important subjects were not included at all; for example the functioning of the Council Presidency was never part of the IGC agenda. Equally the Feira report does not take up the invitation from the Amsterdam protocol to carry out a comprehensive review of the composition and functioning of the Union's institutions. Indeed it expressly excludes such a review: 'It is not the purpose of this Intergovernmental Conference to address, still less to settle, the debate launched elsewhere on the goals of the Union and the future of its institutions'. Nevertheless it goes on to state that such a debate will no doubt continue over the next few years, and 'by opening an in-depth discussion on a number of sensitive issues and trying to find solutions which measure up to the challenges now facing us, this Conference is contributing to the process of constant adaptation of the institutions and the way they operate, without which the Union's immediate future, and, still more, its long-term future would be compromised'. So the Feira report excludes a wider debate for the Nice IGC, yet at the same time foresees the necessity and (almost) inevitability of such a discussion in the medium-term. Already the seeds of a broader constitutional debate have been sown.

Nice: Confrontation under the French Presidency (second half of 2000)

The first six months of 2000 under the guidance of the Portuguese were used to valuable effect to prepare the ground of the IGC. However the negotiations themselves did not seriously get underway until the French took over in July of that year. They were marked by a dramatisation of the arguments and a divisiveness which was to continue right up to the Nice European Council meeting in December 2000, and which coloured the final result.

It quickly became apparent that the Nice IGC would be dominated by differences of view between the large and small Member States. These differences had their roots in the issue of voting in the Council and specifically in the requirement set out in the Amsterdam protocol for the large Member States to be compensated for the loss of their second Commissioner. For the first time Member States' interests, and therefore their negotiating positions, turned out to be consistently determined by their size. This contrasted with traditional negotiations in the Council, or even previous IGCs, where alliances vary according to the issue under discussion, and where this almost never results in a straight division between large and small Member States.

The requirement in the Amsterdam protocol for a trade-off between voting power in the Council and the loss of a second Commissioner looks relatively straightforward. Why then did the IGC find it so difficult to turn this principle into an acceptable deal? This can in part be explained by the fact that the negotiations became blocked as a result of the impossibility of reconciling several contradictory demands, in particular from the larger Member States, and most importantly, from the Presidency itself. In addition, the Presidency's position was complicated internally because of the phenomenon of 'cohabitation': in this case a right-of-centre President Chirac sharing power with socialist Prime Minister Jospin, leading some-times to differences of view within the Presidency itself.

The simplest way of reinforcing the voting power of the larger Member States in the Council is to accept a system which aligns more closely voting weights with population. This can be done through reweighting, or by introducing a double majority system (which means that a majority of both Member States and of the Union's population is required for a measure to be adopted). France, as Presidency, fully backed such a realignment between the larger and smaller Member States, but was unwilling to accept that this should logically extend also to a realignment between the larger Member States themselves, because of its determination to retain parity with Germany. French insistence on this point soured the atmosphere of the IGC by reinforcing the perception that there were different sets of rules for the larger and smaller Member States, and effectively prevented it from reaching a sensible solution on vote weighting. The final compromise took no account of the 20 million population difference between Germany on the one hand and France, UK and Italy on the other, except indirectly through a provision which allows any Member State to invoke the application of a threshold of 62% of the Union's total population for a measure to be adopted. At the same time, the 20 million difference between the latter three countries and Spain and Poland was reflected only marginally. Three years later France abandoned its insistence on parity with Germany when it even-tually embraced the double majority system proposed by the Convention.

The atmosphere was made still more difficult by the reluctance of the Presidency, with the support of several of the larger Member States, to con-template seriously the request from their smaller counterparts for a simple majority threshold in the numbers of Member States (whatever the thresh-old of weighted votes). The argument that this had not been necessary in the past cut little ice with the smalls, for whom this issue increasingly became a matter of principle. In practice such a requirement posed little threat to the large Member States (and was accepted in the end), its real effect being almost negligible since it depends on a hypothetical massed line-up of smaller Member States on a single issue in the Council. The defensive pos-ition of the Presidency on this issue therefore offered little real advantage but at the same time increased existing tensions.

The issue of the Commission was only slightly less divisive. Although the principle of the loss of a second Commissioner was accepted in the end, the longer-term composition of the Commission proved difficult. The Commission is supposed to act in the wider European interest; it cannot therefore take instructions from Member States yet equally cannot operate in a political vacuum. The two contradictory requirements of avoiding nationalisation of the Commission and yet retaining its legitimacy had to be reconciled. At the same time there was a case for not allowing enlargement to lead to a large and unwieldy Commission consisting of too many Commissioners with too few serious dossiers to share between them. That would mean accepting that at some time in the future there would be fewer than one national per Member State.

The divisions between large and small Member States were exposed for the first time half way through the French Presidency at an informal IGC meeting in Biarritz in October 2000. Little progress was made on vote weighting, which meant that President Chirac could only refer in his concluding remarks to the fact that two options were on the table: a simple reweighting or a double majority system (which is neither more nor less than the terms of the Amsterdam protocol). On the composition of the Commission, here also President Chirac concluded that there were two options: either placing a ceiling on the number of Commissioners with a system of equal rotation, or a Commission of at least one national per Member State (although he recognised that the second option raised the problem of the Commission's efficiency). In fact the large Member States were ready in principle to accept a ceiling and equal rotation at a future date, but at Biarritz the President was unable even to conclude that the large Member States could agree to lose their second Commissioner. When challenged by one colleague on this, he recalled (to the irritation of some of the smaller Member States) that acceptance of this principle was linked to an acceptable solution on the Council voting system. The strong sense amongst the smalls that they were going to have their hands forced was to remain until the end of the negotiations. All in all, the prospects for reaching an agreement in Nice were not encouraging.

Nice: the culmination of confusion (December 2000)[8]

The Nice European Council, which brought to a close the French Presidency, was a sobering experience for the Union. Despite the intensive discussions under both the Portuguese and French Presidencies which had led to agreement on a number of less important points, the two principal issues – voting in the Council and composition of the Commission – were as open as they had been at the beginning of the IGC. As a result, the negotiations at the European Council itself were destined to be confused. The meeting was characterised by an unprecedented degree of mistrust, particularly from the smaller Member States, which soured the atmosphere. Yet the pressure to reach an agreement was intense. In the small hours of Monday morning, the fourth day of negotiation, Europe's leaders were brought up against a real possibility that they might fail, and failure would have had consequences going wider than the functioning of the Union's institutions (one member of the European Council drew his colleagues' attention to the likely impact on the euro when the financial markets opened only hours later).

The total impasse which had existed up until then turned into a search for an agreement at almost any price. The result betrayed the lack of any clear sense of direction: the final distribution of votes in the Council rode roughshod over any sense of logic or consistency; European Parliament seats were distributed almost arbitrarily, with the result that they were later challenged and had to be revised in order to increase the numbers for the Czech Republic and Hungary; and an obscure final declaration on the qualified majority threshold took several weeks of subsequent discussion amongst ambassadors to clarify. Not surprisingly the outcome was widely criticised. Never has the result of an IGC been so contested so quickly by both the media and public opinion, both on the method (with some already calling into question the effectiveness of Intergovernmental Conferences, echoing Prime Minister Blair's comment after Nice that 'we cannot continue to do business like this'), as well as on the substance, which was perceived as lacking coherence, unnecessarily complicated, and in general insufficient to face up the challenges of enlargement.

A small chink of light was perhaps cast by the declaration on the future of the Union adopted by the IGC. This declaration, which was in part a response to the sense of failure amongst even the heads themselves, called for a deeper and wider debate about the future of the European Union. In doing so, it acknowledged that Nice itself, whilst charged with tackling the leftovers of Amsterdam, had its own leftovers. The declaration sets out four specific issues ('inter alia') which needed to be addressed: the delimitation of powers between the Union and the Member States, the status of the Charter of Fundamental Rights, the simplification of the treaties and the role of national parliaments. On procedure, the declaration refers to the need for the Laeken European Council to determine the 'appropriate initiatives for the continuation of this process' (of reflection). It therefore contains the seed for the establishment of a Convention, which was the method finally chosen to look at the future of the Union.

The period leading up to the European Council of Nice, the meeting itself and the result, help largely in explaining why the Union finally opted for a more innovative approach to treaty change in the future. But there are in addition more fundamental structural reasons which explain why Europe's leaders took the first steps towards a Convention, and so eventually towards the drawing up of a Constitution.

Post-Nice: a deeper malaise revealed

The failure of Nice cannot be considered as an isolated event. It was rather a reflection or symptom of a wider set of issues which touched on the very nature of the Union itself. Nice had shown that the Union had reached the limits of its capacity to act within the current structures. It served as a catalyst for a deeper analysis by both practitioners and commentators. Why could the Union not continue to do business as it had done in the past? What had changed? And most importantly, what needed to be done in the future?

There are several conclusions which can be drawn about the sort of Union which Europe's leaders faced at their meeting in Nice. Firstly, the number of policy areas covered by the Union, albeit with differing powers and procedures, had reached its limits. The Single Market, with one or two important exceptions, was now largely complete. The Treaty on European Union agreed at Maastricht had created the single currency, which was soon to become a reality. The Maastricht Treaty had also created the important and extensive area of Justice and Home Affairs, and had transformed the notion of European Political Cooperation into a fully-fledged Common Foreign and Security Policy. Both these areas were further developed under the Amsterdam Treaty, which importantly created the post of High Representative for the CFSP, and included specific provisions touching on security and defence policy. In short, there was little scope (and in any case even less political will) to extend further the list of policy areas served by the Union. The main issue now for Member States was rather how to introduce greater coherence into the areas already falling within the powers of the Union. In short, extending the policy frontiers of the Union was now less of an issue than how to manage more effectively the existing limits.

Secondly, there was a general feeling that the Union was also reaching its geographical limits. Negotiations were advancing well with the bulk of countries of central and eastern Europe, a process leading to what many regarded as the long-overdue unification of the continent after decades of artificial separation. In addition, the Helsinki European Council at the end of 1999 recognised Turkey as a candidate country. With several obvious exceptions, the geographical coverage of the European Union was becoming increasingly aligned with the European continent itself. The two issues of policy coverage and geographical scope served to put back on the agenda (with more relevance) the long-standing fundamental question about the ultimate destination of the Union.

Thirdly, several limits had been reached as far as the functioning of the Union and its institutions was concerned. The method by which successive IGCs had modified and expanded the original treaties had resulted in texts which were so complex and byzantine that they were incomprehensible to almost all but the bureaucrats responsible for their implementation. The main reason for this is that the compromises needed to overcome deadlock in IGCs usually involve new mechanisms in addition to those which exist already. The result over the years is a proliferation of instruments and procedures, with complex varieties of competencies, interwoven into a multi-layered text. Set against an ever-increasing pressure for greater transparency and simplicity (seen by many as key to maintaining public support for the Union), it was clear that after more than forty years, such an approach was unsustainable.

An additional factor was an increasing sense that, not only had the Union in some cases reached the limits of its development, it had also developed a tendency, often as a result of far-reaching legal interpretations by the European Court of Justice, to push at these limits in order to extend its powers (a phenomenon known as 'creeping competence'). This gave rise to the feeling that the Union was getting too involved in every aspect of the daily lives of its citizens, and that it should consequently be reined in. The result was the resurrection of the principle of subsidiarity originally created by the Catholic church: that action should only be taken at the level of the Union if the intended objectives of that action cannot be sufficiently achieved at the level of the Member States.

The principle of subsidiarity was enshrined for the first time in the Treaty on European Union, and has become particularly dear to eurosceptics who regard it as a weapon against interference by the Commission in particular. It is therefore all the more surprising that some cite the combination of subsidiarity and the attribution to the Union of powers in such lofty areas as foreign policy and justice and home affairs as evidence that the Union is moving towards a classical multilayered 'federal' model. However this conveniently ignores the fact that both foreign policy and many aspects of justice and home affairs are subject to their own specific rules and procedures reflecting precisely Member States' unwillingness to accept a federal approach.

Finally, as the overall competence of the Union has increased over the years through successive IGCs, so the individual institutions (some more than others) have enlarged the scope of their power of decision. This is especially true of the European Parliament, whose role in the legislative process was given new impetus by the 'cooperation procedure' brought in under the Single European Act in 1987, and more recently transformed in 1992 by the introduction in the Treaty on European Union of the 'co-decision procedure' which puts it on an equal footing in the legislative process with the Council. The existence within the Union of transnational institutions with the power to adopt binding legislation means that it is possible to regard the Union as already containing 'constitutional' elements, and in the view of some, as steadily developing a constitutional order, even under the existing treaties. Some of the academic exercises undertaken, for example, by the European University Institute of Florence[9] demonstrate that it is perfectly possible, simply by a reordering and rationalisation of the current treaties, to create a constitution for Europe, without any change to the Union's existing institutions, powers and procedures.

*   *   *   *   *   *

None of these factors in isolation would have led automatically to the conclusion that the time was ripe for Europe to adopt a treaty establishing a constitution. Indeed, even when taken together, the combination of factors was not enough to overcome the considerable resistance from many Member States. A catalyst was also needed. It required several key individuals to seize the opportunities presented by the confusion of Nice, its root causes and its consequences. It also required a profound conviction in the value of the European project, and an ability to exploit the conditions in which the Union found itself, at best to encourage a sense of enthusiasm for a new way forward, or at least to remove the arguments which had until then bolstered the resistance of the doubters. Enter the Belgian Presidency.

Post-Nice: a Strategy for breaking with the past

Intergovernmental conferences have never been very public affairs. They have met in closed rooms and have not traditionally engaged in any form of collective external consultation. Public interest in early IGCs was negligible, and even in more recent cases has been limited largely to a fascination with the tensions of the closing stages. Only after IGCs have been completed has any real interest in the substance emerged. This has been particularly so in those Member States where a referendum has been the obligatory or chosen route for ratification, and in the case of Maastricht and Amsterdam led to high drama as the ratification process threatened to ditch the new treaties entirely.

Nice laid the basis for moving away in future from a system in which the public were only engaged after the end of the process. The declaration annexed to the Nice Treaty called for a wider and deeper debate about the future of the Union, and invited the incoming Swedish and Belgian Presidencies to encourage wide-ranging discussions with all interested parties. These were formally opened in March 2001. There was a conscious effort to encourage a debate with all sections of society, and various initiatives were taken at the European level such as the creation of a 'Future of Europe' website, although it was widely accepted that the debate had to be concentrated at the national or regional level. It is difficult to conclude that the content of this debate, which continued throughout the Convention, supplemented by various initiatives such as the Youth Convention and consultations with civil society, played a key role in the decision to launch the Convention itself or had any major influence on its outcome. But it had a symbolic impact in that it demonstrated the determination of Europe's leaders to break with the past: there was to be no more secret diplomacy; instead the people were being consulted not just at the end of the process but throughout.

The Swedes ended their Presidency in June 2001 with a report which included pointers for the future. It concluded that there was strong support for the idea that the next IGC should be preceded by an open forum with wider participation, and set out a number of options. Amongst them was the idea of the Convention model, which had been used once in order to draw up the Charter of Fundamental Rights. This first Convention had been successful, but its remit had been tightly drawn; it was also small (and therefore manageable) and responsible for drawing up a text which although highly political, was not intended (at that stage) to have any legal effect. Any

Convention designed to pave the way for an IGC would be different. Nevertheless, the option was on the table, and the Swedish report concluded that the Laeken European Council would have to take the final decision; the process was now firmly in the hands of the Belgians.

The Belgians were convinced that a Convention was the way forward. The experience of the first Convention, despite initial hesitation from several Member States, was regarded as a positive precedent, and the Belgians, historically amongst the most committed to European integration, led the vanguard of those Member States who supported breaking out of the old model of preparing treaty change exclusively via Intergovernmental Conferences.

They did not have to wait long before chalking up their first success. The traditional post-summer break informal meeting of Foreign Ministers (the so-called Gymnich meeting, named after the very first venue) took place in Genval, just south of Brussels, in the first week of September 2001. It was to be decisive. At the close of the discussions, the Belgian Presidency was able to conclude that there were no longer any objections to a Convention along similar lines to that which drew up the Charter of Fundamental Rights. That meant broadly the same composition and structure, with a maximum time frame of 18 months, with work to begin in the first half of 2002. It was also however clear that, whatever the results of the Convention, they could in no way bind the Member States in the subsequent IGC which would still be required.

It was an unexpected and early success for the Belgian Presidency. With a decision in principle taken to convene a Convention, the Presidency could now concentrate on the preparation of the text which would provide the framework and mandate of the Convention. This was no easy task. It had to satisfy both those who wished the Convention to be ambitious (amongst them the Belgians themselves), but at the same time provide reassurance to those who, despite signing up to a Convention, remained sceptical about its added value and sought to keep governments firmly in control of the overall process.

The preparation of the Laeken declaration therefore became a priority for the Belgian Presidency. The ambition was high: to create a document which would be endorsed without difficulty by European heads when they met at the end of the Belgian Presidency, but which the Presidency also hoped would stand the test of time and become a text of historical significance. To oversee the process, the Presidency constituted a group of 'Wise Men' (a technique increasingly used by the Union consisting of inviting a number of 'elder statesmen' to make recommendations on a particular issue). In this case, it brought together the former President of the Commission Jacques Delors, former Belgian and Italian Prime Ministers Dehaene and Amato, former Polish Foreign Minister Geremek and the British MP David Miliband (a close confidant of Tony Blair). Both Dehaene and Amato were subsequently to become Vice-Presidents of the Convention itself and therefore directly involved in turning the mandate which they had had a hand in drafting into concrete results.

The Nice declaration[10], in specifically mentioning only four issues, gave the impression of a mandate which would be very limited in scope. A number of Member States made it clear early on that these four issues, perhaps with one or two limited additions, should constitute the basis for the work of the Convention. At the outset, only a few sought a wider mandate; their argument was that it was difficult to isolate the four Nice issues from many other wider considerations which would inevitably have to be addressed.

Amongst those who wanted as wide a mandate as possible were the Belgians. To achieve their objective, they adopted an approach which consisted of gradually blurring the edges between an explicit mandate for the Convention and the overall content of the Laeken declaration. Almost by sleight of hand, the notion of a mandate was dropped, and the content of the declaration itself became, by default, the basis for the Convention's work. The result was that the Convention felt able to address any issue which had even the most remote link with the text of the declaration. Once it felt it had sufficient endorsement to go ahead on this basis, the priority for the Presidency became the drafting of the declaration itself, an exercise in which Belgian Prime Minister Guy Verhofstadt, as President of the European Council, took a direct and personal interest.

The Laeken declaration, like so many documents produced by the Union, will not enter the literary annals. Its dense structure reflects the laborious conditions in which it was produced as well as the wide range of different sources. These include the group of 'Wise Men' and the Prime Minister's office, as well as a long series of amendments proposed by the Member States both during the European Council President's pre-Laeken tour of European capitals and at the Laeken meeting itself. But what it loses in literary style, it gains in a deft manipulation of language. The latter helped guarantee a successful outcome at the Laeken summit (despite the considerable odds against at the beginning of the whole process); the former ensured that the document would be forgotten almost before the ink was dry.

The deftness of language takes a number of forms. Firstly, the Presidency took on the challenge of the Nice declaration to widen the discussions on the Union by numerous references to the citizen. The temptation not only to flatter the citizen, but even to give him or her a voice in the declaration, was too much for the Presidency to resist. Scattered throughout the Laeken declaration are phrases such as: 'Citizens are calling for a clear, open effective, democratically controlled Community approach' or 'Citizens often hold expectations of the European Union that are not always fulfilled'. As a result, parts of the Laeken declaration read like a register of grievances.

Secondly, there is skilfulness in the choice of themes addressed in the declaration. Many of them are deliberately presented in such a manner as to leave the way open for two very different interpretations, thereby satisfying at the same time both the integrationists and the sceptics. So, for example, the issue of competences leaves open the possibility of assigning new missions to the

Union but also of restoring tasks to the Member States. In the institutional field, the possibility of increasing the authority of the Commission and strengthening the role of the European Parliament is balanced against the suggestion that there might be a greater role for national parliaments. Even the reference to the possible adoption of a constitutional text is countered by the proposal that one of its basic features might be to determine 'the relationship of Member States in the Union', a phrase which pulls the rug from under those who argue in favour of a fully-fledged constitution.

Numerous other self-criticisms (the need for greater legitimacy, transparency, and efficiency) as well as a liberal scattering of somewhat pious-sounding aspirations (the citizens do not want 'a European superstate or European institutions inveigling their way into every nook and cranny of life') served the purpose of disarming a number of potential critics, in particular those from the sceptic camp.

The 'catch-all' approach to the drafting of the Laeken declaration paid off. There was very little discussion on the text itself at the European Council. The groundwork had been well prepared. The declaration contained something for everyone. And the Convention had effectively carte blanche to make whatever recommendations it wanted to. It would be difficult for anyone subsequently to prove that any issue was 'off-limits'.

The main task which leaders were left to deal with in Laeken was to choose the President and Vice-President of the Convention. In this the Belgian Presidency was less successful. With Wim Kok, the Dutch Prime Minister, as his own preferred, but unstated, candidate (despite the fact that Kok himself had not formally declared his candidature), Verhofstadt prepared to launch a table round to ascertain the views of his colleagues. He was immediately bounced by President Chirac who (having done some extensive prior lobbying with his colleagues) took advantage of a point of order to throw the name of former French President Valéry Giscard d'Estaing into the ring. Although some would have preferred a younger candidate, Giscard d'Estaing came with impeccable European credentials, having worked closely with German Chancellor Helmut Schmidt in the 1970's on the creation of the European Monetary System, and was widely seen as the inspiration behind the regular summit meetings of European leaders (now know as 'European Councils').

It quickly became clear that Giscard d'Estaing had sufficient support around the table to be carried. However intensive bilateral consultations were then needed to settle the issue of the Vice-President. The candidature of Dehaene, whom the Belgians had wanted to be Vice-President to Kok, now created difficulties because of a need for political balance (both Giscard d'Estaing and Dehaene being right of centre). The solution was typically European; Guiliano Amato, former socialist Prime Minister of Italy, was asked to work alongside Dehaene as a second Vice-President. The slightly unseemly scramble for names gave little clue that Europe's leaders had probably chanced on a winning combination.

*   *   *   *   *   *

The Laeken European Council was one of the key stepping-stones on the road to a constitution. Not only had the heads decided on a new approach for addressing the issue of the future of the Union, they had, through an ingenious blend of ambition and ambiguity, left the objective of the Convention entirely open-ended. If the Convention wished to do so, it could change the face of the Union, or create the impression that it had changed, or perhaps merely tinker at the edges. But if it was difficult to predict what approach would be adopted, the choice of Giscard d'Estaing as its President meant that the Convention was unlikely to disappear into obscurity.

Less than three months later, the Convention would open with a flourish. The next chapter looks at how the Convention set about its work and the strategy that was adopted to enable it to fulfil its role. At the same time it attempts to separate reality from appearances, and asks what actually took place during the fifteen months between its inception and the final presentation of the results to heads at Thessaloniki in June 2003. In short how did the Convention succeed in delivering its ambitious outcome in the short time available?

3.   The Convention: the gamble pays off

The Convention on the future of Europe was an innovation[11]. When its members and their alternates took their seats in the hemicycle of the European Parliament for the opening session on 28 February 2002, no one knew exactly how the Convention was going to function, how its agenda would be organised, or even what form its final product would take. No one that is except Giscard d'Estaing, the President of the Convention. His address to the Convention's inaugural session[12] gave some clues as to the skill with which he, together with his two deputies, would manage the Convention – its working methods, agenda, and participants – in such a way as to produce a positive outcome.

There was absolutely no guarantee that the Convention was going to be a success. Indeed it was difficult even to decide how success would be defined. The idea of drawing up a single constitutional treaty was ambitious, but was not in itself a definition of success. What of the content? And would the content get through an Intergovernmental Conference? In response to suspicions that he would be tempted to bulldoze his own pre-prepared draft through the Convention, Giscard d'Estaing was deliberately ambiguous on these points. In fact such suspicions were dissipated early on in the process. The Convention required much more subtle handling. Its ability to deliver a product depended above all on a pragmatic approach to its working methods, and flexibility in how it interpreted the mandate which it had been given.

It was however already clear from his opening address that Giscard d'Estaing was ambitious. The Convention was not going to draw up options. It would not run the risk of giving Europe's leaders choices between different approaches. Instead he encouraged the Convention to 'achieve a broad con-sensus on a single proposal' which would 'open the way towards a Constitution for Europe'. The widespread applause from the Convention to this appeal suggested that this approach was widely shared. At the same time, his address gave away little as to what such a proposal might contain.

But whilst the President avoided at this early stage giving any indication of his own preferences on the substance, he already had a clear idea of a strategy for ensuring that the Convention would deliver. His opening address contained several indications as to how he saw the Convention operating: its members should act in a personal capacity and not simply convey instructions from governments, parliaments or others. He reassured the Convention that it would retain overall control of the process; there would be no pre-cooking of the outcome. He outlined three main stages in the work of the Convention: listening, identifying issues, and preparing the Convention's proposal. Finally he emphasised the need to consult widely, in particular by listening to civil society.

This chapter examines these different issues in turn. Together they form a strategy which enabled the Convention to move in only fifteen months from the open-ended mandate of the Laeken declaration to the delivery of a complete Constitution. Specifically it examines the problems faced by the Convention's size and diversity and how these were overcome, in particular through the role of key players in the process. It looks at the importance of a pragmatic approach to the Convention's working methods, and highlights the successful use of time management to control the pace of its work. It also looks at the extent to which the Convention was able to work transparently. In short, it attempts to distinguish appearance from reality, to the extent that these parted company.

*   *   *   *   *   *

One of the most striking differences between the Convention and an Intergovernmental Conference was its composition[13]. An IGC brings together only one group of participants: representatives of the governments which are the signatories to the treaties. The Convention consisted of four very varied groups. Certainly one of them was composed of government representatives (one from each Member State), but they were in a minority compared to the group of national parliament representatives, of whom there were two from each Member State. The two other groups represented the institutions of the Union; one consisting of sixteen members of the European Parliament and the other of two members from the Commission.

An important element in the Laeken declaration on the composition of the Convention was the provision allowing for full participation by both the ten acceding countries and the three candidate countries (Bulgaria, Romania and Turkey). The only difference, which was subsequently (and rightly) ignored, was that they could not block a consensus. Since every member of the Convention also had an alternate, and there were a number of observers, the total number of participants came to well over 200. The combination of size and diversity between the different component groups, as well as the fact that the groups themselves were not homogeneous, meant that the smooth functioning of the Convention was far from guaranteed. But there were several factors which helped to overcome these difficulties and ensure that the Convention delivered a result.

Component groups: starting at different points

The government representatives quickly had to get used to the fact that, unlike in an IGC, they were not in control of the process. They also had to get

used to working in an entirely open environment: the familiarity of the subject matter (for most of them) contrasted with the unfamiliarity of the setting.

For the group of national parliamentarians, both the subject matter and
surroundings were equally unfamiliar. National parliaments have no direct
input into the Union's decision-making process, although they do in some
cases play an important role of scrutiny and oversight of their governments.
As a result, many of their representatives in the Convention initially felt out
of their depth. Most were on a very steep learning curve, operating out of
national capitals, and with no sense of common identity. But this sense of
unfamiliarity confirmed the value of their presence. Most importantly, it
helped the Convention to come up with specific proposals to enhance the
role of national parliaments. More generally it meant that a small cadre of
national parliamentarians would return to their capitals at the end of the
Convention with some familiarity with the Union and its processes. Finally
it helped bolster the argument that the Convention was a more legitimate
and more representative body than an Intergovernmental Conference.

If the subject matter was largely unfamiliar to national parliamentarians, it
was bread and butter to their European counterparts. The sixteen MEPs were
in general steeped in the business of the European Union, and were working
in a familiar culture (and even familiar surroundings) with substantial logis-
tic and intellectual support. The difference in the levels of knowledge between
the component groups, in particular between the national and European parliamentarians, presented some practical difficulties. The proposal by Giscard
d'Estaing to begin the Convention with a 'listening stage' was in part an
attempt to address this difference. The early plenary meetings looked at issues
such as the tasks and objectives of the European Union. Members of the
Convention were asked basic questions such as 'What do you expect of the
European Union?' These discussions, based on background papers drawn up
by the Convention Secretariat, provided opportunities both for those who had
well-developed views to express them, as well as for newcomers to the Union
both to learn and form their own opinions.

The Commission has traditionally been associated with Intergovernmental Conferences (although not formally a negotiating party) and was therefore at ease with its role within the Convention. The experience and
knowledge which it could bring through its two representatives, Michel
Barnier and Antonio Vitorino, both of them supported by a team of advisors
who could in turn draw on the wide-ranging expertise of the Commission
services, was extensive, although the Commission's collective influence on
the Convention's outcome was in the end considerably less than might have
been expected.

Component groups: the differences within

The different characteristics of the component groups was also reflected in
the extent to which they coalesced. Some were more naturally inclined to
organise themselves than others. The European Parliament members, who

were of course well known to each other, met from very early on, and continued to do so throughout the Convention.

The government representatives constituted a more heterogeneous group. Some governments, by nominating persons relatively distant from national power centres, or lacking seniority, appeared to signal from the outset that they were prepared to distance themselves from the Convention's outcome. But as the extent of the ambitions of the Convention became clear, and the argument of legitimacy heightened the pressure to respect the outcome, so attitudes began to change. Most visibly, several governments moved in their Foreign Ministers as Convention members. The appointment in July 2002 by the Spanish government of its representative, Ana Palacio, as Foreign Minister, coupled with her decision to remain in the Convention, encouraged others. So in October, the German Foreign Minister, Joshka Fischer, took his place in the Convention, to be joined soon afterwards by his French counterpart, Dominique de Villepin. The Slovenians and Latvians followed suit. The Convention entered 2003 with no less than eight Foreign Ministers amongst its ranks. The government members met under the chairmanship of their colleague from the Member State holding the Presidency of the Council, and these meetings became increasingly focussed (although more divisive) as the Convention began to tackle the important institutional issues.

The national parliamentarians were equally if not more diverse and took much longer to become organised. Apart from a preliminary meeting to select their two representatives to the Praesidium (see below), it was several months before they met again. This is not surprising given the fact that they were without a natural home or Presidency; in the end the European Parliament acted as a catalyst for further meetings, and even organised joint meetings involving both national and European parliamentarians.

None of the component group meetings had as their aim the coordination of positions; the diversity of views in each of the component groups was simply too great to achieve this. For much of the time their discussions were limited to issues of procedure, or provided the opportunity for a trial run of some of the issues coming up in the next plenary session. Only towards the end, when the main institutional issues were on the agenda, did the component group meetings provide the opportunity for some serious discussions and preparatory bargaining.

The diversity within the component groups was largely a reflection of party political affiliation (as well as, in the case of the government representatives, national differences). The party split introduced a further fragmentation of the Convention in that representatives from the two main political groupings, the Socialists and European People's Party, also met to concert, and in some cases produced joint papers to the Convention. This was particularly the case when the time came to submit amendments to draft articles of the treaty. National differences were highlighted in the meetings of government representatives, although to the surprise of some, divergences of view between the large and small[14] Member States were much more pronounced than the more traditional federalist/sceptic split.

The two Commission representatives had a wide range of natural allies within the Convention. However they were not helped in their task by the constraints placed on them by the college and in particular by the Commission President. The Commission's various written contributions were invariably delayed, and despite much expectation, frequently failed to make a convincing case. Furthermore, the decision of the Commission President to launch in secret a parallel exercise for drafting a completely new treaty turned out to be a major tactical mistake, with the result that the substance of the document was completely overshadowed by the furore over the manner in which it had been produced. Neither Barnier nor Vitorino were fully involved in the exercise, and were embarrassed when the document, curiously code-named 'Penelope', was deliberately leaked.

Giscard d'Estaing, who from the beginning had shown little sympathy for the Commission, from then on treated it with barely concealed disdain. Even its integrationist allies in the Convention were disappointed at the extent to which the Commission had fatally undermined its ability to influence the final outcome.

The multiplicity of divisions and interests amongst the members of the Convention, although giving the appearance of greater legitimacy and inclusiveness than an Intergovernmental Conference, did little to help the efficiency of the process. Yet despite its size and diversity the Convention was able at the end to deliver a result in the form of a single text. There were several reasons for this.

Managing diversity: factors for unity

Firstly, there was a strong sense amongst the Convention's members that they had been selected to take part in a unique process, and one which if successful would go down in the history books. This was a single motivating factor which helped create a genuine sense of 'esprit de corps'. This sense of historical responsibility was not only exploited, but actively encouraged, by Giscard d'Estaing. In his opening speech he told the members of the Convention 'if we succeed, ... you will be able to leave here and return home ... with the feeling of having contributed, modestly but effectively, to writing a new chapter in the history of Europe'.

Secondly, that new chapter was only endorsed at the end by the Convention because there was a second chance. The representatives of the Member States' governments, who had the most direct stake in the outcome, knew that the Convention was not the end of the story. For example the provisions on the institutions, which had been the most contentious part of the draft Constitution, were only agreed because the Member States were secure in the knowledge that they could return to them in the Intergovernmental Conference. Yet the fact that the Convention was not the end of the process cut both ways. Those members of the Convention who might have been

tempted to push for a more ambitious integrationist agenda were also mind-
ful that the Constitution would count for nothing if it were simply to end up
in the Union's archives. So Giscard d'Estaing skilfully used his contacts both
within the Convention, as well as outside with Heads of Government, to
encourage everyone to work towards a consensual approach as the best guarantee of ending up with a product likely to survive the subsequent IGC.

Thirdly, the President's attitude to the different component groups
proved to be an important factor as the Convention entered its final weeks.
He had only sporadic contact with them during the early part of the
Convention when their influence was, in any case, limited. Yet he made little
effort to hide a natural sympathy for the government representatives, whose
sponsors alone would determine whether the Convention's product eventually saw the light of day in the subsequent Intergovernmental Conference.
That changed with the discussions on the institutions. The hostility of many
of the government representatives to some of the President's own proposals
on institutions, together with the reopening of the split between the larger
and smaller Member States, led to him becoming increasingly disillusioned
with the Member States. By the end of the Convention he found to his surprise that he had more allies amongst parliament representatives.
Furthermore, support for his ideas from parliamentarians lent legitimacy
which could be deployed to useful effect.

Finally, the decision to avoid voting in the Convention helped give the
appearance of a greater degree of consensus that was frequently the case.
Voting would have brutally exposed differences of view both within the
component groups and between them. Instead the approach based on seeking consensus tended to encourage the identification of points in common,
naturally allowing a positive result to emerge. In this way the component
groups were never allowed to dominate the proceedings by constituting
caucuses within the Convention. The decision to avoid voting, taken during
the early discussions on the Convention's working methods, was instrumental in securing the success of the Convention.

So the potential difficulties posed by the diversity of the Convention's
composition proved to be surmountable. The very natural human desire to
be part of a success story was key. Equally important in the whole process
were the role of key players within the Convention, the management of its
timetable and its working methods.

The key players

The Praesidium

It is impossible for a body of more than 200 people to draft texts, negotiate
and cut deals. For this reason, the Laeken declaration foresaw the creation
of a 'Praesidium' in order to 'lend impetus' to the Convention, and to 'provide it with an initial working basis'. From the outset it was clear that the
Praesidium had to steer the Convention sufficiently to enable it to operate

effectively, and yet avoid criticism that it was attempting to manipulate the discussions and the outcome.

In order to do this the Praesidium itself had to be considered to be legitimate in the eyes of the Convention. Laeken stated that it should comprise, apart from the President and two Vice-Presidents, three government representatives (from the three Member States holding the Council Presidency during the course of the Convention), two representatives of national parliaments, two European parliamentarians and the two Commission members. Once the nominations to the Convention had been made, the composition of the Praesidium was therefore automatic except in the case of the national and European parliamentarians, where the relevant component group met to select their two representatives. The only addition was the nomination as guest (and subsequently full member) of Alojz Peterele, former Slovenian Prime Minister, following lobbying from the candidate countries that they had no presence in the Praesidium. The resulting composition was equally as diverse as the Convention as a whole, and like the Convention, the level of knowledge varied considerably. But it had the advantage of size; with only thirteen people round the table there was an opportunity for serious discussion, and when necessary, hard bargaining.

The Convention members had been encouraged by Giscard d'Estaing to act in a personal capacity. Whilst the same applied to members of the Praesidium, there was equally an expectation from the Convention as a whole that they would to some extent reflect views expressed within their component groups, or at the very least act as a channel of communication between the groups and the Praesidium. This certainly happened in the case of the two MEPs and Commissioners. The government representatives also proved to be a useful source of information for the Praesidium on the views of their group, particularly once the discussions moved on to institutional issues. But with no common position on most issues, the three government representatives remained free to press their own national case within the Praesidium. Least successful in this regard were the two national parliamentary representatives, who emerged as being out of touch and out of sympathy with many of the views expressed within their component group. As a result they encountered particular difficulties with their peers in the closing few weeks of the Convention.

The President and his two deputies

One of the masterstrokes of the Laeken meeting was its decision on the appointment of the triumvirate of the President and his two deputies. The nomination of Giscard d'Estaing did not initially go uncriticised. Some felt that the choice of a former French President already in his seventies and not known for his ability to rub along with all sections of society sat uneasily with the objective of bringing Europe closer to the citizen. Nevertheless his brilliance of mind and deft handling of the plenary sessions of the Convention were received with a mixture of frustration and admiration, and by the end of the Convention even his sharpest critics were ready to admit that it was thanks largely to him that the Convention had delivered.

The qualities of Giscard d'Estaing were complemented, and his excesses tempered, by his two deputies. Giuliano Amato, former Italian Prime Minister and Professor of constitutional law, known by the sobriquet *il dottore sottile* (the subtle doctor), brought to the Convention a sharp intellect, an encyclopaedic knowledge and a dry sense of humour. He consistently argued his corner with gentle but firm persuasion, and was responsible for securing some important compromise solutions in the Praesidium. Jean-Luc Dehaene, formerly Prime Minister of Belgian, whose bulldozer build disguised considerable tactical finesse, combined a deep-rooted commitment to European integration with a high degree of political realism. Direct and down to earth, he was largely responsible for driving through the initiative to create the post of Foreign Minister. The three men apparently had little in common except a strong commitment to the success of the Convention. Although Giscard d'Estaing and Amato were commuting to and from Brussels, all three quickly learnt to work together and to value each other's qualities, frequently meeting together before Praesidium meetings. When they could agree on a particular approach, they would lead the Praesidium from the front, although their very different styles helped camouflage the extent to which they had adopted a common strategy.

The Secretariat

The Convention was supported by a small secretariat of 15 administrators headed by Sir John Kerr (now Lord Kerr of Kinlochard), former head of the UK diplomatic service. Apart from providing basic secretarial support such as writing minutes and ensuring the logistics, the secretariat drafted all the papers which constituted the basis for the Convention's discussions, as well as, in the later stages, the first drafts of the articles of the new Constitution. Its composition, drawing on staff from the three main EU institutions as well as several from the Member States, ensured that its products remained balanced and objective. Its value depended crucially on the good relationship between the President and the Secretary-General, which developed out of a mutual respect for each other's qualities.

Working Methods: calculated pragmatism

The working methods of the Convention were key to its success. Since the Laeken declaration said virtually nothing about how it was to function, some basic rules were needed. The first draft rules of procedure circulated to the Convention deliberately avoided detailed provisions on decision-making. Many members of the Convention, particularly those from a parliamentary background, not surprisingly wanted to introduce more parliamentary-type procedures, including specifically rules on voting. They saw the first set of draft rules as giving too much influence to both the President and the Praesidium. Giscard d'Estaing was adamant that there should be no voting, believing (almost certainly correctly) that this would severely hamper the chance of getting a single text at the end, and preferring that the Convention should operate by consensus. He called on everyone's good sense to avoid endless discussions on rules when there were more important issues of substance to be dealt with. He got his way since, although some changes were introduced to curb the powers of the Praesidium, voting was avoided and so flexibility maintained. As if to underline the point, the 'rules of procedure' were subsequently to be known as the 'working methods of the Convention'.

These early moves on working methods were vital. They helped ensure that deals struck within the Praesidium were not subsequently consigned to oblivion by the Convention as a whole. The Praesidium was not operating in a vacuum; it was able to take account of the views expressed in the Convention and adapt its texts accordingly. In fact the Praesidium texts were frequently criticised in equal measure by different opponents for different reasons. Hundreds of written amendments to each treaty article were countered by other amendments seeking exactly the opposite changes, thereby cancelling each other out. In this way, the Praesidium was able to deflect criticism from itself, whilst retaining overall control of the process.

Time Management: watching the speed

'I would like to reveal to you, if you allow me, one of the factors which helped us succeed. It is a factor which has not been so obvious, but to which you have all been exposed: the good use of time'. So declared the President in his final speech to the closing session of the Convention.

The management of the Convention's relatively limited time-span was crucial to its success. The frequency of meetings varied little over the entire fifteen month period, with plenary sessions taking place on average once a month. The Praesidium normally met twice a month, once just before each plenary and once in between, although some additional meetings were needed once the Praesidium started drafting articles. If the frequency of the meetings remained largely unchanged, the pace of the work was carefully calibrated. The overall strategy of lengthy discussions during the first few months, accelerating gradually during the period when the working groups were at work, and culminating in a concentrated period of negotiation on the most sensitive issues at the end, paid off. Within the framework of that overall strategy, time was managed equally well for tactical reasons. Discussions were accelerated when they became too contentious, or slowed down when it was important to prevent the Convention from being distracted by unhelpful issues. Sometimes tight deadlines had to be fixed in order to allow written amendments to be adequately taken into account in preparing revised proposals. Finally, the extension of the Convention's

work by one month gave the impression of providing an opportunity for
further negotiation which turned out to be largely illusory.

The listening phase

As already highlighted, Giscard d'Estaing had a clear strategy for the
Convention's work. The first phase, which ran from its opening in February
2002 until the summer break in July, he designated as the listening phase. Its
main purpose, as already mentioned above, was to bring everyone up to the
same level of knowledge.

The relatively slow pace of the listening phase led gradually to a sense of
frustration from more experienced members of the Convention. The
response from the Praesidium was to propose the establishment of working
groups which were designed to examine topics in greater detail than was
possible in the Convention plenary, and to report back with specific recommendations. The establishment of the first six working groups was
agreed at the May plenary session. These were to cover mostly legal and
structural issues – subsidiarity, the place of the Charter of Fundamental
Rights, the EU's legal personality, the role of national parliaments and complementary competences – although following pressure from the socialist
group in the European Parliament channelled through Klaus Hänsch, one of
the EP's representatives in the Praesidium, an additional group covering
economic governance issues was also set up.

There was also pressure from some Convention members to begin work
on a draft treaty, and one specific request that the Commission be invited to
undertake this task. The President informed the plenary in July 2002 that the
Praesidium had rejected this latter suggestion, saying that it would be tantamount to the Convention shirking its responsibilities. Instead he
announced that, following the reports in September from the working
groups on legal personality and the Charter, the Praesidium would at the
late October plenary session make proposals to the Convention for an outline treaty structure. The July plenary also approved the establishment of
four more working groups covering external action, defence, simplification
of legislative procedures and freedom, security and justice. With ten working groups under way, and the promise of a draft treaty outline in the
autumn, Giscard announced that the July plenary brought to a close the 'listening phase'. With the promise of a busy autumn, Convention members
were free to leave for their summer holidays.

The analysis phase

The pre-summer stirrings of impatience meant that the second phase of the
Convention's work, that of 'analysis', needed to begin in earnest. For the rest
of 2002, from September onwards, the ten working groups kept the members of the Convention fully occupied (or at least as occupied as they could
be given that the majority of them had full-time responsibilities elsewhere).

A further group was established in November to look at social policy following strong pressure from some Convention members, and despite an attempt by the President to diffuse this pressure through a debate on social issues in plenary. The conclusions of the working groups, after discussion in the plenary sessions, were to provide the foundations on which the Constitution would be constructed.

This work at the coalface was given a fillip in October when, as promised, Giscard d'Estaing presented his draft outline treaty. This set out a list of articles with, in the case of Part I, a very brief description of the content. Well received by the Convention, its timing proved to be perfect. It gave the necessary encouragement to those who had doubted that the Convention's pace was sufficient to meet the deadline of June 2003. As an official draft endorsed by the Praesidium, it cut across other outline Constitutions or (in some cases) complete texts which some of the more enthusiastic Convention members had been drawing up on their own initiative over the summer. It gave new impetus and significance to the work of the working groups. Finally, but quite accidentally, it pulled the rug from under the feet of the Commission when its now infamous 'Penelope' text was circulated in December.

The drafting phase

The actual drafting of the treaty itself did not start until early 2003. It began slowly, partly because the Praesidium itself became quickly bogged down in the early treaty articles, particularly those defining and setting out the different types of competences. These proved to be some of the most difficult to settle, and went through some substantial changes before the overall text of the Constitution was agreed. The pace of the drafting period was carefully controlled. Drafts were circulated to the Convention, following which time was allowed for the submission of amendments, and for summaries of these amendments to be prepared and distributed in advance of the next plenary session. Given the huge number of amendments received (the institutions' articles alone were the subject of more than 650 proposed amendments), the plenary debates (in which speaking time was strictly limited) were vital in allowing the Praesidium to identify those points which were actually a priority for Convention members.

Key to the timing of this final phase of the Convention's work was the delay in submitting the most sensitive articles on the institutions. Although the Convention had held one plenary debate on institutional issues in January 2003, the President had resisted pressure to establish working groups on institutional issues. Instead he personally drew up the first draft of the institutional articles which were submitted to the Praesidium on 22 April. After a long Praesidium meeting, and some changes of substance to the text, a revised draft was presented to the plenary on 24 April. This left only seven weeks for the Convention to reach agreement on the most problematic area of the Constitution, and one on which there had been virtually

no real preparatory work. It looked at times as though Giscard d'Estaing
was pushing his luck. In the end brinkmanship paid off.

When the President presented the outcome of the Convention's work to
the European Council meeting in Thessaloniki on 19 June 2003 he secured
their agreement to the continuation of the Convention's mandate until the
middle of July, although this extension was restricted to purely technical
work on drafting Part III of the Constitution (the part covering the Union's
policies). The extension had already been anticipated by the Convention. It
had almost certainly helped secure an agreement on the basic text in
advance of Thessaloniki, not least because of expectations by a number of
Convention members that the extra few weeks would provide the opportunity for some important changes to Part III (notably the extension of
Qualified Majority Voting to new policy areas) which would help offset
some of the less attractive institutional provisions which they had grudg-
ingly accepted. In the event, only a limited number of changes were made
during these last few weeks. The tactic of securing an extension therefore
helped in getting an agreement in June and provided the opportunity for
some useful tidying up of the text, but the constraints imposed by the
Thessaloniki European Council ensured that there was little chance of
introducing further substantial changes.

The Convention and public opinion: the fabrication of interest

One of most vaunted aspects of the Convention was its capacity to reach
out, stimulate and reflect public opinion. Here was a body which unlike
Intergovernmental Conferences would consult widely and, through the participation of parliamentarians, would be able to take on board the aspirations and concerns of the Union's 450 million citizens.

Giscard d'Estaing recognised immediately the importance of being seen
to consult. In his inaugural speech he insisted that 'Everyone must have the
opportunity to be heard, which of course presupposes effective, decen-
tralised organisation, making possible a dialogue with no ideological or par-
tisan barriers. Similarly, there is a desire for interactive surveys, enabling
civil society to react to some of our future proposals'.

The translation of these aspirations into reality was on the face of it
impressive. Apart from the Convention's own website, a separate site
known as the 'Forum' enabled non-governmental and other organisations to
express their views on the work and objectives of the Convention. In
addition, a special plenary session took place in June 2002 dedicated to civil
society. The purpose was to provide the opportunity for a direct dialogue
between the Convention and non-governmental organisations. A similar
exercise was conducted with young people through the organisation of a
'Youth Convention' which took place in July 2002, and which reported back
to the Convention proper. At the same time, national government and parliamentary representatives were encouraged to stimulate debates at the

national level. The President himself even participated in a 'webchat'. The people were being consulted.

It is difficult to demonstrate whether the various initiatives undertaken to consult more widely actually affected the final outcome. Many of the demands from non-governmental organisations were for purely declaratory language, with few of them wishing to engage in a substantive debate on policy. The dialogue with civil society was criticised for being restricted to those within the EU circuit ('Brussels talking to Brussels'), and even Giscard d'Estaing was disappointed that the Youth Convention, which had been his personal initiative, came up with rather unimaginative and bureaucratic proposals ('Eurocrats in short trousers'). Perhaps more serious was the charge that the debates at the national level never fulfilled their potential for sensitising the wider public within the Member States to the Convention and the challenges which it was trying to address.

Transparency: a selective strategy

A policy of communication went hand in hand with transparency. One of the purposes of establishing a Convention was precisely to break away from the closed-door practices of intergovernmental conferences. So all the Convention plenary sessions were open to the public and retransmitted via webcam, and all Convention documents were published on a dedicated Convention website. The public could no longer claim that it was uninformed.

However the Convention could only work effectively if there were some limits to transparency. Members of the Praesidium in particular had to be able to express themselves freely at Praesidium meetings. During the discussions on the rules of procedure, there were a number of attempts to oblige the Praesidium to operate more or less in the open. These came to nothing and the requirement for confidentiality was never subsequently challenged from within the Convention. A complaint to the European Ombudsman by the European Citizen Action Service (ECAS) about the lack of openness in the Convention, and the Praesidium in particular, was rejected. The sole concession was that short summary records of the outcome of Praesidium meetings were posted on the website, but to avoid prejudicing the whole process, this was only done once the Convention was over.

In general the Convention probably succeeded through a judicious mix of transparency and confidentiality. Confidentiality was essential if the Praesidium was to be free to negotiate and draft texts, and yet subsequently take collective responsibility for them before the Convention as a whole. Transparency was an inseparable part of the Convention process. It provided the opportunity for open debate and a much wider consultation than was the case in the past. That in turn gave the final product a legitimacy which it was difficult for Member States to ignore when they eventually sat down in the subsequent IGC. Who would dare overturn a document on which the public had been so widely consulted?

However some questioned the legitimacy of the Convention (although interestingly they did so in private only). They argued that the composition of the Convention was largely indiscriminate, and that its legitimacy was therefore spurious. For them, only an IGC, composed of representatives of democratically elected governments of the Member States, had the proper authority to decide to alter commitments binding on sovereign nation states. Of course the Convention was to be followed by an IGC, but as later chapters will show, political pressure left governments with surprisingly little scope to reshape the Convention's product.

The result: consensus achieved but never defined

Two fundamental issues had to be addressed in order for the Convention to reach a successful outcome. Firstly, a choice had to be made on the shape of the final product; was there to be a composite document, with different options to be presented to governments, or would the Convention aim for a single treaty text? Secondly, and linked to the first point, how would the Convention decide on the outcome? If voting was excluded, the product would need to have the support of a broad consensus. At first sight, the early choice of Giscard d'Estaing, which was widely supported, to deliver a single text without options, sat uneasily with the requirement for consensus. How therefore did the Convention reach agreement by consensus on a single text in the form of a Constitution?

The outcome: what form?

It quickly became clear that there would be little if any opposition to the suggestion that the end result of the Convention's work should be a Constitution. This was confirmed when the President's outline text received such widespread support from the Convention in October 2002. One of the main reasons for this was that a Constitution meant different things to different people. For some, a Constitution would draw a line in the sand: the Union's powers would be fixed once and for all. For others, a Constitution would provide a new framework for a new Union, opening up the possibility of it evolving into a structure more closely resembling a federal state.

If there were any differences of view during those early few months of the Convention, they were not so much about the nature of its final product, but rather about its scope. When the Praesidium began to reflect on the possibility of the Convention drawing up a Constitution, its members had for the most part in mind a text setting out some of the basic objectives, principles, powers and institutions of the Union (i.e. what eventually became Part I of the Constitution), but leaving to one side the detailed provisions governing the Union's policies. The main reason for this was that it was simply not considered feasible within the time available. Giscard d'Estaing however was from the very beginning more ambitious. He wanted the Convention to produce a complete text, partly because he considered that the Convention would not otherwise have properly fulfilled its mandate, and partly because he wanted a text which the subsequent Intergovernmental Conference would not be able to circumvent on the grounds that it was incomplete.

His approach was widely, and increasingly, shared by the Convention. The sense of shared participation in an historical task, nurtured by Giscard himself, and the *esprit de corps* which had built up, manifested itself in a commitment to achieving an ambitious result. This endured throughout the life of the Convention, even when fundamental differences arose over specific issues.

The outcome: how to get there?

The President's case for avoiding voting in the Convention rested largely on the imbalance between the different component groups. He was probably concerned in particular that the government representatives, being overall in a minority, could be outvoted (although by the time the Convention came to discuss institutions he may well have regretted this). Instead of voting, the Convention was to decide by consensus, although nowhere was this defined. When Jean-Luc Dehaene was asked once what it meant, he replied that once you try to define what a consensus is, you can be sure you will never reach one.

In practice, it was always Giscard d'Estaing himself, in drawing the conclusions at the end of each plenary session, who decided whether or not consensus had been reached. The advantage of such an approach was that the outcome of the Convention's discussions on any specific issue was never finally closed. All issues became part of an overall package which was adjusted to take into account different views until the very last day of the Convention. Consensus on one point was sufficiently fluid to allow for modifications if needed in the light of consensus on another point, until the President himself judged that the overall text represented a sufficient balance of interests. Avoiding voting helped bridge significant differences on some issues, leading to a more balanced result which was more likely to stand up to the subsequent Intergovernmental Conference. So Giscard d'Estaing could conclude at the end that an overall consensus existed, and that the Convention had therefore completed its work.

*   *   *   *   *

The success or failure of the Convention depended very much on process. Giscard d'Estaing above all understood how to manage a large and disparate group, and specifically how to make effective use of the timetable which he had been given. Whilst he had his own views, in some cases strongly-held, on many issues, in most cases he wore these lightly, and preferred instead to use his ability to manage the process to ensure that the Convention ended up at least not too far from where he wished. The result was, he said at the Convention's close, not perfect, but more than could have been hoped for.

Process led to an outcome, but it did not guarantee a sensible outcome. What were the Convention's clear successes? Where did it attempt to address issues but fall short of its ambitions? And where did it fail, either in coming up with a sensible outcome, or in delivering a result which stood up to the subsequent Intergovernmental Conference? These are the subjects of the next three chapters.

4.   The fundamentals of the Constitution: a success story

On 13 June 2003 the Convention was brought to a close with champagne and a rendering of Beethoven's 'Ode to Joy'. Even the few ardently sceptical members of the Convention present that day in the hemicycle of the European Parliament found it difficult to deny that the delivery of a complete draft treaty establishing a Constitution for Europe represented a considerable achievement. Few would have thought it possible when the Convention began its work fifteen months earlier. In contrast to the sharp criticism directed by the press at the Nice Treaty, the Constitution was in general fêted as marking an important step in the development of the European Union. Only the most churlish and hard-bitten commentators sought to diminish the Convention's achievements.

On the whole, the governments also held back on their criticisms. When Giscard d'Estaing presented the text of the Constitution to Europe's leaders at their meeting in Thessaloniki the following week, it was received with broad acclaim. There were few dissenting comments. The European Council collectively agreed that the Constitution marked an historic step in the direction of furthering the objectives of European integration and that it was a good basis for the Intergovernmental Conference. In fact in many ways it proved to be more than a good basis, since most of the text went unchallenged by the Intergovernmental Conference. Indeed the subsequent focus on a few key problematic issues frequently led governments and commentators alike to lose sight of the big picture. The Convention text, in its overall construction, as well as for a very large part of its content, survived intact. As a result, when finally adopted in June 2004, the Constitution was remarkably similar to the product presented to Europe's leaders almost exactly a year previously to the day.

The purpose of this chapter is to identify and analyse the successes of the Convention. That means providing an objective assessment of those parts of the Constitution which offer solutions to the problems which the Convention was called upon to address. But since politics is about real life, it also has to take into account the extent to which these solutions stood the test in the subsequent Intergovernmental Conference. Much of the success of the Convention concerns the fundamentals. Fundamentals are principally about clarifying the relationship between the Union and the Member States, and the structure of the Union itself. They include the decision to reorganise completely the existing treaties, to institute a single 'Union' in place of, rather than alongside, the existing European Community, to define in simple terms the powers of the Union, to simplify its instruments and procedures, to improve the efficiency and legitimacy of its decision-making, and last but not least, to give the end product the title of 'Constitution'.

Subsequent chapters will look at the policies of the Union, where the results of the Convention were more mixed, and at the Union's institutions, where the Convention largely missed the opportunity to provide acceptable and long-lasting solutions.

Giving Europe a 'Constitution': an exercise in constructive ambiguity

One of the most surprising aspects of the Convention was the ease with which it accepted the notion that its product should be classified as a Constitution. Those who initially had hesitations eventually went with the flow; UK Foreign Secretary Jack Straw simultaneously endorsed and deflated the idea by stating that even golf clubs have constitutions. Yet the very label 'Constitution' introduces a fundamental ambiguity over the nature of the exercise. There is a paradox in that the notion of a Constitution, which is normally considered as axiomatic, here is open to different interpretations. For some it signifies the relaunch of a new integrationist agenda, for others it means that the limits to integration have been reached.

This ambiguity is encapsulated in the full title, which reads: 'Treaty establishing a Constitution for Europe'. In the published version of the Convention text, even the typography becomes a political tool, since the title is printed with the first three words in small black lettering, whilst the reference to 'Constitution for Europe' is set out in large bold coloured typescript.

Yet despite the ambiguity, the fact that the Convention chose to use the title of 'Constitution' cannot be dismissed as insignificant. The choice of name is important, particularly when combined with the decision to introduce symbols such as the flag, anthem and motto. It is never easy to argue that something is different from its label: when is a Constitution not a Constitution?

In addition, the decision to divide the text into separate parts strengthens the argument that the product is constitutional in nature. The draft outline Constitution presented by Giscard d'Estaing in October 2002 foresaw the entire text being divided into three parts, with the first part containing the more important provisions relating to the Union's objectives, powers, institutions, instruments and procedures. The second part would contain the detailed provisions on policies, and the third part the usual final provisions. This structure was unchallenged, and so served as the basis for the Convention's work. The only subsequent change was that, with the introduction of the Charter of Fundamental Rights as Part II of the Constitution, the final version is divided into four parts rather than three, with policies and final provisions becoming Parts III and IV respectively.

The aim of this approach was to respond to the multiple calls for an understandable and accessible text. So Part I sets out in simple terms what the Union does and how. As such it contains a number of basic elements which can be considered constitutional in nature, whilst the remainder of the treaty is for practitioners, experts or the simply curious. This approach drew inspiration in part from the work undertaken by the European University Institute, which had demonstrated that it was perfectly possible to separate out the 'dignified' elements from even the existing treaties and present them in a single coherent text.

The claim of Giscard d'Estaing that the Constitution should be pocket-sized was vindicated when a small format version of Parts I and II of the Constitution was published soon after the Thessaloniki European Council. With the addition of Parts III and IV the text became much more voluminous, and less accessible. However many of the criticisms of the length of the text are ill founded. The most substantial part of the Constitution is that on the Union's policies (Part III). National constitutions do not require an enumeration of the policy areas falling within their ambit since by definition nation states are sovereign in all areas. The Union operates on the principle of powers attributed to it by the Member States. The precise nature and scope of these powers are essential for clarity in the functioning of the Union. Those who make unhelpful comparisons between the length and limpidity of the Union's Constitution and national constitutions are forgetting this basic principle. It is not a strong argument against the use of the term 'Constitution'.

Yet for reasons set out in an earlier chapter, a convincing case can be advanced that the existing treaties are at least partly 'constitutional' in nature. So what is the legal effect of using the title 'Constitution' for the first time?[15] The formal answer is not a lot. Fundamentally, the nature of the Union is unchanged, and in several important aspects remains different from a nation state. The Union for example is not sovereign but can only act in accordance with powers attributed to it under the treaties by the Member States. More importantly, whatever the title, the Constitution remains a treaty between independent nation states ('High Contracting Parties').

Some members of the Convention, led by Vice-President Amato, sought to exploit the use of the term 'Constitution' in the title to try to introduce more far-reaching 'constitutional-type' provisions (for example the introduction of majority voting for future treaty change). Such proposals, which would have transformed the European Union into a very different body from that which exists today, received little political support. Amato's ideas constituted an audacious attempt to use the title to change the substance. But they got short shrift, and only served to highlight the ambiguity of the term 'Constitution'.

Yet the very ambiguity of the title may help in ratification. Member States are free to interpret the term as they choose. The ambiguity may even play a role in debates within individual Member States. Even if the title 'Constitution' may be unpalatable to some, it may yet help to convince them that the Union has reached its final destination.

What is the Union? – the search for an honest definition

Defining the European Union has for the past fifty years been the search for the holy grail for practitioners and academics alike. How to encapsulate something unique, complex, dynamic and meaning different things to different people? The Union has never fitted neatly into one of the many categories of constitutional law (federal, confederal etc). For those wanting to duck the issue, the Union is simply an unidentified constitutional object. But ducking issues was not the Convention's style.

The dynamic nature of the Union (or Community as it was originally) is encapsulated in the opening words of the Treaty of Rome: 'determined to lay the foundations of an ever closer union among the peoples of Europe'. This provision in the preamble has remained intact ever since. The iterative nature of the Community has however been a sensitive issue. Just how sensitive becomes clear with the adoption in 1986 of the Single European Act. Article 1 of the SEA states (in the English version): 'The European Communities and European political cooperation shall have as their objective to contribute together to making concrete progress towards European unity'. In the French version the last two words are: 'l'Union européenne'. A quick glance across the different language versions reveals not only a range of expressions, but even a judicious use of capital letters and lower case, in each case deliberately intended to address specific national sensitivities!

The Praesidium recommended that since the Constitution was designed to last for many years, the term 'ever-closer union' was no longer appropriate. Despite some calls for its reinsertion, it disappears from view for the first time since 1957.

The first attempt by Giscard d'Estaing at a definition was included in the outline Constitution of October 2002 which was endorsed by the Praesidium. The EU was 'A Union of European States which, while retaining their national identities, closely coordinate their policies at the European level, and administer certain competences on a federal basis'. This is not far removed from Jacques Delors' definition of the Union as a federation of nation states. Except that for Giscard d'Estaing the nation states come first and the federation second. The order is not without significance.

The first draft of article 1, when presented to the Convention at the end of January 2003, was very similar to that in the outline, except that it began with the phrase 'Reflecting the will of the peoples and the States of Europe to build a common future....'. The only substantive change introduced subsequently was the removal of the word 'federal'. This was anathema to the UK, and following direct intervention by Prime Minister Blair at a meeting with Giscard d'Estaing in London on 19 May 2003, was replaced by the phrase 'in the Community way' (subsequently modified in the IGC to read 'on a Community basis'). Apart from sounding odd, the Convention's decision that the European Community would be entirely subsumed within the Union means that the phrase has little meaning. Perhaps that is part of its charm. The final text is a bold if imperfect attempt to define the undefinable:

'Reflecting the will of the citizens and States of Europe to build a common future, this Constitution establishes the European Union, on which the Member States confer competences to attain objectives they have in common. The Union shall coordinate the policies by which the Member States aim to achieve these objectives, and shall exercise on a Community basis the competences they confer on it.'

But the very fact that for the first time a definition exists is important. Firstly, it serves to stabilise the identity of the Union, and in doing so, implicitly puts a brake on any significant moves towards further integration, at least for the foreseeable future. The removal of the phrase 'ever closer Union' emphasises this point even more strongly. For several Member States the interpretation that the Union has more or less reached its destination is an important argument in support of the Constitution. It is a point which was eventually reflected in the conclusions of the European Council in June 2004 following the adoption of the Constitution: '(The Constitution) completes the process which began when the Treaty of Rome established the basic framework for European integration'[16].

Secondly, the definition in the Constitution implicitly accepts that the Union will continue to function according to two methods operating in parallel. The reference to coordination recognises that there are some policies, which although now firmly embedded in the treaties, nevertheless have their own particular procedures and are rooted in a more intergovernmental approach. The 'Community based' policies on the other hand are those which have traditionally been the core of integration, subject to a range of specific provisions such as that which confers sole right of initiative on the Commission.

This dual approach has its origins in a system which had existed for many years, but which was only formalised for the first time in the Treaty on European Union agreed in Maastricht in 1992 which adopted the so-called 'pillar' approach. The Maastricht Treaty isolated the more traditional 'Community' policies in a first 'pillar', separating them from the policies and procedures for the Common Foreign and Security Policy (CFSP) and Justice and Home Affairs (JHA) which were covered in two separate 'pillars'. Although the three pillars were distinct, they all fell within the overall framework of the new (at that time) organisation known as the European Union, and shared a number of common provisions such as a single institutional framework. The pillar separation was necessary because a number of Member States would only accept the inclusion of CFSP and JHA if they could remain entirely 'uncontaminated' by the Community method. Other more integrationally minded Member States considered that this approach would in due course lead to an eventual consolidation of all policy areas under the 'Community method'. The Constitution is more realistic.

Thirdly, the opening reference in the Constitution to the will of the citizens and states of Europe makes explicit for the first time the principle of dual legitimacy of the Union: the fact that the Union derives its authority from both the Member States and the peoples. The inclusion of this principle is important in helping to justify some of the more specific provisions of the

Constitution, in particular the new definition of qualified majority voting (see chapter 6), and the generalisation of the 'legislative procedure' (previously known as co-decision) under which the Council and Parliament have an equal say in the adoption of EU legislation. Dual legitimacy was also used by some in the Convention to support the case for balance between the main institutions. So the creation of the post of permanent President of the European Council was justified on the grounds that it was an appropriate reflection of that part of the Union's legitimacy which is derived from the Member States.

The definition of the European Union drawn up by the Convention required considerable conceptual thought, and the final text owes much to Giscard d'Estaing himself. Whilst not perfect, it attempts for the first time to impose some sense of order. Its basic concept of a Union based on the dual legitimacy of states and citizens will no doubt have consequences for the future, not least through the establishment of jurisprudence. In particular it is likely to act as a brake on those who wish to diminish the role of the Member States and take the Union in a much more overtly federalist direction.

The Union's powers: what are they and how are they attributed?

One of the more important issues highlighted in the Laeken declaration is that of the 'competences' (or 'powers') of the European Union. Indeed there is an entire section with the leading title: 'A better division and definition of competence in the European Union'. At the moment it is almost impossible for the non-expert to deduce from the treaties what powers have been attributed to the Union, and to what extent. There are several reasons for this. Firstly there is currently no list of competences; they rather lie hidden within the detailed policy provisions of the existing treaties. Secondly, the extent of competence in a given area is in part determined by how far the Union has chosen to exercise through legislation the potential powers attributed to it. Thirdly, the European Court of Justice has established an impressive corpus of jurisprudence, which impacts directly on the extent of the Union's powers.

The results of the Convention's deliberations take the form of the affirmation of several basic principles underpinning the Union's powers, indicative lists of these powers separated by category, and the establishment of a mechanism providing for political oversight of the application of the principle of subsidiarity.

As mentioned above, the Union operates on the basis of powers attributed to it by the Member States. In the Constitution the principle of attribution is made explicit for the first time[17]. Whilst this might seem obvious, such a reference is highly symbolic. In doing so, the Constitution acknowledges the primacy of the Member State in the genesis of the Union: in the beginning was the nation. The Constitution also reaffirms the twin principles of subsidiarity and proportionality in the exercise of the Union's powers. Cherished by the sceptics, they are designed to ensure that the Union only acts when it can offer real 'added value' at the European level, and that when it does so, the extent of the action is limited to that which is absolutely necessary to fulfil the stated objectives.

The principles of subsidiarity and proportionality are not only enshrined in the Constitution, but are given extra force through the introduction of an additional legal instrument attached to the Constitution in the form of a protocol. This protocol requires the Commission to justify its legislative proposals against both principles, and obliges it to reconsider any proposal to which a third of national parliaments have raised objections on the grounds that it does not respect the principle of subisidiarity. This procedure, known colloquially in the Convention as the 'yellow card', was one of the more significant results of the working group on the role of national parliaments chaired by British parliamentarian Gisela Stuart. Its most direct benefit will be to improve national parliamentary scrutiny of legislative proposals, and in doing so should help narrow the divide between national legislatures and the Brussels policy-making process.

The Convention also established lists of the Union's competences sorted according to three main categories[18]. These categories, whilst in common use by practitioners and academics, have never before been formalised in treaty form. The first category concerns areas (such as trade policy) in which the Union has 'exclusive competence'. This means that the Union alone has the power to act in these fields. So for example, the Member States may not enter into trade agreements with third countries (this has been the case since the creation of the European Community). The second category, which includes the majority of policy areas (e.g. internal market, agriculture, transport etc), is known as 'shared competence'. Here the Member States may exercise competence, but only to the extent that it has not been exercised by the Union. The final category concerns areas of supporting, coordinating or complementary action. Here the Member States continue to have the power to act, yet the Union also has the possibility of parallel action, although within clear limits. For example, harmonisation of Member States' laws or regulations in these areas is explicitly excluded. Examples are health, education and culture.

The Constitution recognises that there are two separate areas: the coordination of economic and employment policies and the Common Foreign and Security Policy, which function according to rather specific arrangements and which therefore fall outside the three main categories.

Taken together these provisions constitute a significant advance on the existing treaties. For the first time the respective responsibilities of the Union and its Member States and the principles which underlie them are clearly set out in a basic text. This facilitates understanding and brings greater legal certainty. The frequent attempts (usually by the Commission) to push forward the boundaries of Union competence, often on the grounds of a spurious hierarchy of 'Community' over 'national' legitimacy, will no longer be possible. The 'grey zone' of uncertainty which was a constant source of friction between the Union and its Member States has been considerably reduced.

Standardising the Union: the pillars are toppled

As already described above, the Constitution's definition of the Union clearly supposes that it will continue to act according to different sets of procedures depending on the policy area. Yet the Convention was equally clear that the formal separation into three 'pillars' had no place in the Constitution. This meant that there is no longer any juxtaposition in the text between blocs of provisions each operating in legally watertight compartments. Instead there is a single consolidated text divided only by subject matter. Removal of the pillars entailed a harmonisation of legal instruments and procedures across the full range of Union policies, particularly evident in the area of Justice and Home Affairs. Furthermore it ended the separate legal personality of the European Community: from now on there would only be one legally recognised organisation (the 'European Union') with a single legal personality[19], thereby simplifying relations with third countries and other international organisations. All these moves, although apparently arcane, help to clarify and simplify the functioning of the Constitution.

Despite this, total standardisation proved beyond the grasp of the Convention. For reasons which were both practical and political, the Union would not operate completely on the basis of a single method. As the definition of the Union in article 1 recognised, there was still more than one approach. The pillars had been toppled, but their shadows remained.

It is quite natural that, given the vast range of subjects now covered by the treaties, a 'one size fits all' approach makes little sense. The same procedures and instruments cannot be applied neatly to such diverse policies as foreign policy, police cooperation, and the preservation of marine biological resources. This differentiation of approach according to subject matter is in some cases functional, based on the simple recognition that different policies call for different approaches. In other cases it is political, when there is particular sensitivity in a given area. Under the Common Foreign and Security Policy, for example, important differences remain: Member States insist on retaining the right of initiative alongside that of the Commission (unlike in 'Community' policy areas where the Commission enjoys sole right of initiative), Qualified Majority Voting remains the exception rather than the rule, and there are specific provisions governing the respective roles of the European Parliament and the Court of Justice.

The Convention, whilst recognising in its definition of the Union and description of competences that the Union would continue to function in different ways, made every effort to create a single legal framework and standardise the instruments and procedures which apply to the wide range of policy areas. It probably went as far as it could within the current practical and political constraints.

Simplification of decision-making instruments

Over the years the Union has accumulated a large number of different procedures and instruments through which it carries out its business. This complex web contributes to making the workings of the Union almost impenetrable to outsiders. The Convention saw simplification as one of its key objectives, and set up a working group on the issue under the chairmanship of Amato, although its remit covered not just the simplification of the Union's instruments and procedures, but also the strengthening of democratic legitimacy (the fact that the two concepts sometimes sit uneasily together went largely unremarked). The recommendations of the working group were ambitious, and were fully endorsed by the Convention. They included a reduction in the number of legal instruments from 15 to 6. There would be four types of binding acts: laws and framework laws (both legislative instruments), decisions and regulations. In addition there would be two types of non-binding acts: recommendations and opinions. Under legislative acts, a new hierarchy would be established, with delegated acts under the responsibility of the Commission and monitored by the legislator, and below that implementing acts of the Commission. Finally, the co-decision procedure (by which the Council and the European Parliament act as co-legislators) was to be renamed the legislative procedure, and the co-operation procedure would be abolished[20].

Whilst there was perhaps a tendency for the Convention to inflate its own success in this area by overplaying the real complexity of the current system, there can be little doubt that the reduction in the number of legal instruments, as well as the change of name in most cases, helps the legislator, the practitioner and the judge alike. Clearer legal instruments make for better and more understandable policy implementation. Combined with the clarification of the division of competences, the simplification of instruments, particularly in its establishment of a clear hierarchy, helps provide a better articulation between the action of the Union and that of the Member States.

Amato was fond of saying that there is nothing more complicated than simplification. In the past the treaties had demonstrated that there is nothing simpler than making things complicated. In this area at least, the Constitution had made real progress.

The Charter of Fundamental Rights: cautious evolution

The original outline treaty of Giscard d'Estaing referred to the possibility of including the Charter of Fundamental Rights in the Constitution, but left it to the working group to confirm whether this should happen, and if so, how. The Charter had been drafted by an earlier Convention and solemnly proclaimed at the Nice European Council. Its inclusion in the Constitution would be significant in that it would give the text legal force for the first time.

The working group recommended incorporating fully the text of the Charter into the Constitution. In so doing, the group stressed that its incorporation would add no new competences to the Union, and that the substance of the Charter (with the exception of a few technical amendments) would not be altered. It also underlined that the provisions of the Charter concerned only the Union's institutions and the Member States when they are implementing Union law.

The incorporation of the Charter was broadly endorsed by the Convention, and most Member State governments considered it quite natural that a Constitution should include provisions on basic rights. However the UK was never totally happy with the assurances given that the Charter could not be interpreted to cover national legislation. It continued to ask for more secure guarantees well into the IGC, as described in chapter 8.

The Preamble: literature revered

Treaties and constitutions normally begin with a preamble; two good reasons not to make an exception in this case. Nothing stirred the Praesidium into action more than the idea of drafting a preamble. Literary talents were rediscovered. Several versions reached the table of the Praesidium, but it was quickly clear that the President's text was the version which would be submitted to the Convention. When it emerged from the Intergovernmental Conference, the preamble was remarkably unscathed.

Comments on the text focussed largely on the absence of a reference to God or to the Christian heritage of Europe. Several government representatives criticised the text as being too focused on the classical roots of European culture and the enlightenment, as well as being too complacent (there was virtually no reference to the darker side of Europe's history). Intense lobbying from the Vatican and other religious denominations made no difference; the text endorsed by the Convention was virtually unchanged. Nevertheless the same criticisms persisted in the Intergovernmental Conference.

Some in the IGC dared to suggest that the preamble should be scrapped entirely. Many saw in their own language versions a text which was self-conscious, subjective and frankly in many cases unreadable, begging the question as to whether the problem was one of translation from the French. It was not.

Yet the mood in the IGC was one of resignation, coupled with a curious reverence for the origin of a text which bore so clearly the marks of its author. So, very few changes were made, and those who sought a reference to Europe's Christian heritage were to be disappointed. In the end the most important change resulted from the decision by the IGC to sacrifice the quotation from Thucydides which Giscard d'Estaing himself had chosen to open the preamble. Only the Greek and Cypriot delegations mourned its passing. Everyone else considered it pretentious, inaccurately translated, and inappropriate (not least given Thucydides' profoundly undemocratic credentials). Extraordinarily, the Presidency was at one point tempted, at the request of the Greeks and the Cypriots, to replace it with an alternative quote from Thucydides. Someone somewhere had missed the point.

Continuing a process: extending QMV and co-decision

A continuing theme of successive Intergovernmental Conferences has been the increase in the number of areas to which Qualified Majority Voting (QMV) applies. It is a direct response to calls for more effective decision-making in a steadily enlarging Union, and reflects an increasing readiness by Member States to accept the possibility of being outvoted in a larger number of policy areas. In practice, the Council tries as far as possible to avoid voting, preferring to reach compromises which are acceptable to all. The importance of QMV is therefore less about forcing Member States to accept something they don't like, but more about creating a dynamic for compromise: QMV obliges Member States to engage in the negotiating process.

The Convention considered that enlarging the scope of QMV was vital if the Union were to continue to deliver policies effectively. Equally, it saw the extension of co-decision (renamed as the 'legislative procedure' in the Constitution) as key to reinforcing legitimacy. The result was twofold: the Convention introduced over 50 new cases where QMV is applied, of which over 40 are also subject to the legislative procedure – a substantial advance for the Union. It also created a lighter procedure for introducing QMV in the future, although still only by unanimity.

The extension of QMV went too far for the Intergovernmental Conference, which reintroduced unanimity in several key areas, notably tax, own resources[21] (the Union's system for raising finance) and the multiannual financial framework[22]. Despite these reversals (which for several Member States - in particular the UK - were essential for the Constitution to be acceptable), this is an area in which the Convention was almost certainly able to deliver more than a classical IGC.

Enhanced Cooperation[23]

The existing treaties contain a number of separate provisions on enhanced cooperation to take account of the different arrangements in each of the three 'pillars'. However the basic principles are the same: enhanced cooperation is intended to offer the possibility for a smaller group of Member States to take forward cooperation amongst themselves in order to further the objectives of the Union as a whole. These provisions have never been used. In the Convention, several Member States, in particular France and Germany, concerned at the risk of policy sclerosis in a much enlarged Union, attached particular importance to maintaining and strengthening these provisions.

As a result, the Constitution consolidates the current arrangements on enhanced cooperation. It requires a minimum of a third of all Member States to launch enhanced cooperation, extends its coverage to include security and defence issues for the first time, and allows the participating Member States to decide that Qualified Majority Voting should apply, even if the treaty base foresees decisions by unanimity. Whilst much play has been made in general terms of the importance of enhanced cooperation for the future successful development of the Union, there have been few serious suggestions as to what policy areas such cooperation might cover. It is therefore unclear whether the Constitution will provide a new basis for stimulating enhanced cooperation, or whether the new articles will remain dormant like their predecessors. This issue is addressed in the final chapter.

* * * * * *

The basic aims of the Convention come under three broad headings. Firstly, a more formalistic aspect which consists of reorganising and simplifying the existing treaties which over time have become increasingly unreadable as the Union has expanded and its tasks widened. Secondly, addressing the policies of the Union; and thirdly, improving the functioning of the institutions and the relations between them.

From the description set out above, it is clear that the Convention was successful in delivering the first of these, even if this is sometimes at the cost of some ambiguity of interpretation.

The Constitution is a complete rewrite of the basic texts in a form which is more readable, coherent and 'user-friendly'. This is particularly the case with Part I which sets out the basic elements of the Constitution. This is a substantial part of the Convention's work which should not be under-estimated. It is also an aspect which earlier Intergovernmental Conferences had attempted to address, but without success. Why was the Convention able to deliver when so many IGCs had failed?

Firstly, many of these issues have simply been regarded by the Member States as too big to handle. Any attempts to tackle some of the fundamentals invariably ran up against major political difficulties, and IGCs simply backed off. It was easier to live with the status quo. In short, the Member States have not had sufficient political will or interest to address these issues head on.

Secondly, IGCs have traditionally been concerned with updating existing treaties. The burden of proof has always fallen on those who wish to introduce changes – how do they improve the current system? By contrast, the Convention was starting from scratch; the onus fell on those who wished to be less ambitious to say why.

Thirdly, Intergovernmental Conferences had less time to address these issues. The use of the expertise of working groups in the Convention was key to cutting through, for example, much of the deadwood of outdated instruments and procedures. Equally these groups had the time to reflect on and prepare viable alternative recommendations. So time and resources played a role.

The next two chapters look at the other two areas of the Convention's work: those which touch upon the substance. In the area of the Union's policies, the changes introduced were limited. Many of the existing legal bases were simply incorporated wholesale into the Constitution. The next chapter looks at where changes were introduced and why. This is then followed by an assessment of the important area of institutions, where many of the solutions put forward by the Convention failed to address the issues satisfactorily, and in many cases where the subsequent Intergovernmental Conference substantially amended the Convention's proposals.

5.   The Union's policies: mixed results

The previous chapter showed that the Convention successfully delivered a text that contains many positive innovations in the areas of fundamentals. Equally, the next chapter will highlight the shortcomings of the Convention text, most of them related to the functioning of the institutions.

The purpose of this chapter is to examine Part III of the Constitution, which consists of the detailed provisions governing the attribution of powers to the Union and their scope. It constitutes the legal basis on which the Union acts across the full range of policy areas, and is therefore critical to what the Union does, and how it does it. Yet anyone familiar with the existing treaties will be surprised that even a casual glance at Part III of the Constitution reveals a text which is instantly recognisable. This is because the majority of legal bases were simply taken over wholesale from the existing treaties.

This chapter will look firstly at the limited number of policy areas that were examined in detail by the Convention. This means assessing the outcome of the five working groups that were established to look at specific policy areas, and the extent to which their recommendations were endorsed by the Convention. Also important is whether the Intergovernmental Conference made any further substantive changes in these areas. Secondly, the issue of other policy areas needs to be addressed. Was leaving the majority of provisions largely untouched a consequence of the Convention's mandate or a lack of time? Or was it a deliberate choice by the Convention? In which limited number of other areas were changes made and why? Finally this chapter looks at the effect on the overall impact of the Constitution. As far as the Union's powers are concerned, is it the revolution which some claim? Or is it rather the case that the Union is limited to doing more of the same, but perhaps does it rather more efficiently?

* * * * * *

The Convention's mandate certainly did not exclude it from examining the provisions that constitute the basis for the Union's action in different policy areas. As described in chapter 2, the Laeken declaration is an extraordinarily wide-ranging document. It sets out a series of questions (more than fifty in all) in a rather unsystematic manner, with the result that it is difficult to argue that there was much that was 'off-limits' for the Convention. The

Laeken declaration is quite explicit in its expectation that the Convention look at the Union's powers in the area of external policy, as well as the range of issues falling under the broad heading of justice and home affairs. It also refers to public expectations that the Union take action to tackle unemployment, poverty and social exclusion, and that it address issues such as environmental pollution, climate change and food safety.

The Laeken declaration suggests that the scope of the Union's powers or competences is directly related to the issue of their clarification and simplification. Both aspects were tackled early on in the Convention. Discussions on the Union's powers or 'missions' took place at the April 2002 plenary on the basis of a questionnaire drawn up by the Praesidium. The questionnaire included some basic questions as to whether the Union should be doing more or less, coupled with the issue of whether the competences of the Union should be spelt out explicitly in the treaties or not.

At the end of the April plenary session, Giscard d'Estaing concluded that the current remit of the Union had not been fundamentally called into question. A majority of those Convention members who took the floor had however called for a strengthening of the Union's missions in the two areas of Common Foreign and Security Policy (CFSP)[24] and Justice and Home Affairs (JHA)[25]. A smaller number also wanted to reinforce the economic governance of the Union.

These priorities were reflected in the choice of themes for the working groups, of which the first wave of six groups was established at the May plenary. The original intention had been to restrict this first set of working groups to issues related to legal and structural issues rather than policies. However, as has already been seen, the Praesidium gave in to pressure to create in addition a group on economic governance, and agreed that it should be chaired by Klaus Hänsch.

The second wave approved in July 2002 included groups on the EU's external relations, on defence, and on freedom, security and justice (another term for JHA). A final group on social Europe was set up as an afterthought, and then only after further pressure from the socialist political family within the Convention. All these groups reported back to the Convention with their recommendations during the course of the autumn and winter of 2002, ending with the report of the social Europe working group which finally issued at the beginning of February 2003.

This chapter will look in turn at the results of these different working groups, and examine the extent to which they led the Convention to amend the scope of the Union's action in each policy area. The question is an important one: ultimately it is about the additional powers, if any, which the Member States are ready to give up for the sake of an effective policy at the European level.

External Relations

In the area of external relations the Laeken declaration is remarkably long on prescriptions and surprisingly short on questions. Under the heading of 'Europe's new role in a globalised world', it asks two questions. One is rhetorical (does Europe not, now that it is finally unified, have a leading role to play in a new world order?), and the other (what is Europe's role in this changed world?) it answers itself, seeing the Union as an enlightened 'power' acting in support of the greater 'good'. Further down, the declaration picks up the need to improve synergy between the High Representative and the competent Commissioner; it appears almost as an afterthought.

The Convention did not take issue, either in its early discussions on Europe's missions or in the debate on the EU's external action at the July 2002 plenary, with the need for the EU to play a leading role globally. Nor did it disagree with the high-minded responses of Laeken on the nature of this role. Its main concern was related to Europe's ability to act coherently given its varied and compartmentalised procedures within the area of external action. It specifically picked up with zeal the challenge of improving synergy between the High Representative for CFSP (Javier Solana) based in the Council, and the Commissioner responsible for external relations (Chris Patten). Improving coherence and consistency became the principal objectives of the working group on external action chaired by Jean-Luc Dehaene.

It is perhaps astonishing that in the area of external action the risk of incoherence is built into the existing arrangements. The Maastricht 'pillar' system was designed precisely to ensure that the Common Foreign and Security Policy was kept quite distinct from the so-called 'Community method' and vice-versa. These differences have already been alluded to in earlier chapters. On procedures, the main difference is that the Member States rather than the Commission are in the driving seat for CFSP, and as a general rule decisions are taken by unanimity rather than Qualified Majority Voting. Conceptually CFSP sits uneasily alongside the more traditional 'Community' policy areas, largely because the Union's objective in CFSP is to achieve a 'common' rather than a 'single' policy. The distinction is important; it means that once agreed, a common policy does not lead to a transfer of power to the Union, nor does it prevent the Member States from continuing to act, provided they do so within the parameters of the common policy. At the same time, paradoxically, there are no limits to the potential scope of a common foreign policy – everything is possible if the political will exists.

The particular characteristics of CFSP and its consequent isolation from the rest of Union action would not be a problem if foreign policy itself could be ring-fenced. But it cannot. The Union's relations with the rest of the world are multi-faceted. Key areas, in particular trade policy, are 'Community' policies, where the Commission's role is critical. The Union's substantial development and cooperation budget can be deployed as an effective instrument in relations with many third countries. It lies firmly in the hands of the Commission. So also do large areas of economic, financial and technical cooperation with third countries. In addition the increasingly international scope of many traditionally internal policies (for example environment and transport) further underlines the growing importance of the

Commission in determining the Union's external policy. The result is that whilst Member States are the driving force behind CFSP, the fact that so many tools to implement foreign policy lie in the hands of the Commission means that neither can afford to ignore the other.

In addition to the lack of coherence between different aspects of the Union's external action, the rotating six-monthly Presidency undermines the ability of the Union to pursue a consistent foreign policy and hinders continuity. Although the creation of the post of High Representative for CFSP in the Amsterdam Treaty (1997) was an attempt to address this, the Union's external representation in CFSP remains primarily in the hands of the Council Presidency. The Member State holding the Presidency can put its stamp on the Union's foreign policy agenda by bringing its own priorities to the table. As a result, third countries and international organisations are not only confronted by several different interlocutors – Presidency, High Representative and Commission (the first of whom changes every six months) – but often have to try to make sense of fluctuating policy priorities.

The only place where the Union's policies, instruments, and procedures come together is at the level of the European Council, where the President of the Commission sits as a full member. The Amsterdam Treaty sought to take advantage of this by creating an instrument known as the Common Strategy. By cutting across different competences, it provides the European Council with the possibility of defining in a single document the Union's overall policy towards a particular geographical area or theme. The Common Strategy offers the added advantage of opening up the possibility of limited use of QMV in its implementation. However the Common Strategies so far (covering Russia, Ukraine, and the Mediterranean region) have fallen short of expectations. They have lacked bite, have ended up being negotiated with partner countries rather than standing as autonomous statements of the Union's strategy, have not adequately addressed the problem of coherence in implementation, and were deliberately drafted to circumscribe the use of QMV. The current strategies are not being renewed when they expire.

Faced with incoherence built into the system, the Convention had two choices: to change the system radically, or try to make the best of a bad job. The obvious solution would have been to remove the distinctive features of CFSP and bring it within the 'Community method'. But political constraints meant that this was a non-starter. The alternative of repatriating more traditional Community policies, such as trade, to Member State control would have been tantamount to beginning the dismantlement of the European Community, and was therefore out of the question. The radical solution was therefore not an option.

Even the decision by the Convention to bring to an end the 'pillar' structure (as covered in the previous chapter) had to take into account political and practical constraints. In the case of the Union's external relations, these were all too clear. Whilst there was a willingness to consolidate the existing treaty provisions (the working group explicitly recommended[26] that all the articles from the existing treaties be grouped together in a single section of the Constitution), the fundamental differences had to remain. The text may therefore look tidier; underneath very little has changed. In fact, when the Convention came to draft the articles on external action, it did so against the background of the war in Iraq. This served as a dramatic illustration of the political limitations of CFSP, and as a result the Convention took the line of least resistance and largely reproduced existing treaty language (including its imperfections). However it did add a useful new set of principles and objectives (based very closely on the working group's recommendations) underlying all aspects of the Union's external action.

If both the basic structure and the treaty text were to stay largely unchanged, the Convention had to look for other ways to improve coherence. Faced with the impossibility of merging the two different aspects of external action, the Convention began to look at possible ways of improving coordination between the two individuals personifying these two aspects: the High Representative for CFSP and the Commissioner responsible for external relations. At the same time, the Convention recognised that lack of continuity could only be addressed by tackling the problem at its source: the rotating Presidency.

On the first of these, the working group's report contained several options, from a minimalist approach (improving the level of operational cooperation) to a maximalist solution of integrating the functions of the High Representative into the Commission (which would imply full 'communitarisation' of CFSP and which was therefore a non-starter). The middle option, giving the two functions to the same person, whilst maintaining their specific characteristics, was known as 'double-hatting'. This idea, which already represented a compromise within the working group, was given a boost in the Franco-German paper on institutional questions which was issued at the beginning of 2003 and rapidly gained ground within the Convention as a whole. Its charm lay in its ability to please both schools. The integrationists stressed the importance of the 'double hat' being a full Vice-President of the Commission, bound by collegiality for issues falling within its competence. Others were reassured that the specific characteristics of CFSP would be maintained.

On the second issue of how to improve continuity in the Union's foreign policy, the working group recommended that the High Representative (or the 'double hat') take responsibility for the external representation of the Union. Perhaps even more importantly, the Convention endorsed the idea that the High Representative should chair the Foreign Affairs Council (which the working group recommended should be finally separated from the General Affairs Council). Taken together, these two changes are probably more significant than the moves to introduce coherence between the Council and Commission. Solana had always had more problems with the six-monthly rotating Presidency than he ever had with Patten (where the respective roles were more or less clear). Probably few in the Convention imagined that the IGC would be ready to accept the consequences of its recommendations in the area of CFSP: the end of a role for the rotating Presidency, and the incorporation of the powers of the Commission as an institution into those of the Foreign Minister (as one of its Vice-Presidents).

The IGC broadly accepted all the Convention's recommendations in this area, so the Constitution includes the 'double hat', baptised (to the irritation of some, in particular the UK) as the 'European Union Foreign Minister'[27]. The UK in turn irritated others in the Intergovernmental Conference by persisting in calling for (and eventually obtaining) a small but significant change in the text to help reduce the risk of the Minister being confronted with a conflict of interest (see chapter 7). The Constitution also provides the legal base for the establishment of an External Action Service which will combine the structures for external policy preparation currently in the Commission and Council Secretariat. It will include staff from both institutions as well as from Member State diplomatic services. The purpose of the External Action Service is to provide policy support for the Minister, although exactly what form it will take is left open.

The post of Foreign Minister is one of the main innovations of the Constitution; how exactly it will work is not clear. Since its inception the Union has operated on the basis of a clear separation of functions between the institutions. The constructive tension that results from this creates the dynamic that enables the Union to deliver results. The post of Foreign Minister cuts across this dynamic in the name of coherence. Whether there turns out to be a problem of conflict of interest will probably depend more on how the future incumbent (since confirmed as Javier Solana, current High Representative for the CFSP) chooses to see his role, as well as on the eventual structure of the External Action Service, than on the details of the text of the Constitution.

Defence

The Laeken declaration virtually ignores defence as an issue, but for Giscard d'Estaing it was important enough to require the creation of a working group[28]. The choice of Michel Barnier, a member of the Commission, to chair the group surprised some. The almost complete lack of a role for the Commission in the area of defence meant that as an institution it had virtually no scope to influence the outcome. Nevertheless Barnier himself proved to be a driving force in some of the key ideas developed by the group.

The main issue for the group was how to ensure an effective security and defence policy in an enlarged Union[29]. The very different commitments of the Member States (for example, some neutral, others members of NATO), their varied levels of military capabilities and their different historical attitudes towards the projection of military force, are likely to make it increasingly difficult to secure unanimous agreement to launching military operations. Yet unanimity cannot be circumvented in an area so close to national sovereignty. How then to square the circle?

The answer lay in an innovative construction known as 'structured cooperation'. Inspired by thinking amongst French and British officials, it foresaw that a group of countries with enhanced military capabilities could cooperate amongst themselves 'with a view to the most demanding missions'. Although not formally exclusive (other Member States were free to apply to join subsequently provided they met the criteria), the group acted without consulting non-members and yet operated in the name of the Union. Therein lay a paradox. Equally paradoxical was the suggestion that the Member States would decide both on the founding members of the 'club', but would at the same time define its entry criteria (would individual Member States really agree to rules by which they themselves would be automatically excluded?). Barnier liked to describe structured cooperation as the 'Eurozone of defence', prompting some to comment that the analogy was no better than the construction itself.

Equally sensitive was the more specific issue of mutual defence guarantees. Although the Convention endorsed the recommendation of the working group for a 'solidarity clause' invoking mutual assistance in the event of a terrorist attack, a comprehensive mutual defence clause was not going to run. A curious alliance of atlanticists (led by the UK) and neutrals, whilst reluctantly accepting that a group of Member States could amongst themselves sign up to a mutual defence guarantee, insisted that this should be open to all but imposed on no one. The Convention agreed. At the same time the reference in the existing treaties to the progressive framing of a common Union defence policy was maintained.

It was clear from the beginning of the IGC that the structured cooperation provisions were not only not going to be accepted as they stood, but were also linked to the issue of mutual defence guarantees. Early on in the IGC, France, the UK and Germany took it upon themselves to try to come up with an overall deal on both issues. The UK's interest in structured cooperation lay in getting others to spend more (and more effectively) on defence. It could not demand this and not at the same time yield to French pressure for a more generalised mutual defence guarantee. After lengthy trilateral negotiations, the article on structured cooperation was amended and complemented by a draft protocol. Its purpose was now limited almost exclusively to improving capabilities (important, but rather different from the Convention text), and the somewhat heterodox construction put forward by the Convention was modified to bring it more into line with the standard provisions on enhanced cooperation. At the same time, the mutual defence guarantee was extended to apply to all, although hedged with an indirect reference to the neutrals, and an acknowledgement of the importance of NATO for those states belonging to it.

An essential element in these negotiations was the proposal (pushed by the French) to establish an EU 'operations' cell within the military staff. This was a sensitive issue, since it had the potential to drive a wedge between the two agreed options of running EU operations either through NATO or a national Headquarters. It was also an issue which had nothing directly to do with the Constitution. The UK fought to limit the size and scope of such a cell. The final decision to establish a 'cell', but with a restricted remit, was the result of a trade-off between the French and the UK, but became in the process part of the wider compromise package on security and defence in the Constitution.

Nothing stirred up United States interest in the Constitution more than defence. Concerned that its own influential role in European defence through NATO would be undermined, the US viewed the initial structured cooperation provisions with suspicion, considering that they ran the risk of creating 'caucuses' within NATO. At the same time the Americans had a strong interest in circumscribing the role of the 'operations' cell. Interestingly, they were much less concerned by the prospect of mutual defence commitments (which in any case still existed elsewhere in the form of a remnant of the effectively moribund Western European Union). The final package largely allayed their concerns: the IGC must have got something right if both the French and the US were happy.

An Area of Freedom, Security and Justice

In tackling issues related to freedom, security and justice (otherwise referred to as Justice and Home Affairs), the Convention must have felt it was pushing at an open door. Opinion polls had consistently shown that there was substantial public support for a greater EU role in confronting problems such as terrorism, organised crime and illegal immigration. In the early debates in the Convention many speakers underlined the need to strengthen the Union's capacity to act in this area.

Given that these problems were not just long-standing, but had also been given a new urgency following the attacks of 11 September, why had the Union not fully lived up to expectations? The answer, paradoxically, is that in this area, the public was probably ahead of their governments. Entrenched interests within interior ministries in particular had led to treaty provisions which, largely because they required unanimity, were destined to hinder rather than help. There was then frequently insufficient political will to overcome the hurdle of unanimity in specific cases.

The working group[30] on this subject was chaired by John Bruton, former Irish Prime Minister and a representative from a national parliament on the Praesidium. He was clear from the outset that he wished the working group to be ambitious.

Ambitious it certainly was. Yet the group recognised that most of the powers needed by the Union to act in this area already existed. The problem lay rather in the cumbersome procedures (not least the continuing extensive requirement for unanimity) which so often prevented these powers from being exercised effectively.

Certain aspects of JHA (visas, asylum, immigration and judicial cooperation in civil matters) had already been 'communitarised' under the Amsterdam Treaty. But the areas of police and judicial cooperation had been considered too sensitive to be included. The collapse of the pillars in the Constitution in effect extends the process of 'communitarisation', and although some specific rules continue to apply to JHA, these are relatively limited, and certainly less pronounced than in the area of CFSP. The Convention decided to drop some of JHA's more idiosyncratic and heavy features such as the instrument, itself known as a 'convention', which required ratification by Member States before it could enter into force. The principal remaining feature peculiar to JHA is that the Commission's right of initiative in the area of police cooperation and judicial cooperation is shared with the Member States, although the Constitution requires any initiative to have the support of at least a quarter of their number.

This continuation of a process of 'communitarisation' of JHA is reinforced by the Convention's proposals to follow the trend to extend the application of both Qualified Majority Voting and the legislative procedure (i.e. co-decision) within this area. Both were proposed for legislation on asylum and immigration policy, the mutual recognition of judicial decisions in civil matters, and facilitating cooperation (including through the adoption of minimum rules) in criminal matters. The last point proved a step too far for several Member States in the Intergovernmental Conference, not least because of concerns about the very different practices that exist under the common law system. However faced with opposing pressure from others (notably France and Germany) not to backtrack in this area, the Presidency was obliged to table a compromise in the IGC which retained but hedged the application of QMV (see chapter 8).

A further innovation by the Convention was the proposal to allow for the creation of the post of the Office of European Public Prosecutor. Although requiring a decision by unanimity, it proved highly sensitive for several Member States. The final outcome of the IGC retains the proposal, but limits the Prosecutor's scope for action, at least initially, to combating crimes affecting the financial interests of the Union.

Economic Governance

Klaus Hänsch's working group[31] on economic governance quickly entered a minefield. At the heart of its discussions was a fundamental question about the powers of the Union in determining economic policy. The responses were very different depending from which side of the political spectrum you came. The right maintained that a single monetary policy determined by the European Central Bank should be balanced by flexibility in economic policy, so that whilst some limited coordination (through for example the Broad Economic Policy Guidelines and the Stability and Growth Pact) could be helpful, further steps to harmonise economic policy instruments at the Union level were unwelcome. The left considered that a centralised monetary policy required much stronger economic policy coordination, which meant first and foremost a greater role for the Commission.

Whilst the arguments went backwards and forwards, the working group never fully broke out of this basic dilemma. The final report contained little by way of concrete recommendations but read more like a record of the discussions. Giscard d'Estaing was however determined that there should be some progress. The Convention finally agreed on a number of relatively minor amendments which slightly enhanced the power of the Commission to ensure compliance with the Broad Economic Policy Guidelines and the Stability and Growth Pact. It also introduced a very limited and carefully hedged application of QMV in specific areas of cooperation in tax matters. Finally the Constitution recognises for the first time the existence of the Eurogroup (the Economic Ministers from the Eurozone), and slightly extends the powers that these ministers have to take decisions on their own.

Even these limited proposals in most cases went too far for the Economic Ministers, who, meeting in the ECOFIN Council, attempted to influence the work of the Convention, and subsequently took it upon themselves to instruct the IGC to return to the status quo. Foreign Ministers meeting in the IGC were reluctant to push for many of the (in some cases, minor) amendments proposed by their colleagues, and stuck largely with the Convention text. The main exception was tax, where the UK, backed by several others, insisted that there should be no move at all in the direction of QMV.

One unnoticed but valuable piece of work in this area was undertaken by legal experts supporting the Convention. They completely revised and updated the entire section on the transition to the Euro, removing the many obsolete provisions. This major technical work contributed to a text that is clearer and reflects the present rather than the past.

Social Policy

The working group on social policy[32], like its counterpart on economic governance, enjoyed only limited success. It was chaired by Greek MEP George Katiforis, a distinctly left-leaning academic, whose main published work: 'An introduction to Marxist economics', appeared just as the planned economies of eastern Europe were on the point of collapse.

Giscard d'Estaing only agreed to establish the working group under pressure from a hard core of proponents of a stronger 'social Europe'. It was invited to look at the Union's values and objectives, and at the legal bases governing social policy – should they be amended, and specifically should there be an extension of QMV?

The recommendations of the group on the Union's values and objectives came too late to be included in the first draft articles, but subsequent amendments introduced many of the group's desiderata. On competences, there was broad consensus in the group that the existing scope for action in the social field was adequate. The battle lines were instead drawn over the issue of the possible extension of QMV. In the working group, a small group of Member States, led by the UK, strongly opposed any further extension, arguing that this was not necessary since the relevant article already included a 'bridging clause' allowing the Council, by unanimous decision, to introduce QMV in the future without treaty change.

Views in the group were split over the sensitive issue of Services of General Interest (meaning those which are subject to certain public service obligations), with some arguing that the current provisions were purely declaratory and should remain so. However those pushing for a greater recognition for such services were rewarded by a small addition to the existing text providing the basis for legislation in this area.

Overall the group had some influence over the statements on the Union's values and objectives, but in the case of the substantive articles on policy, the Convention ended up largely reproduced the existing treaty provisions.

The arguments on social policy were not however entirely over. In the IGC Belgium proposed the insertion of a general clause at the beginning of Part III of the treaty stating that in any action undertaken under Part III, the Union would take into account various requirements linked to social policy. This clause was accepted by the IGC although, because of its lack of precision, it is not clear how exactly it will operate in practice.

* * * * * *

The five policy areas covered by the working groups accomplished some valuable work. In the areas of external relations and Justice and Home Affairs in particular the Constitution represents a significant advance compared with the existing treaties. Outside these five areas the changes are minimal. There were skirmishes over the article on common commercial policy, and after much to-ing and fro-ing a new legal base on energy was added. But for the most part the provisions in Part III are familiar because they are largely unchanged. Given the emphasis placed at the beginning of the Convention on the Union's missions, on substance rather than institutions, what had happened?

Firstly, the early discussions in the Convention on Europe's missions revealed that few wished to call into question the Union's existing remit. Indeed the small group of sceptics who called for a roll-back of the Union's powers could not agree amongst themselves on which ones, and their dissenting 'minority report' produced at the end of the Convention failed to gain the support of a single government representative. Equally, only in two specific areas was there a significant call in the Convention for a strengthening of powers: CFSP and Justice and Home Affairs. This is reflected in the outcome.

Secondly, as has been raised in an earlier chapter, the Union has probably reached its policy limits. It is difficult to imagine many entirely new policy areas where the Union can provide objective and significant added value. Even if they exist, it is even less likely that the political will exists for a significant new transfer of sovereignty to the European level.

Thirdly, the policy bases as currently drafted provide the necessary powers for the Union to accomplish what is required. Some members of the

Convention (notably the Swedish government representative) called for a revision of the articles on agriculture, arguing that they reflected an outdated vision of agriculture policies rooted in the 1950's. The Praesidium wisely resisted this. In an ideal world, updating the articles would have tidied up the Constitution. But the articles had not prevented the Union from fundamentally changing the Common Agriculture Policy, and do not prevent it from going further in the future should it wish to do so. Operationally therefore there was no reason to change. In addition, given the sensitivity of agriculture for some Member States, it is unlikely that the Convention would ever have reached agreement on a text, and if it had, it would have stood little chance of surviving the IGC.

This point serves to underline the difference between the legal bases in the treaty and the choice of policy. Some in the Convention blurred the lines between the two and tried to change policy through the Constitution. Part III of the Constitution is about giving the Union the power to act and determining the limits and methods of that action. Policy choice comes later. The choice of policy depends on circumstances, needs and political will. These can and do change frequently. The Constitution is more permanent.

Finally, it became clear that the changes in Part III were as much, if not more, concerned with facilitating the powers already attributed to the Union as changing the powers themselves. This is an important distinction. The Union already has the power to harmonise taxes. It is unlikely ever to be able to do so for as long as decisions on tax are taken by unanimity. Many of the moves in Part III are related more to the issues covered in the previous chapter: the extension of QMV in order to facilitate decision-making, and the extension of co-decision for reasons of increased legitimacy. Although the Convention had decided that the Union's powers should remain largely unchanged, it equally decided that it should be given the means to use those powers more effectively. For the IGC sometimes that meant too effectively, with the result that there was a return to unanimity in a number of key areas. With a Union of twenty-five Member States, that constitutes almost a guarantee of inertia.

Part III of the Constitution does not open the floodgates to new intrusions by the Union into every aspect of the lives of the citizens of Europe. There are no new wholesale transfers of sovereignty to the Union level. There are instead significant advances designed to help the Union operate more efficiently where those powers exist already. If that is a revolution, it is a rather quiet one.

6. The institutions: missed opportunities

If the Convention was successful in delivering a Constitution which was sound on fundamentals, and which made limited but important advances in the area of policies, it found it more difficult to meet expectations in its proposals for the future functioning of the institutions. The purpose of this chapter is to examine the results of the Convention on these issues. To what extent did they respond to the challenges of ensuring that a Union of 25 or more Member States functions effectively? What were the particular sensitivities which affected the outcome? Did the Convention's proposals on institutions stand up to the subsequent IGC? Were opportunities missed, and if so why?

The European Union has frequently been criticised, with some justification, for being too obsessed with its own internal functioning. The citizens, the argument goes, want to see results; they expect the Union to deliver policies which make their lives more secure and more prosperous. They care neither about the niceties of inter-institutional relations nor the details of the decision-making process. True, up to a point. For those immersed in them, institutional issues can take on the challenge of a vast game of chess and provide sufficient intellectual distraction that they risk becoming an end in themselves.

But institutional issues do matter. Policies cannot be delivered without efficiently functioning institutions, nor do they stand up if they do not have the guarantee of sufficient democratic legitimacy. This was recognised in the Laeken declaration, which invited the Convention to address a series of questions under the heading of 'More democracy, transparency and efficiency in the European Union'.

Giscard d'Estaing accepted that institutional arrangements were a means rather than an end. That is why he insisted that the Convention's opening sessions should concentrate on asking about the Union's missions and tasks. Institutions should follow. However, as described in chapter 3, this was also a tactical point. He wanted to avoid creating working groups on institutional issues, believing that they would be unlikely to come up with clear recommendations, and that in any case institutional issues were of sufficient interest to the Convention as a whole to make it difficult to constitute a legitimate working group on the basis of limited membership. Postponing any discussions on institutions gave Giscard d'Estaing the opportunity to work up his own ideas and present them directly to the Praesidium in the form of draft treaty articles.

Many of the Convention's proposals on institutions failed to meet expectations in two ways. Firstly, a number of them were either rejected or substantially revised by the subsequent IGC. That is not in itself a substantive criticism. Nevertheless neither is drawing up a Constitution simply an academic exercise. The extent to which the Convention's proposals stood up has to be taken into account. Many of them did not. Which is not to say that the alternatives agreed in the IGC were necessarily any better. Where they differ substantially, the details will be examined in a subsequent chapter. Secondly, a number of the Convention's proposals do not objectively meet the twin requirements of efficiency and legitimacy which the Convention set itself, or at least they do not meet them any better than the current arrangements.

The following is an assessment of each of the main proposals on institutions as put forward by the Convention.

The Legislative Council: a short-lived solution

The Council meets in different formations, bringing together the relevant specialist ministers depending on the subject matter. The Council's Rules of Procedure provide for the Council itself to decide on the list of formations. There are currently nine. Each formation has both legislative and policy-making responsibilities (although to differing degrees depending on the subject matter) within its area of responsibility. Each has tended to operate independently of the others, leading to criticism that the coherence of the Council as a whole is undermined.

The Convention's response was to single out two Council formations in the Constitution and give them a decisive role. These were the Foreign Affairs Council (which the Constitution states shall be chaired by the EU Foreign Minister), and the 'Legislative and General Affairs Council'. The Constitution leaves it up to the European Council to decide on other formations.

The 'Legislative and General Affairs Council' had a curious birth, starting life as simply the 'Legislative Council'. Vice-President Amato vigorously promoted the idea of a separate Legislative Council for reasons which were both practical and ideological. He argued that the separation and consolidation of the legislative activity of the Council into a single formation (even if relevant ministers would not be prevented from following in the Legislative Council proposals falling within their area of responsibility) would help ensure consistency and quality of legislation across all sectors. He also saw it as providing the opportunity for opening up the work of the Council when exercising its legislative function. Less obvious was the fact that such a move would constitute the genesis of a second legislative chamber, thereby discreetly reinforcing one aspect of the Union's tentative federal structure.

Government representatives in the Convention in particular said that they would never be able to sell the idea of a Legislative Council to their colleagues, since it constituted too much of an intrusion into their own internal organisation and so into domestic politics. By way of appeasement of the critics, the Praesidium proposed combining the Legislative and General Affairs Councils. However rather than addressing the substantive criticisms, this move only muddied the situation further by aligning two completely separate functions of the Council: legislative and policy-making (which is the primary role of the General Affairs Council). By this stage the government representatives were resigned to waiting for the Intergovernmental Conference. Sure enough, the Legislative Council became the first scalp of the IGC, surviving only hours after the opening ceremony. Importantly, however, the provision that the Council should meet in public when legislating was retained.

The definition of Qualified Majority Voting: simplistic but seductive

The Convention text proposes a system of voting in the Council by qualified majority which requires a double majority of both Member States and the Union's population (with the thresholds set respectively at 50% and 60%). The subject proved highly controversial, both in the Convention itself and in the Intergovernmental Conference. Indeed the issue not only dominated the Intergovernmental Conference but threatened to derail it definitively.

The voting system is sensitive since it concerns the relative powers of Member States. It constitutes the ground rules which determine the degree to which each Member State can influence the decision-making process within the Council. This in itself has become more important as decisions in the Council are increasingly taken by Qualified Majority. Given the sensitivity of the issue, it is surprising at first sight that the Convention chose to replace an empirical system which had served the Community well since its inception.

From the very beginning Qualified Majority Voting was based on a system of vote weighting, with each Member State being attributed a certain number of votes reflecting various criteria, not least (but not exclusively) that of population. So the Community of six attributed four votes each to France, Germany and Italy, two to Netherlands and Belgium and one to Luxembourg. It required twelve votes out of a possible total of seventeen to achieve a qualified majority. For a long time the Council used QMV as an instrument to help achieve consensus but avoided actually putting issues to a vote. As a result, the system, whilst not perfect, was relatively uncontroversial.

For a long time it remained uncontroversial. The system was simply adjusted as the Community enlarged: new Member States were attributed an appropriate number of votes and the threshold was adjusted accordingly. It first hit a snag with the accession in the mid 1990s of Austria, Finland and Sweden, by which time the use of QMV had been considerably extended as a result of the Single European Act (1986) and the Treaty on European Union (1992). Although initially the attribution of votes to the three new Member States was queried, the main focus of the discussions subsequently moved to the thresholds required for adopting legislation (or conversely for blocking it). Although proportionately the same with fifteen Member States as with twelve, the UK, supported by Spain, objected on the grounds that, with a higher number of Member States, their ability individually to block decisions was reduced. For the first time, a simple extrapolation of the weighting system was being called into question.

The solution, known as the 'Ioannina compromise', named after the provincial capital of Epirus in Northern Greece, was not particularly elegant. It stated that if the number of votes of Member States opposing a particular proposal fell between 23 (the old blocking minority) and 26 (the new blocking minority), then Member States could request that the Council try to reach an agreement which would respect the old qualified majority threshold. The Ioannina compromise constituted a political rather than a legal solution. Yet it is significant in that it was the first manifestation of an undermining of the weighted vote system, and a preview of the grosser aberrations introduced under the Nice Treaty which resulted in the whole system of vote weighting falling into disrepute.

At Nice the empirical system was tested to its limits. As already described in chapter 2, France adopted a contradictory approach which consisted of arguing for a proportionately higher number of votes to be attributed to the larger Member States compared with their smaller counterparts, yet at the same time (because of its insistence on retaining parity with Germany) accepting little if any recognition, in the attribution of votes, of the differences between the larger Member States. One of the consequences of this was that Spain and Poland fared particularly well under the Nice Treaty. Not surprisingly they proved the most resistant to the move to the double majority system proposed by the Convention.

Vote weighting served the Community well for several decades. As a system it was, and remains, transparent, potentially fair and easy to use. It fell into disrepute because it was abused for political ends. The system having been discredited, it is not surprising that the Convention turned to alternatives, and specifically the main alternative already floated, but rejected, at Nice: the double majority system. The main arguments in support of the double majority system were that it was simple to understand, and perhaps more importantly that it was durable. Gone would be the time when Europe's leaders had to spend hours or even days in increasingly difficult negotiations on the attribution of votes each time the Union enlarged. An additional argument which appears attractive at first sight but (as will be shown later) is ultimately less convincing, was that the double majority system was fairer because it was a reflection of the fundamental principle of the Union's double legitimacy: Member States and population.

For these reasons, the system of double majority quickly gained a large degree of acceptance in the Convention. Not surprisingly, representatives from Germany, which stood to benefit the most from the new system, were amongst its more vigorous proponents. More surprising perhaps was that this enthusiasm was quickly shared by the French, who at Nice had been the most implacable opponents of double majority. In the subsequent

Intergovernmental Conference, France and Germany argued together that maintaining the double majority system was for them a sine qua non for the adoption of the Constitution.

Perhaps even more surprising than the acceptance by the French authorities of the double majority system was that the initiative behind it came from Giscard d'Estaing himself, who had apparently fully shared the official French view before the Nice meeting in 2000 that there should be no move away from parity with Germany. In an interview given to *Le Figaro* in October 2003, the French MEP Jean-Louis Bourlanges exposed with intellectual rigour the disadvantages for France of moving to the double majority system. Quoting Voltaire in conclusion, he says that 'le drame de la France, c'est de changer souvent d'idée fixe'.[33]

The system of double majority adopted by the Convention was not the straightforward double threshold of 50% as proposed by the Commission and supported by many of the smaller Member States, but rather a requirement for at least 50% of Member States representing at least 60% of the Union's population. The higher population figure was introduced by the President to reflect the political reality that the smaller Member States would be in a majority in the enlarged Union of twenty-five. Nevertheless the double majority system in any format was far from universally welcome. At a meeting of government representatives during the closing days of the Convention, a straw poll confirmed that eighteen of them preferred to stick with the Nice system!

Against this background it is not surprising that the double majority system was strongly contested within the Intergovernmental Conference, as is explained in detail in a subsequent chapter. Some opposed it for clear reasons of national interest (for example Spain, Poland and most of the smaller Member States); others outside the IGC challenged it on grounds of principle. The IGC began, but never completed, the substantive discussions which the Convention should have had. If the debate had been brought to its natural and logical conclusion, the Constitution, on this issue at least, might have looked rather different.

The Presidency: an uncertain solution

Some of the drawbacks of the six-monthly rotating Presidency of the Council have already been highlighted in the previous chapter. Its disadvantages are most obvious in the area of foreign policy, but lack of continuity (despite being addressed in part through multiannual programming) is seen by many as a problem across the board. The main advantage of the rotating Presidency is that it provides a useful, if brief, opportunity to advertise the European Union at a national level.

The Convention chose to tackle the issue of the Presidency from the top down. One of its main innovations was the creation of the post of full-time President of the European Council, a proposal which went largely unchallenged in the Intergovernmental Conference and which therefore remains as one of the more important new institutional provisions of the Constitution.

Giscard d'Estaing, who claimed with some justification to have been the creator together with Helmut Schmidt of the European Council in the seventies, sought generally to raise its profile in the Constitution. But the description in his original draft of the European Council as the 'highest authority of the Union' was too much for the Praesidium to stomach. It was deleted, and the articles on the European Council were moved to after those on the Parliament. Interestingly, the description of the European Council in Article I-45 of the Convention text as consisting of representatives 'accountable to national parliaments' would have excluded the French President and had to be amended by the IGC in the final version of the Constitution. Apart from this correction, the Convention's proposals on the President of the European Council were endorsed by the IGC without modification.

For Giscard d'Estaing, the creation of a full-time President of the European Council was an important element in raising its profile. It was certainly not an uncontroversial proposal. It was supported originally by only a handful of larger Member States, and regarded with considerable suspicion by many members of the Convention on the grounds that it would shift power from the Commission to the Council. Even Germany was initially very reticent, and only accepted the idea as part of an overall deal on institutional issues with France (the counterpart being agreement that the EU Foreign Minister should be one of the Vice-Presidents of the Commission), and once it was satisfied that the text limited as far as possible the future President's role.

Whatever the role of the future President, the decision by the Convention to create the post provided some with the ammunition to claim that at last the unhelpful and complicated arrangement whereby the Presidency of the Council rotates every six months would cease. Such claims are somewhat misleading for several reasons.

Firstly, the function is deliberately unclear. Those who were originally opposed to the idea, and then became resigned to it, turned their attention to ensuring that the Constitution attributed to the President the minimum powers possible. However, the resulting minimalist approach of the Convention text conceals the fact that in reality there were two very different visions of the President's role. Taken at face value the text provides for little more than the task of chairing meetings of the European Council. Which begs the question as to how this (presumably) senior figure is going to occupy himself or herself for the remaining three hundred and fifty days or so of the year.

For the supporters of the idea, the role of the full-time President is central to the running of the Council as a whole. His tasks would inevitably include (even if not stated in the Constitution itself) the setting of the wider agenda of the European Union and oversight of its implementation at political level.

The existence of these two rather different concepts of the post means that the full-time President of the European Council constitutes one of the great unknowns of the Constitution. Nevertheless political realism will almost certainly mean that the post will be neither purely ceremonial nor a European version of General de Gaulle, but lie somewhere between the two.

Secondly, whatever the outcome, there is always a risk that the relationship between the President and his counterpart at the Commission, as well as with the EU Foreign Minister (given that the permanent President of the European Council has some responsibilities at his level in the area of the external representation of the Union), could give rise to problems. In which case, far from facilitating the current system, the creation of the post of permanent President could risk, at least initially, complicating it further.

Thirdly, and most importantly, whilst the Convention provided for greater continuity at the level of the European Council, it avoided addressing the separate but related issue of the Presidency of the Council and its many preparatory bodies. Apart from the Foreign Affairs Council (which is to be chaired by the Foreign Minister), the Convention text limited itself to stating that: 'The Presidency of Council of Ministers formations.....shall be held by Member State representatives within the Council of Ministers on the basis of equal rotation for periods of at least a year'. The details of how this would operate were left to a decision of the European Council. The result is that the Convention neatly sidestepped the issue of the Council Presidency.

The text of the Constitution therefore provides the outline (but nothing more) of two rather different models of the Presidency: a full-time individual for the European Council appointed for two and a half years, and a national rotating system for the rest (with the exception of the Foreign Affairs Council). Since there is an obvious functional link between the European Council and the different formations of the Council, in particular the General Affairs Council (which the Constitution states is responsible for the preparation and follow-up to meetings of the European Council) the absence of specific provisions on the relationship between the two models of Presidency begs the question as to how they are to interact.

The Intergovernmental Conference attempted to fill in the gap left by the Convention on the Presidency of the Council. It looked at two basic approaches, both described as 'teams' (an alternative proposal for electing Council chairs had very little support). The first provided for groups of Member States working together for a fixed period and sharing fully the responsibilities of the Presidency function, in particular the chairing of Council formations. The second, although described as a 'team presidency', is in reality a continuation of the current six-monthly rotating system, albeit with some provisions for better coordination between the three consecutive Member States making up each 'team' in order to improve continuity. Despite the fact that the existing system has been extensively criticised, the IGC chose the second option. However it did not shed any further light on the relationship between the Council Presidency system and the full-time President of the European Council. In practice the only organic link between the two will be via the Secretary-General of the Council, whose role as a result will almost certainly be enhanced considerably.

The Commission: a solution en trompe l'oeil

The Commission represents the common European interest and its members are supposed to be independent. Nevertheless, the Member States attach importance to the presence of their nationals in the Commission, regarding them as providing a two-way street of information, and as giving legitimacy to the Commission's proposals. At the same time, with the Union growing to twenty-five and more, the Commission will find it increasingly difficult to function efficiently with at least one Commissioner from each Member State. The challenge for the Convention was how to square legitimacy with efficiency.

The Nice Treaty already provides an answer of sorts. It foresees that from 2004 each Member State will retain one Commissioner (meaning that the larger countries lose their second Commissioner). However once the Union consists of twenty-seven Member States, the number of Commissioners will be less than the number of Member States. Nice leaves open the exact number of Commissioners, but is clear that the system will operate on the basis of equal rotation.

The Praesidium chose a rather different approach. Giscard d'Estaing succeeded in persuading its members that in the interests of efficiency, the overall size of the Commission should be restricted (the Praesidium text set a ceiling of fifteen including the President). The Praesidium also accepted that the Commission President should be able in addition to appoint 'associate Commissioners', without the right to vote. As a result the Praesidium text represented an endorsement of the President's view that the legitimacy of the Commission lay in giving almost free rein to its President to choose its members.

The Convention balked. A large number of its members still preferred a Commission composed of one national from each Member State. At the very least those Member States with no national in the Commission proper should be entitled to an 'associate Commissioner'. In which case there should be some guarantees over access, which explains why the main focus of objection to the Praesidium text was the lack of any reference to a system of equal rotation. The President's own pronouncements raised rather than lowered suspicions that this was not an oversight but deliberately intended to open up the possibility of the larger Member States having greater access to the Commission than their smaller counterparts. Legitimacy was turning out to be in the eye of the beholder.

Whilst none of the smaller Member States wished to see differentiated access to the Commission, there was a variety of views over its eventual size. The applicant countries underlined the domestic political significance of maintaining the right to have a national in the Commission indefinitely. The result would be an ever-increasing Commission, even if nuanced by proposals such as that put forward by the Praesidium for a two-tiered approach. The smaller founding Member States (i.e. the three Benelux countries) regarded the Commission as their natural ally and considered that it therefore needed to operate as efficiently as possible. They argued strongly for a reduced Commission.

But the 'one Commissioner per Member State' group were in the majority, and once the pass had been sold by the Praesidium, albeit in the form of a two-tier system, this majority sought to whittle away at the differences between the two types of Commissioners, insisting at the same time on (and obtaining) the inclusion of a reference to a system of equal rotation. In the final Convention text, the right to vote was the only factor which distinguished 'full' Commissioners from the rest. Even their similarity of title – 'European Commissioners' and 'Commissioners' – suggested that they had more in common than had originally been intended. Furthermore the Convention foresaw that, mainly to address the concerns of the new Member States, the two-tier system would only come into effect in 2009.

The outcome of the Convention was rather different from the original vision of Giscard d'Estaing. Instead of being reduced to manageable proportions, the Commission would increase steadily as the Union enlarged. Furthermore the Convention text was clear that access to the nominally more important posts of Commissioners with voting rights was based on the principle of strict equality, the implementation of which was to be determined by a decision of the European Council. Those who hinted at the time that this decision could in some way override the principle of equality, which is set out (together with details on its application) in the text itself, were guilty of wishful thinking.

There were a number of ambiguities and weaknesses in the Convention proposal, some of which deserve to be highlighted.

Firstly, the only fundamental distinction between the two types of Commissioners was that of the right or not to vote. Yet all participated in Commission discussions. Voting was the end of a process in which all would have taken part. It is artificial to imagine that the views of non-voting Commissioners would have been simply ignored once it was time to take a decision. In reality there would have been virtually no difference between the two types of Commissioners.

Secondly, the ceiling of fifteen voting Commissioners (including the President and the Foreign Minister) was an arbitrary figure and took no account of future enlargement. The number of non-voting Commissioners would have therefore increased over time, making it difficult to implement the rules on equal rotation.

Thirdly, the Convention text nowhere defined the tasks and prerogatives of the non-voting Commissioners. Although it is likely that their views would have been fully taken into account, the formal absence of a vote even on subjects within or related to dossiers attributed to them would have constituted a recipe for frustration. In the longer-term, the two-tier system built potential conflict into the functioning of the Commission.

Fourthly, the rotation system automatically excluded the possibility of a second mandate, even for a Commissioner who had proved to be exceptionally able. This risked putting additional pressure on individuals who knew that their term was limited to five years to act less in the European interest and rather to pursue national objectives, thereby undermining the independence of the Commission.

The Convention correctly identified the need from the beginning for a Commission which could act efficiently and provide legitimacy. Reconciling these two principles proved problematic. It is difficult not to draw the conclusion that in attempting to meet both objectives, the Convention actually delivered on neither.

The European Parliament: the semblance of a solution

The allocation of seats in the European Parliament to the Member States (just like the attribution of votes under the vote weighting system in the Council) has traditionally taken the form of tables attached to successive treaties, with the figures extrapolated on the occasion of each new accession. Like the attribution of votes (and for similar reasons), the allocation of seats at Nice contained enough aberrations for the Convention to adopt a different approach. Specifically it decided to avoid getting into negotiations on numbers.

Instead the Convention set out some basic principles underlying the attribution of seats. The overall size of the Parliament was set at a maximum of 736, and the minimum number of MEPs per Member State at four. Representation was to be 'degressively proportional'. The actual decision on attribution is left to the European Council on the basis of a proposal from the Parliament itself.

The decision to set principles rather than numbers is significant. Experience has shown that the weight of a Member State's representation in the Parliament is regarded by Member States as being as much of an issue of power as the weighting of votes. As such, the two issues have historically become interlinked. Nowhere was this more the case than at Nice, where Germany benefited from an increase in EP seats as compensation for accepting parity on voting with France, and Spain had to make do with proportionally fewer MEPs as a result of its increase in votes in the Council. Yet the two issues are not totally comparable. In the Council each government representative represents one view and speaks with one voice. The Parliament is different: Member State governments cannot oblige or even expect their nationals of varying political persuasions within the EP to rally together in support of any particular issue, even one which touches directly on national interests.

The original text from Giscard d'Estaing referred simply to the principle of proportionality, with a minimum threshold of four MEPs per Member State and a cap on the overall size of the Parliament of 700. Proportionality is not qualified, and it is therefore reasonable to suppose that Giscard d'Estaing intended it to be applied directly. This would have resulted in a very different allocation from that under the existing system, with the larger Member States making significant gains. Aware that this would cause problems, the Praesidium agreed that the reference to proportionality should be conditioned by the inclusion of the word 'degressive' in order to protect the interests of the smaller Member States. In any case, some argued, if vote weighting in the Council took account of both the Member State and population factors, so should the attribution of seats in the Parliament.

In fact, it is perfectly possible to interpret the three elements in the original proposal from Giscard d'Estaing as together constituting a system which is already degressively proportional. Such was the intention of the EP itself when it floated (unsuccessfully) exactly this same proposal to the previous IGC in 2000. How can it be degressive? As a starting point, each Member State is attributed four seats. Over and above this, an additional number of seats is attributed to each Member State in direct proportion to their population such that the total number of seats respects the overall ceiling of 700. Under this system, the minimum number of four seats attributed to every Member State constitutes the degressivity key.

So the inclusion of the word 'degressive' in the Convention text is ambiguous. Does it merely clarify the President's original text, or could it be interpreted to mean that there should be a double degressivity key? Since it is for the Parliament to come up with a proposal, the European Council will have to wait and see.

The Convention raised the President's proposed overall cap on the size of the EP from 700 to 736. However even the degressively proportional system as set out above, whilst resulting in an objectively fairer system, would have still severely penalised many of the middle-sized Member States (precisely those who lose out under the double majority voting system), and given additional seats to the largest Member States, in particularly Germany, which has already done very nicely under the double majority voting system.

The IGC, more by luck than design, redressed the situation[34]. At the insistence of the smaller Member States, the minimum number of MEPs per Member State was raised to six. At the same time the overall ceiling of the Parliament was increased to 750. More importantly, Germany let it be known (as part of a wider negotiation) that it could live with a lower number of EP seats (even lower than its existing allocation of 99). As a result the final text of the Constitution states that no Member State shall be allocated more than 96 seats. Unwittingly, the Intergovernmental Conference almost certainly made the whole system more politically palatable, although the Parliament now has significantly less scope when drawing up its proposal than in the original Convention text.

The Congress: a solution which never saw the light of day[35]

The Congress is the only institutional proposal from Giscard d'Estaing which never saw the light of day in any form. Conceived as an assembly bringing together both national and European parliamentarians, it appeared in the first draft of the articles on institutions but was never welcomed by the Convention. The President proposed that sessions of the Congress should take place at least once a year, and that it could be consulted by both the President of the European Council and the President of the Commission. Its

main objective was to improve the Union's legitimacy by bridging the gap
between Brussels and national capitals, and in particular to give national parliamentarians a stake in the Union. However he also envisaged that it might
be given some specific tasks in relation to the nomination of the President of
the European Council as well as in future revisions of the Constitution.

European parliamentarians in the Convention were largely hostile, sens-
ing an attempt to usurp their own prerogatives by reinstating Member
States' influence via the back door. The President's subsequent proposal that
the Congress should be chaired by the President of the European Parliament
did little to help. More widespread opposition was based on the criticism
that there was no convincing case for a new institution. In general the
Convention saw little need to give serious consideration to the possible
merits of the proposal. As a result the Congress, which could probably have
made a useful contribution to improving relations between the European
Parliament and its national counterparts, was destined not to survive.
Whilst members of the Praesidium had in general also been sceptical about
it, respect for its ownership meant that a sense of embarrassment rather than
triumph accompanied its final demise. The Congress was eventually laid to
rest just as European and national parliamentarians had discovered the
value of joint meetings in the margins of the Convention. The irony was not
lost on Giscard d'Estaing.

Other Institutional issues

The Convention made only minor changes to the provisions on the Union's
other institutions and bodies. It decided to raise the profile of the European
Central Bank by making it an institution and giving it a separate article in
Part I of the Constitution, although the content of the article is based closely
on existing treaty provisions. The European Court of Justice was the subject
of an ad hoc discussion group, which made a number of recommendations
about its role and functioning. These were largely taken up by the
Convention. The Court of First Instance was for example renamed the 'High
Court', and an appointment panel was created to assist in the selection of
judges. The Convention also usefully widened the scope of the right of
access by individual citizens to the Court.

Conclusion: missed opportunities

Institutional issues proved to be the main battleground of the Convention.
They dominated the discussions during the final few weeks of its work, and
at times looked as though they might prevent the Convention from delivering a complete text. Had the Convention not been followed by an IGC, there
would almost certainly have been no agreement. A majority of Member
States was ready to acknowledge that the draft Constitution had successfully delivered on a wide range of issues. Few were under any illusions that
the part on institutions would survive the subsequent IGC intact. At the end

of the Convention, consensus was achieved but never defined. Giscard d'Estaing was satisfied, and justifiably so, yet at the same time his bluff had been called: in reality it was the government representatives rather than he who had decided what was meant by consensus.

There are several reasons why the Convention failed to produce acceptable and durable solutions on institutions. Firstly, institutional questions, by their very nature, are about power: the balance of power between the Member States, and between the institutions. Since the Union is the creation of its members, issues of power can only be decided by the governments of the Member States. The Convention as an instrument, despite all its claims about legitimacy, could never second-guess the Member States. So its outcome on institutions was always likely to be an approximation based partly on wishful thinking.

Secondly, the issue of institutions was particularly sensitive for the acceding Member States, which were in the process of ratifying their accession treaties. Their acquired rights on issues such as the size of the Commission and the Qualified Majority Voting system were now being called into question. Not surprisingly they preferred to stick with the status quo. From their point of view, in the area of institutions in particular, the timing of the Convention was far from ideal.

Thirdly, Giscard d'Estaing chose very different tactics on institutions: there were to be no working groups, and apart from a single debate in plenary in January 2003, the first serious discussions on institutions were when the Convention was presented with draft articles towards the end of April. This tight timing was partly due to factors beyond his control. He attached importance to a planned discussion with the European Council on institutional issues before presenting his proposals. Because of the Iraq war, this was postponed and only took place finally in the margins of the signing ceremony for the new Member States in Athens on 16 April 2003. In the event, the meeting provided little useful input beyond endorsing the proposal for the creation of the 'double hatted' Foreign Minister, but it meant that the Convention had very little time left to debate seriously the proposals on institutional issues.

The tight timing, although in part dictated by external factors, was nevertheless quite useful for the President. It put additional pressure on the Convention, and the absence of any serious debate on institutional issues meant that he himself could set the agenda. He needed to do this since his own proposals were bound to create some controversy. Running like a thread through them was his own strong conviction that the legitimacy of the Union depends less on the equality of Member States than on a reflection of the respective power and influence which they can bring to bear, a view which was not surprisingly anathema to most of the smaller and middle-sized Member States. The result was an inevitable confrontation between the 'smaller' and 'larger' Member States, with little opportunity for detailed analyses of the problems which might have helped avoid the rapid politicisation of the discussions.

Fourthly, in the absence of the opportunity for the Convention to carry out a detailed analysis of the options on the key institutional issues, the recent past, and in particular the memory of Nice, provided a potent backdrop for the Convention's discussions. For example, on QMV, a narrow vision of national interests meant that it proved impossible to address the aberrations of Nice within the context of a weighted voting system. The choice was then simple: either stick to Nice or invent an entirely new system. The Convention chose the latter, but did so without having to address the consequences.

Fifthly, the discussions on institutions were not helped by the President of the Commission, who was so keen to kill off the idea of a full-time President of the European Council (fearing that it would lead to a stronger Council and so – erroneously – to a weaker Commission) that he promised to back those who wanted to retain one Commissioner per Member State. His strategy failed on both counts.

Finally, the perception of the Convention that it needed to respond to and satisfy public opinion led it to adopt solutions, which were either simplistic (in the case of double majority voting) or ambiguous (in the case of the composition of the Commission). The experience subsequently in the IGC showed that for governments paying lip service to public opinion is rather less important than defending the national interest. Simplicity is always a valuable goal, but it usually comes at a price.

* * * * * *

Despite best intentions, the Convention did not fully meet expectations in the area of institutions. In part that was a function of the nature of the Convention itself. But it is also arguable that it was partly because the Convention departed from procedures which had successfully delivered in other areas. The Convention process had many advantages. It had the time and resources to examine issues in depth. It could take a fresh approach to many issues unencumbered by the need to protect inherited rights and powers. It also had the potential because of its size to favour the common good over and above narrower national and institutional interests. Had these advantages been better exploited, it is possible (although by no means certain) that the Convention's proposals on institutional issues might have done the Union a greater service. Whether that would have meant also that they would have proved more resilient to change by the IGC is another issue.

7. The Intergovernmental Conference: return to Realpolitik

The six-monthly Presidency of the Council culminates in a European Council meeting which is the opportunity for the Member State holding the Presidency to vaunt its achievements and bring to a successful close its period of tenure of the office of Presidency. The Thessaloniki European Council in June 2003 was no exception. Yet one of the most important points on the agenda at Thessaloniki was largely outside the control of the Greek Presidency and one for which it stood to gain little credit. Giscard d'Estaing was to present to Europe's leaders the results of the Convention on the future of the European Union.

As seen in the previous three chapters, the draft Constitution came as a package, with its fundamentals, providing for the first time a comprehensive and understandable overview of what the Union was supposed to do and how it was supposed to do it. It made some small but important changes in the area of the Union's policies, and it offered up alternative (and in some cases quite radical) proposals as to how the Union's institutions were to function in future. It was the culmination of fifteen months of work by more than two hundred individuals gathered together from very different backgrounds, but bound together by the common sense that they had had the opportunity (in the words of Giscard d'Estaing) 'to touch the hem of history'. It was the end of an adventure.

But not quite the end. Giscard d'Estaing had previously requested (and obtained) from the Greek Presidency a commitment that the Convention should continue for a further three weeks. However the Thessaloniki conclusions were clear that this should be limited to some 'purely technical work on drafting Part III'. As already seen, the extension turned out to be largely tactical; the additional few weeks made little difference to the final text as it was approved by the Convention on 10 July 2003 (with perhaps one important exception in the area of trade in services, where the French were able at least in part to secure some safeguards in the very sensitive area of 'cultural exception' – the practical effect being that European film industry is offered some protection against its US counterparts). The members of the European Council themselves clearly already considered it to be the end. After the President had presented the Convention's work with his customary aplomb, there was a series of interventions, carefully ordered by the Greek Presidency, welcoming the draft Constitution. Few dared to enter a dissenting voice to the otherwise resounding clamour of praise for the product of a body which they themselves had established. The occasional note of warning for the Intergovernmental Conference did not go unnoticed, but no one wanted to undermine the Convention's achievement, for which its President could take considerable credit.

After Thessaloniki, it was left to Giscard d'Estaing to hand over the complete draft Constitution to Italian Prime Minister Berlusconi in Rome on 18 July. The Rome meeting was purely ceremonial. This time it really was the end of the Convention, but certainly not the end of the Constitution. Indeed the ceremony itself constituted a rite of passage between the Convention and the subsequent Intergovernmental Conference, which alone could decide whether to endorse, amend or reject the Constitution.

Why Rome? Intergovernmental Conferences are chaired by the Member State holding the six-monthly office of Presidency of the Council. Since it was the turn of Italy to hold this office for the second half of 2003, it found itself also in charge of presiding over, and therefore largely responsible for, the IGC. The intention of Italy was to wrap up the IGC under its own Presidency, reaching agreement on a final text by December 2003. In the event, it was to fall to the Irish, who followed the Italians, to bring the IGC to a close.

This chapter is the story of the Intergovernmental Conference. Why was it so different from previous IGCs? What went wrong in December 2003? And how did the Constitution finally fall into place at the closing European Council under the Irish Presidency in June 2004? These are serious questions; the Convention was not the end of the process. Indeed its product was (according to the Thessaloniki conclusions) only 'a good basis for starting the Intergovernmental Conference'. At times it seemed that it would not even be that, and that the Convention could end up being an interesting but ultimately futile experiment. The story of the IGC is the story of how the draft Constitution was given the chance to grow up. The ideals of the Convention were to be tested in the school of 'realpolitik'. The end result bore both the wisdom of maturity and the scars of self-interest. However, the Constitution survived, and survived largely intact.

* * * * * *

Whilst the European Union might be regarded as a product of enlightened self-interest, successive Intergovernmental Conferences have demonstrated clearly that the Member States, however enlightened they may be, continue to pursue self-interest with determination. If the day-to-day business of the Union is a game in which each tries to secure an outcome which serves both European and national interests, Intergovernmental Conferences are about setting the rules of the game. There is little opportunity subsequently to go backwards since IGCs are governed by cumbersome procedures in which unanimity is the rule. So for the Member States, getting it right in an IGC is absolutely crucial.

This IGC was different from others in that it was preceded by the Convention, yet it remained, like others, dominated by 'realpolitik'. This combination produced a curious mixture of two apparently contradictory phenomena.

Firstly, it became clear very quickly that there was considerable pressure to limit as far as possible any changes to the Convention text. A number of Member States considered that the Convention text should not be reopened. What could the IGC achieve that had not already been done by the Convention? Why reopen the product of fifteen months hard work by such a diverse (and in the view of many, legitimate) body?

Secondly, it was clear that, despite the pressure not to reopen the text, there were a number of key issues (not least the institutional questions) which were simply not going to get through the IGC in the format put forward by the Convention. The combination of these two factors led to an IGC in which Member States were resigned to the bulk of the Constitution going through unamended (even when they might have wished to see some changes to the text), but dominated by difficult negotiations on a small number of significant points. The message was clear: choose the few points that really matter to you – leave the rest well alone.

The Convention text: setting the agenda of the IGC

The political pressure to limit changes to the Convention text came from both outside the IGC (notably from a large swathe of Europe's press), and also from within the IGC where it was defended with insistence by Germany and France in particular, but also by Belgium and (although holding the office of chair of the Conference) Italy. Germany in particular took an absolutist position by claiming to be ready to sign up to the Constitution unamended (although this did not prevent it from later defending vigorously requests for some important changes to the Convention text). The few serious dissenting voices, such as Finland and Austria, found it difficult initially to make themselves heard. This was partly because the one Member State (UK) which could be expected to press for a more thorough review of the Convention text, decided at this stage that discretion was the better part of valour. Later on it was to annoy many of the other IGC participants with its long lists of requests for amendments. But for the moment it kept its own counsel.

The political pressure not to amend the Convention text was stronger than the Thessaloniki description of the draft Constitution as a 'good basis' for the IGC would seem to suggest. There are several reasons for this. Firstly, against the expectations of many, the Convention had produced a single text. Giscard d'Estaing had rightly assessed that a Convention result with options would have opened the way for the IGC either to ignore or reject much of the Convention's work. A single text increased the political pressure not to reopen. Secondly, the fact that two of the largest Member States, France and Germany, defended so strongly the Convention text put significant pressure on others to follow suit. Thirdly, the legitimacy argument was used to considerable effect (and probably explains in part the initial reticence of the UK to press for its entire wish-list of amendments). The participation of national parliamentarians in the Convention, and the much-vaunted openness of its process, put governments under notice that a wholesale redraft would not be acceptable. Finally, all governments remained bruised by the experience of Nice. Most knew that any unravelling of the Convention text would carry the risk of a re-run of Nice. This was certainly something to be avoided, even at the price of swallowing some of the less palatable aspects of the Convention text.

The consequences of this political pressure were far-reaching. Whole swathes of the Convention text were never discussed within the IGC and as a result survived unscathed. Even many issues which had long been highly controversial, such as the legal personality of the Union, were accepted without comment. It is difficult to imagine this happening in other circumstances. It quickly became clear that the Member States, who had themselves created the Convention 18 months earlier, were destined to live with, and therefore endorse, much of the Convention's outcome. It was not how many of them had seen it at the time.

The Convention text: determining the organisation of the IGC

The political pressure brought to bear by the Convention on the IGC also had a direct impact on the way the IGC was organised. It led the Italians, as Presidency of the IGC up to the end of 2003, to make a number of far-reaching procedural proposals. The Italians foresaw in particular that the opportunities for reopening the Convention text should be kept to a minimum. That meant limiting the number of meetings of the IGC, and placing a tight deadline on the completion of its work. Hence the objective of concluding the IGC by the end of 2003 (which since it did not formally open until October that year meant limiting its lifetime to only two months – short by the standards of earlier IGCs). More radically, the Italians adopted a narrow interpretation of the Thessaloniki conclusions: the Convention text was not just the basis of the work of the IGC but should remain unchanged for as long as there were no good reasons for doing otherwise. The Italians considered that it was up to individual Member States to make the case for changes, and to rally sufficient support for them.

Not surprisingly, the defence of national interests ensured that this approach was never fully respected (even the most ardent supporters of the Convention text wobbled when confronted with the choice between their position of principle and issues of national sensitivity – Germany over the Stability Pact and France over the budget being obvious examples). Nevertheless the Italian approach imposed a sense of discipline which, for the reasons just outlined, no one fundamentally called into question (wags readily recalled the lesson from French history that the Convention was followed by the reign of Terror!), and there is little doubt that in practical terms it helped the IGC (eventually) to reach a successful conclusion.

Limiting discussion on the Convention text meant that Member States had to exercise a degree of self-discipline and prune their lists of problems as drastically as possible. Since this exercise was essentially political, the Thessaloniki European Council saw little need to extend the activities of the IGC beyond the political level. The main work was therefore to be kept at the level of Heads of State or Government, with preparatory work being undertaken by Foreign Ministers. So unlike previous IGCs there was to be no technical level preparatory group, since the Convention had already carried out all the necessary preparatory work, and in any case, what was the justification for letting civil servants call into question the results of such an eminently political and legitimate body as the Convention? This time, the politicians were to be in charge.

Well almost. In fact, although such an approach appeared on the face of it to be rather attractive, it proved in practice difficult to apply strictly for at least two reasons. Firstly, it quickly became clear that ministerial meetings, if they were to be at all productive, required a minimum of preparation. The Italians, who originally insisted that, as Presidency, this was their responsibility and theirs alone, accepted that more inclusive preparations were needed if ministers' time was to be used productively. They also realised that many of the more mundane issues raised by Member States (despite the constant exhortation to exercise self-discipline) could in fact be addressed without recourse to a political level discussion.

Secondly, most Member States accepted that, separately from any political problems they might have with parts of the Convention draft, it was important to carry out a thorough review of the text in order to correct a number of technical errors and improve the legal drafting.

In order to carry out its role as Presidency, the Italians had asked for the name of an individual in each capital who could act as a contact point on IGC matters. In most cases these were Directors-general of EU affairs in foreign ministries. Once the Italians accepted that some form of collective preparatory process (albeit informal) was required if ministerial meetings were to be effective, it naturally turned to this group, who became known as the 'focal points', and who met twice during the Italian Presidency. These meetings were tightly controlled: their mandate was to clear the ground around the list of problems already established at political level. New problems could not be added. In fact the Irish subsequently gave slightly greater leeway to this group and used it actually to negotiate and resolve a number of issues. This was partly a matter of choice by the Presidency, and partly because the habit of working together over time introduced a greater sense of confidence. The requirement for focal points to be based in capitals was designed to keep the preparatory process as close to ministers as possible, thereby reinforcing the notion that the IGC was still being conducted at political level. An interesting consequence of this was that COREPER, the powerful Brussels-based committee of Member States' ambassadors to the EU, was almost entirely excluded from the IGC, although many of its members were active individually behind the scenes.

The focal points could assist in preparing ministerial meetings, but they were not suited to carrying out a detailed technical review of the Convention text for two reasons. Firstly, such a review required both time and considerable legal expertise. Most members of the focal points had neither. Secondly, the review needed to be strictly controlled so that it did not stray into political issues. So the technical review process had to be (and be seen to be) kept quite separate from the main work of the IGC. The answer lay in the creation by ministers of a second group, this time Brussels-based and consisting almost entirely of lawyers. To reinforce the point that this group was technical rather than political, the Italians asked Jean-Claude Piris, Legal Advisor to the Council, to chair it. The group was rigorously controlled; any attempts to introduce political issues were quickly ruled out of order. However, as in the case of the focal points, familiarity encouraged greater flexibility, with the result that a limited number of sensitive issues were discussed and resolved by the group. The definition of a 'political' issue became a function of the ability of the technical group to address it.

Despite the creation of these two groups, any fear that the IGC would be taken over by civil servants and lead to a complete reopening of the Convention text proved groundless. But the absence of any formal preparatory processes placed a greater burden on the Presidency (both the Italians and subsequently the Irish), as well as the Secretariat to the IGC which was provided, as is traditionally the case, by a small team from the Council Secretariat.

Autumn 2003: the IGC gets underway

The Italians launched the IGC in Rome in October 2003 at the level of Heads of State or Government, and arranged that it should be followed immediately by a meeting of Foreign Ministers. Traditionally IGC meetings have included representatives of the Commission and of the European Parliament (although neither has the ability to block a consensus). In the case of the post-Convention IGC, Vitorino and Barnier continued to represent the Commission, and Mendez de Vigo (subsequently replaced by Brok) and Hänsch participated on behalf of the Parliament. Less traditionally, the IGC also included observers from the three candidate countries, Bulgaria, Romania and Turkey, reflecting the fact that they had participated fully in the Convention.

The inaugural meeting was followed by further ministerial sessions, two meetings of the focal points, and a summit meeting in October. Despite this, there was comparatively little to show for the efforts of the Presidency when Foreign Ministers began to arrive in Naples at the end of November for a full two-day session (known as a ministerial conclave) designed to prepare the ground for the final summit in Brussels only ten days later. But the

Italians, although discreet, had not been idle. Whilst there were still no proposals on the table to attempt to resolve the larger institutional issues, a systematic approach designed to settle some of the less obvious but still political issues, had borne some fruit.

The Presidency had circulated just prior to the Naples meeting a document which attempted to capture the progress which had been achieved. Setting aside the key institutional issues, this was a fairly comprehensive set of proposals for amendments to the Convention text intended to respond to the various (in some cases conflicting) requests from delegations. The Italians had already tested some of these proposals on the Member States, and could therefore reasonably assume that they would not give rise to major difficulties. Others had not yet been seen by delegations, but nevertheless constituted a genuine attempt to meet their differing requirements.

The Naples meeting probably achieved more than the Italians had hoped for and others had expected. There was only limited reopening of points already tested with delegations, and significant progress was made on many others. Even where differences of view persisted, the meeting enabled the Italians in very many cases to have a clear idea of what a possible solution might look like. In the days following the Naples meeting, the Italians worked on a revised version of the document which was eventually submitted to Member States just before the 12-13 December summit meeting in Brussels.

This (so-called) 'post-Naples document', although now largely forgotten, constituted an important staging post in the life of the IGC, being particularly useful for three reasons.

Firstly, it dealt satisfactorily with a number of important political issues, with the result that some of the Italian proposals remained unchallenged and unamended throughout the remainder of the IGC. The package on defence is a key example. As described in chapter 5, the outcome of the trilateral consultations between France, the UK and Germany paved the way for the introduction of some fundamental changes to the provisions on 'structured cooperation', including a protocol on the details of how it would function, as well as the inclusion of revised wording on mutual defence. After some fine-tuning on the mutual defence provisions to respond to some residual concerns from the neutral Member States, the text was to remain carved in stone.

Similarly lasting arrangements were found to accommodate the very specific concerns of Denmark over its existing opt-out in the area of Justice and Home Affairs. This had to be extended and modified if the Danes were to accept the much more ambitious provisions in this area foreseen by the Convention. Yet this was far from a unilateral issue. It was never certain that others would be willing to accept an opt-out with such far-reaching consequences, raising the spectre, as it did for some, of a European Union in which Member States pick and choose those policies in which they wish to participate. Some deft foot-work by both the Presidency and the Danes guaranteed that this also would be an issue which could be put to bed before the December summit.

Secondly, the post-Naples document was useful in addressing requests for amendments intended to clarify or iron out wrinkles in the Convention text. These were requests which went beyond the technical clarification exercise, but at the same time did not necessarily call into question the basic provisions of the Convention text. Examples include the articles relating to the functioning of the 'double-hatted' Foreign Minister. The UK in particular had repeatedly highlighted the risk of a conflict of interest between the Minister's responsibilities before the Council and his obligation to respect the collegiality of the Commission. The small but significant amendments introduced into the post-Naples text recognise this risk, and shift the Minister's allegiance slightly in the direction of the Council, but without calling into question the basic nature of the 'double-hat'. No one raised any fundamental objections to this change, which remained part of the overall draft package until the end of the IGC. Similarly, the provisions on judicial cooperation in criminal matters were not in principle contested, but several delegations were concerned that the introduction of QMV in a number of particularly sensitive areas was a step too far. Others considered that the extension of QMV constituted one of the main achievements of the Convention in the area of policies, and that it should therefore be maintained. An ingenious solution, known as the 'emergency brake' and described in the next chapter, allowed the IGC to square this particular circle.

The third element of the post-Naples package was a significant number of more minor proposals which in themselves were unlikely to attract much attention from those outside the IGC, but which nonetheless responded to points of real difficulties for one or more delegations, and just as important, when taken together, began to give the complete set of proposals the appearance of an overall compromise package. Examples include a limited but balanced set of proposals on maters relating to economic and financial issues, and some amendments to various policy articles such as those in the areas of transport, research and development, energy and public health. Equally, the package attempted to respond to some very specific requests from individual Member States such as the introduction of provisions on the protection and welfare of animals (Italy), the status of overseas territories (France), and the future institutional arrangements on the accession of Bulgaria and Romania. In most cases these additional provisions were introduced with little if any opposition from others.

If the Naples meeting had, to the surprise of some, made real progress, and if the Presidency's package of proposals as set out in the 'post-Naples' document looked reasonably encouraging, why did the summit meeting only days later end in such fiasco? What went wrong, and could things have been done differently?

The Brussels IGC meeting (12-13 December 2003): flamboyance and fiasco

The relatively positive outcome of the Naples meeting helped create an atmosphere of expectation for the Brussels summit which was encouraged by some pre-summit spin by Italian Prime Minister Berlusconi (who was to chair the summit) which was at best overly optimistic, and at worst simply reckless. In fact, it quickly became clear that the chances of reaching an over-all agreement by the end of the Italian Presidency were slim. The December summit was destined to fail for a number of different reasons.

Firstly, despite the progress achieved at the Naples meeting, as reflected in the 'post-Naples document', a critical number of important and politically sensitive issues had simply not been addressed at the Naples meeting, and were therefore notable by their absence in the post-Naples document. Foremost amongst these was the question of the extension of Qualified Majority Voting. Most delegations had a number of points on which they could not accept the introduction of QMV (and some issues for some dele-gations were so-called 'red lines' – deal-breakers). Some (notably Belgium, but also France and Germany to some extent) adopted a position of prin-ciple of supporting extending QMV as far as possible in order to reduce the risk (as they saw it) of sclerosis in an enlarged Union. Somewhere between these two positions a compromise had to be found. No real progress had been made in testing out where such a compromise might lie. And given the importance of the issue, a solution was unlikely to fall into place at the summit without prior groundwork.

Secondly, and similarly, insufficient efforts had been deployed to resolve the even more complex institutional issues. The smaller Member States remained intransigent in the face of increasing pressure to move to a smaller Commission, and the Spaniards and Poles not only showed no signs of movement on the double majority system of voting within the Council, but even toughened their approach. Despite Berlusconi's assurances that com-promise was in the air ('I have at least four proposals in my pocket') it rap-idly became clear that the rather vague ideas being floated were not sufficiently developed to enable an overall deal to fall into place. Not only had the IGC discussions on institutions been sketchy and unproductive, but the pre-summit contacts at the level of Heads of State or Government had been cursory, incomplete, and lacking in any serious discussion on possible compromise options.

Finally, it was soon evident that the absence of an agreement would rather suit a number of delegations for domestic political reasons. President Chirac in particular was facing the prospect of a serious setback in forthcoming regional elections, and many others were not looking forward to the likely outcome of the European Parliament elections scheduled for early June 2004. The French, working in tandem with the Germans, were able to adopt a high moral tone in objecting to any 'watering-down' of the Convention text, and yet secure their twin objective of postponing agreement for electoral reasons, whilst still able to let the blame for failure fall largely on others (this explains why Chirac subsequently remained adamant that the Irish should not conclude until their summit in June 2004, scheduled *after* the European Parliament elections).

These three factors together almost guaranteed that the December summit would fail. There was virtually no substantive discussion in plenary; instead the Presidency spent most of the Friday afternoon and night (12 December) as well as some of the Saturday morning engaged in increasingly futile bilateral meetings. Futile both because some delegations were not seriously prepared to work towards a deal, and because the Presidency, having little to offer by way of serious compromises, locked into listening mode, only responding to assure all its interlocutors that their key demands would be met, even where these were mutually incompatible. The flamboyance and bravado of Prime Minister Berlusconi did nothing to disguise the increasing sense of confusion; by Saturday it was clear that no agreement was going to be reached.

At the time, many saw Berlusconi's role as the main contributing factor to the failure of the Brussels summit. It has in turn coloured the whole perception of the way in which the Italians handled the Intergovernmental Conference. This is not completely fair. Much of the preparatory work in the IGC under the Italians had been both constructive and useful, if incomplete. However Berlusconi could probably have put much more effort into consulting at his level prior to the December summit. Equally the useful work accomplished by the Italian Foreign Ministry had not been sufficiently exploited by the Prime Minister's office and therefore rendered the IGC less effective when it moved up to summit level. However the combination of circumstances set out above make it far from certain that agreement would have been possible in December whoever had been in the chair. Nor should it diminish the extensive progress made under the Italians; progress which gave the next Presidency a head start when they took over the IGC in January 2004.

The December summit conclusions acknowledged failure, and invited the incoming Irish Presidency, on the basis of consultations, to assess the prospects for further progress in the IGC. It was asked to report back in three months. It was the very minimum, and at that stage there was little indication that the IGC would be able to recoup, let alone build on, what had been lost in December. The Irish, who had planned on simply having to work on their own domestic ratification, now found themselves not only without a Constitution, but responsible for deciding whether the Union was ever likely to have one.

The Irish Presidency (January - June 2004): picking up the pieces

It fell to the Irish not only to pick up the pieces from the confusion of the Brussels summit, but to report back to the next European Council in March 2004 as to whether they could be stuck back together again. Recognising the useful work undertaken by the Italians, the Irish took the 'post-Naples document' as their point of departure. Not that this document had ever been officially approved (indeed a golden rule of IGCs is that nothing is agreed until everything is agreed), but it provided a helpful snapshot of the highpoint of the negotiations under the Italians. The problem with the 'post-Naples document' concerned less what was in it than what had been left out.

Between January and March 2004 the Irish entered into a series of discrete and highly productive meetings with all the other Member States at every level. These included intensive contacts between the Irish Prime Minister (or Taoiseach), Bertie Ahern and his counterparts. Normally such emphasis on bilateral meetings would have raised considerable suspicions amongst the smaller Member States that they were going to be confronted with a deal pre-cooked by their larger partners. Such suspicions were allayed by the scrupulous attention paid by the Irish to ensuring that all were treated equally, and by their policy of being completely open about their approach. The fact that Ireland itself fell within the camp of smaller Member States helped considerably. The handling alone helped re-establish a climate of confidence which had been so obviously lacking at the December summit.

The practice of discreet bilateral contacts within wider multilateral negotiations is well-known within the EU. Sometimes known as 'confessionals', since they allow Member States to come clean about their real intentions, they put the Presidency in a strong position to work up compromises which meet the many varied requirements of different delegations. The IGC had already demonstrated the difficulty of negotiating with twenty-five Member States: ministers were increasingly resorting to repeating their well-known national positions in plenary meetings rather than engaging in face-to-face negotiations. This put pressure on the Presidency to make increasing use of bilaterals. In fact in the first three months of 2004, the Irish used bilateral contacts exclusively as they tried to assess whether there was any serious prospect of the IGC being successfully completed. It put them in a strong position subsequently when they came to map out a path towards an eventual compromise on the Constitution. At the same time, through careful handling, Member States were reassured that this was an open and inclusive process.

The bilateral contacts enabled the Presidency to confirm how far the 'post-Naples document' represented an acceptable compromise. More importantly (and for the first time since the IGC opened) they provided the opportunity for the Irish to test out possible options on the main outstanding institutional questions. The tactics employed by the Irish were crucial, but also benefited from external developments totally outside their control. Most important amongst these was the 11 March terrorist attack in Spain which led directly to a change of government, Prime Minister Zapatero's new socialist government proving to be more ready to accept a compromise on Qualified Majority Voting than that of his predecessor Aznar.

Events in Spain demonstrated again that control of a negotiating process, however effective, is only ever partial. External events can be a major factor of influence, both positive and negative. Given the number of participants in the Union's negotiating process, the impact of external developments can be considerable. For example, domestic events (not least elections) can radically alter a single Member State's negotiating position which in turn can change the whole atmosphere of the negotiations. More generally, events outside the Union can either put a brake on future action or act as a catalyst for major developments.

The combination of skilful handling by the Irish Presidency and the coincidence of events in Spain led to an upbeat report by the Irish to the European Council meeting in March 2004. No one demurred from the general assessment that the IGC should be concluded under the Irish Presidency, and specifically that agreement should be reached 'no later' than the next European Council, scheduled for 17-18 June 2004. Despite the inclusion of the reference to 'no later than', several leaders made it clear that they would not countenance any attempt to accelerate this timetable. For them it was politically important to maintain some negotiating room during the end-game. For domestic reasons this was easier once the European parliamentary elections (taking place only the week before the June European Council) were over. Again political reality took precedence over principle. Long forgotten were the Thessaloniki European Council conclusions, which stated that the IGC should agree the Constitutional Treaty 'in time for it to become known to European citizens before the June 2004 elections for the European Parliament'.

March to June 2004: The final push

The Irish were left with three months to bring the IGC to a conclusion. Ironically, the problem now looked as if they might have too much time rather than too little. The intensive bilateral consultations during the first three months of 2004 had provided the Presidency with a very comprehensive picture of Member States' positions on all issues. So much so that the parameters of an eventual agreement were already fairly clear by March, and even more so now that there appeared to be a rather more amenable partner in Madrid. The UK continued to have a number of serious problems (for some of their partners, the list of UK problems seemed to grow longer rather than shorter as the IGC progressed), but they had a sympathetic ear in Dublin, and both countries had the benefit of a long tradition of mutual problem-solving born of years of difficult negotiations over Northern Ireland. More difficult was to deliver some of the smaller Member States (in particular Austria and Finland) although again the Irish had an advantage in coming from the same camp. On institutional issues the Poles remained the most unpredictable, as they did right up to the very end. Strangely, given the political pressure to keep textual changes to a minimum, the main defenders of the Convention text found it increasingly difficult to sustain their position of principle. The reason was simple: other delegations all had demands on which they had little room for manoeuvre. The choice was not between the Convention text unchanged or amended, but rather between an amended text or no text at all.

In the run-up to the June summit, the positive and effective approach adopted by the Irish gave rise to optimism. At the same time, all delegations were aware that, having signed up to getting agreement in June, the political pressure not to fail was enormous, not least because realistically there would be no second (or rather third) chance. Yet despite all these reasons for optimism, sharp differences, in particular on institutional issues, remained. Success in June was certainly not guaranteed. No text at all was still a real possibility.

The tactics of the Irish in these last three months consisted in building on the earlier bilateral contacts by restarting the full negotiating process. This included a meeting of the focal points in Dublin in early May, and a resumption of ministerial meetings in the margins of the monthly General Affairs and External Relations Council. The Irish Prime Minister also engaged on an intensive round of consultations with his fellow leaders, travelling throughout Europe almost without a break for about four weeks. Both the meetings and the consultations helped the Presidency to cross-check the conclusions it had drawn from the earlier bilateral contacts, and gradually to narrow down the range of differences of view. This narrowing-down was reflected in the documents which were submitted to Member States: the total list of proposed amendments to the Convention text was divided up into two separate lists. The 'closed' list contained issues which the Presidency could realistically expect not to be reopened (even if no formal agreement had been reached). The very fact that an issue was included in this list put pressure on delegations not to raise it. The second 'open' list contained unresolved issues on which further discussion was certainly necessary. The purpose of the exercise was to transfer gradually as many issues as possible from the 'open' to the 'closed' list. Through clever handling, the Presidency managed to use this approach to whittle down the number of open issues for the final negotiation to the absolute minimum.

When leaders gathered in Brussels on 17 June 2004 the 'open' list was limited primarily to institutional issues. Yet even here the way forward was relatively clear, for the simple reason that there were only a very limited number of ways to meet as far as possible the often conflicting demands of delegations. But institutions had always been the issue which would be settled at the very end; the issue on which delegations would hold out longest in the hope of obtaining more. It needed the drama of a summit meeting to conclude, and it required Europe's leaders themselves to take responsibility for the final compromises which would be necessary for success. The alternative would have been to accept full responsibility for failure.

*   *   *   *   *

The next chapter examines the impact of the IGC on the substance of the Convention's text. It inevitably concentrates on the institutional questions, since these turned out to be the most difficult. But even in this area, many of the key features of the Convention text remained intact. The final glosses to the text as a whole were as limited as they are frequently inelegant. But they allowed the IGC to reach agreement. The penultimate chapter will then take a step back and look at how well the Constitution as a whole stands up to close scrutiny.

8. The Intergovernmental Conference: the end product

Long after the Intergovernmental Conference was underway, and even after it had been brought to a successful close, the basement storage areas of the Council building in Brussels were still housing pallets containing thousands of copies of the draft Constitution drawn up by the Convention. Overtaken by events, and gathering dust, this surplus stock bore witness to the transience of the Convention text. The fact that the Convention had produced a complete Constitution led many to overlook the fact that the process was not yet over. The subsequent Intergovernmental Conference would both render the Convention text outdated, and yet at the same time breath into it the potential for life. The Convention text, its many annotated versions, its commentaries and critiques, passed into history on 18 June 2004. Together these now constitute a valuable archive on the proceedings and outcome of the Convention. But the text that matters is that approved by Europe's leaders on that day. That is the text which is due to replace the existing treaties once it comes into force.

Few outside the rarefied world of European studies are likely to carry out a detailed comparative study of the two texts. Those that do might well be surprised. In the first place, the most striking feature is their similarity. The strategy agreed by the Member States of exercising self-discipline paid off; the text was not fatally reopened. Its fundamentals remain largely untouched, and its structure and much of its content is that agreed on by the Convention.

The second surprise might be that the most apparently far-reaching changes are not in fact the most significant. Changes to the order of articles, the reversal of sentences, the rewording of crucial provisions; these are the results of the legal experts' group who worked throughout the autumn of 2003 to remove inconsistencies and improve the clarity and legal security of the text. Their task was complemented by the legal-linguists who carried out a further technical review of the text once it had been approved. This included a useful renumbering of the entire Constitution so that it reads consecutively across all four parts. More noticeable still is the addition of a second volume of the Constitution, twice as thick as the text itself, which contains a raft of protocols and declarations annexed to the treaty. Many of these are existing texts which had to be amended by the legal experts in order to align them with the provisions of the Constitution, and which were at the same time updated and consolidated. This was essential work, but work which the Convention did not have the inclination, time or expertise to carry out.

Hidden amongst the many superficial amendments to the main text are a number of substantive changes. Some were introduced to clarify the Convention text, whilst others alter it significantly. Many were agreed with little difficulty, a number are the product of hard-fought compromise. A few were critical to ensuring that the Constitution was agreed at all.

This chapter offers an overall assessment of these substantive changes. It looks at what lay behind them and what effect they will have on the way the Union functions once the Constitution comes into effect. Some of these changes have already been covered in previous chapters and will be referred to here for the sake of completeness. Others have been touched upon, but not developed in any detail. They are grouped under the successive headings of fundamentals, policies (both the substantive provisions and the scope of Qualified Majority Voting) and institutions.

The largest part of the chapter will be devoted to institutions, and within that to the issue of the definition of Qualified Majority Voting. There are good reasons for this. It was by far the most sensitive issue in the Intergovernmental Conference; sufficiently important for some delegations to stake the whole Constitution on a satisfactory solution to this one problem. Even late in the evening of 18 June 2004, it was still not certain that the compromise carefully crafted by the Irish Presidency on this issue was going to work.

The Fundamentals: fundamentally unchanged

Nowhere was the stricture to avoid reopening the Convention text respected more than in the area of fundamentals. The reason is clear. The fundamentals constitute the framework of the Constitution, in particular Part I. Touch one piece and you run the risk of bringing down everything else with it. There are a number of issues which in the Convention had proved to be very sensitive, and had been hard fought over. The issue of the primacy of EU law is one example. Despite the fact that EU law has always had primacy over national legislation (indeed the functioning of the EU, as a law-based organisation, depends on it), advertising it for the first time caused ruffled feathers in the UK and Portugal, even amongst practitioners who knew very well that the Constitution was simply stating the obvious. Although in the Convention the article on primacy was accepted as part of the overall package, the UK in particular remained uncomfortable with it being so obviously flagged up. Yet it resisted the temptation to push for a reopening of the article in the Intergovernmental Conference, and settled instead for a short declaration which it considered provided the necessary reassurance.

The first few articles of the Constitution, on values and objectives, had also been negotiated long and hard in the Convention. The result is not particularly elegant, but it is balanced, and everyone can find something satisfactory in the text. Again, no one saw any advantage in reopening substantive discussions in an area where nearly everything had already been said. The Intergovernmental Conference introduced only two minor amendments. For the rest, and for almost all the fundamentals, the Intergovernmental Conference passed over them in silence.

Many delegations must have wished that this had included the issue of the Charter of Fundamental Rights. Although stressing that it had no intention of reopening the substance of the Charter, the UK managed to irritate almost everyone else by insisting on an abstruse (but for the UK significant) point related to the scope of legal interpretation of its provisions. The issue was eventually settled through a minor change to Part II of the Constitution and a declaration. Although the Charter appeared to be a rather British obsession, the amendments made by the IGC subsequently provided useful reassurances to the French Constitutional Court when it came to examine the text of the Constitution.

Of wider significance was a request from the Portuguese that Part I of the Constitution should contain a reference to the equality of Member States[36]. This was a sensitive issue, reflecting a profound sense of unease that on institutional issues in particular the larger Member States had an increasing tendency to ride roughshod over their smaller partners. But treating the equality of Member States as an absolute would clearly not work: in many ways the Member States are very obviously not equal. The final text refers instead to the need for the Union to respect the equality of Member States before the Constitution. A legal truism, but nevertheless a further small piece in the jigsaw of securing overall agreement on the Constitution.

With the exception of these few points, the fundamentals remained untouched, although it is not clear that everyone at the time was fully aware of the extent to which some of these issues could subsequently be exploited by political opponents. As a result, when the Intergovernmental Conference began to discuss other issues where the political stakes were much higher, it was already clear that the backdrop of the basic structure, as agreed by the Convention, would remain largely unchallenged. This at least provided some sense of security when the discussions on institutions in particular threatened to derail the entire process.

The provisions on policies: some minor skirmishes

As described in chapter 5, in the area of substantive policy provisions, the results of the Convention were modest. The changes introduced by the Intergovernmental Conference to the Constitution were even smaller. Some minor skirmishes led to limited adaptations to the text, but much of it went unchallenged.

Some of the skirmishes have already been covered in earlier chapters. Defence was perhaps the most sensitive area where the Convention provisions were not going to stick. But the deal discreetly negotiated by France, the United Kingdom and Germany offered an acceptable alternative. On foreign policy, despite some uneasiness amongst the British in particular about the whole concept of the 'double-hat', it quickly became clear that there was little appetite for reopening what was considered by many to have been a balanced deal within the Convention.

The IGC had little difficulty in agreeing to amend some of the more ambitious Convention provisions in the area of economic policy and to return to the status quo (although these reversals never went quite far enough for Finance Ministers). However a small core of economic issues remained on the table to the very end of the IGC. These had less to do with the Constitution itself than with the quite separate confrontation over the Stability and Growth Pact, and specifically the concerns amongst some medium-sized and smaller Member States (and the Commission, which took the Council to the European Court of Justice on this issue) that there was one rule for them and another for the larger Member States. There was a long standoff between the Dutch and Germans before the two were persuaded to try to settle their differences bilaterally. As so often in such cases the solution was a lengthy, inelegant and redundant declaration. But it did the trick. With that, some other smaller issues, for example a minor extension of the powers of the Eurogroup, fell into place.

On other policy provisions, the changes were also relatively minor. At the insistence primarily of the Greeks, a new article on tourism was included, reflecting the fact that it featured in the list of competences in Part I. On the article on the Common Commercial Policy, the Swedes led a group of Member States who wanted to clarify that the basic provision whereby trade agreements are decided by QMV could not be used to undermine the unanimity rule for other sensitive policy areas (e.g. social, education and health) where these form part or whole of an agreement.

The article on energy was particularly sensitive for the Dutch and the British who sought to circumscribe its potential scope by explicitly excluding energy exploitation, choice of energy source and the supply structure. For the Commission, which was already able to make proposals on energy policy using alternative legal bases, this constituted a sufficiently retrograde step for them to argue that the new article should be deleted altogether. It stayed in the end, with provisions which were slightly diluted, but which provided adequate reassurances for the Dutch and British.

More significant than these detailed changes was the decision by the IGC to introduce a simplified procedure for revising the policy articles in Part III through a decision of the European Council, so avoiding an Intergovernmental Conference. This was a sensitive issue which was only agreed on condition that any such revision could not extend the competences of the Union, and that it would still require ratification by the Member States.

The IGC had no real difficulty in agreeing the necessary modest changes to the Constitution's policy provisions. This was not the case for the extension of Qualified Majority Voting, which looked initially as though it could be one of the two main issues (along with institutions) to block agreement on the Constitution entirely.

The provisions on QMV: different forms of retreat

The Convention had attached more importance to facilitating policy-making than changing the legal bases themselves. As a result the Convention text had provided for an ambitious extension of Qualified Majority Voting, including in some particularly sensitive areas. Several delegations made it clear from the outset that in a number of cases there would have to be a return to unanimity. So clear in fact that the expected clash on this never materialised, as it became obvious that some retreat to unanimity was the inevitable price which its opponents would have to pay for the Constitution.

Although the Convention had been ambitious in its extension of QMV, many of its members had wanted to go even further. At one extreme, some had argued that there was no place in a Union of twenty-five plus for decisions being taken (or rather not taken) by unanimity. Many others considered that there were some particularly sensitive issues on which Member States could simply not accept being outvoted. An important element in reaching a compromise between these two positions was the simplified procedure for extending QMV through a unanimous decision of the European Council.

Given the agreement that the Convention text was the starting point for the IGC, it was clear that Member States would be under strong pressure to accept the Convention's recommendations on QMV. Yet it was equally clear (not least because the UK left no one with any doubts) that there would have to be some retreat in key areas. The result exposes the reality that on this issue, perhaps more than on most others, those Member States with the most ambitious objectives found themselves with relatively little bargaining power, as it came down to the choice between modest advances or no advances (and no Constitution) at all.

At one end of the scale were the slightly surreal discussions on decision-making in the area of the Union's Common Foreign and Security Policy. This was traditionally the last bastion of unanimity, and the Convention made no serious attempt to go further than the current very limited and circumscribed scope for recourse to QMV. However the Italian Presidency took their lead from a small minority of Member States who are traditionally much more ambitious. With considerable flourish, the Italians decided before the Naples conclave to propose introducing QMV into the Constitution for all proposals emanating from the Foreign Minister. This would have been sheer provocation to the large number of delegations for whom unanimity in CFSP is sacrosanct, had it not been so clear that this was almost entirely for tactical reasons. Instead these delegations simply sat back and waited for the proposal to be withdrawn. It lasted until well into the Irish Presidency but was never seriously destined to be part of the final package. It was an entirely fabricated retreat.

Whilst it was always clear that there would be areas where a return to unanimity was unavoidable, most delegations accepted that they could not press their case for unanimity in some areas without making real efforts to accept the maintenance of QMV elsewhere. So trading one area against another was the basis of the eventual overall compromise. However in a few cases the pressure both from delegations wishing to keep QMV and from those seeking to revert to unanimity was sufficiently and equally strong to force the IGC to look for more innovative solutions. An example is judicial cooperation. Here several delegations (in particular the UK, Ireland and Austria) were concerned that the introduction of QMV was a step too far. This was not simply a political issue, but for some raised substantive problems related to the nature of their legal systems (in particular the common law system). Yet several other delegations considered it essential to maintain QMV and were therefore equally determined not to go back on the Convention text. How to square the circle? The answer lay in an ingenious solution which became known as the 'emergency brake'. In its first manifestation this provided for the maintenance of QMV, but allowed any Member State, if it considered that a proposal in this area would affect fundamental aspects of its legal system, to suspend the legislative procedure and refer the matter up to the European Council.

There were immediate objections: the right of appeal could be used simply to block – was this more a 'handbrake rather than a footbrake'? In response, a time limit was introduced in order to avoid deadlock. Still there were objections: if there were problems specific to one or more Member State, why should all the others be prevented from acting? The reply to this was to introduce an automatic right for other Member States to proceed with enhanced cooperation. This final construction was unofficially baptized as the 'brake/accelerator'. It combines the protection sought by some from being outvoted on a sensitive issue, but at the same time puts these same Member States under considerable political pressure to agree to an outcome in order to prevent others going ahead with enhanced cooperation (which they would generally prefer to avoid). The same 'emergency brake' mechanism was applied to the provisions on social security, although without the 'accelerator'.

It is in the economic area (in its broadest sense) that the retreat to unanimity is most obvious. Tax was the ultimate 'red line' of the UK, although they had considerable support from others, not least a number of new Member States. Despite the fact that the Convention text, through a somewhat curious construction, made only very limited moves towards QMV, it was clear from the outset that for some there could be no change from the existing treaties. No one doubted the seriousness of this position; it fell into place as part of the final package with scarcely a murmur.

Equally sensitive for the UK was the proposed use of QMV on how the 'Own Resources' system (the method by which the Union is financed) functions. Anything which risked the UK being outvoted and so open up the real possibility of it losing the rebate secured by Margaret Thatcher twenty years earlier was anathema to Her Majesty's Treasury. The final text locks decisions on the functioning of the Own Resources system into a prior decision on the system itself. That decision is taken by unanimity and therefore provides the necessary guarantees sought by the UK.

Whilst 'Own Resources' are about financing the Union, the rules on spending are equally sensitive. Every seven years the Member States enter into protracted negotiations to fix the maximum levels of expenditure by policy area which the Union can incur for the next seven-year period. The Convention took the view that these negotiations (rechristened as the Multiannual Financial Framework), already difficult with fifteen Member States, would only be possible with twenty-five or more if they could be resolved through a decision taken by Qualified Majority. In the IGC the main contributors to the EU budget were determined to guard their position by reverting to unanimity. Paradoxically, many of the net recipients also saw unanimity as a means of protecting their interests. It was one of the clearest examples for the proponents of QMV of the short-sightedness of sticking to unanimity.

The discussions on QMV in the economic and financial area became linked to the slightly different issue of the procedures in the Constitution for reaching agreement annually on the Union's budget. The Convention had decided that the budget rules should be simplified by removing the current distinction between compulsory and non-compulsory expenditure and the different procedures which apply in each case. The effect of removing this distinction was to give the Parliament the last word in the decision-making process, thereby bringing the European Parliament in line with the practice by which legislatures traditionally have the final say on budgetary issues.

Whilst some Member States in the IGC were happy to accept this, a larger number successfully rallied to put the Council back on at least an equal footing with the Parliament. They did so for different, even contradictory, reasons. France for example wanted to be able to ensure that spending levels on areas of vital national interest, most importantly agriculture, could not be undermined by the European Parliament. Others such as the UK saw it as an opportunity to ensure budgetary rigour by restraining the Parliament's natural tendency to encourage higher expenditure.

The results of the IGC in this area were mixed. It had always been inevitable that there would be a return to unanimity in some key areas. Yet this should not be allowed to obscure the very real advances achieved by the Convention, the large majority of which were untouched by the IGC. Expanding the scope of QMV has been one of the threads running through the history of the European Union. If it is becoming increasingly difficult to remove the remaining traces of unanimity, this is not as a result of greater stubbornness on the part of Member States, but rather because as the list of issues becomes gradually shorter, so their sensitivity increases; many of the provisions still subject to unanimity are considered to touch at the heart of national sovereignty.

Institutions: making or breaking the Constitution

Whilst the scope of QMV was a sensitive issue, and could have blocked a final agreement, it was not complicated. With the exception of those areas where it was decided to apply the emergency brake mechanism, the IGC had a simple choice between unanimity or QMV. The compromise lay in determining which policy areas lay on which side of the dividing line. This was not the case with institutional issues. Whilst many of them were just as sensitive, if not more so, the solutions were much less obvious.

The fate of several of the main institutional issues has been covered in an earlier chapter. The demise of the legislative Council, the reinstatement of the rotating Presidency under a different guise[37], and the haggling over the numbers of European Parliament seats[38]: all of these occupied the IGC at different stages and for different periods. The Convention's proposal to create a full-time President of the European Council[39], although resented by many Member States, went unchallenged in the IGC, but remained a potential weapon in the hands of some of the smaller Member States and could have been used to devastating effect had other issues (for example the balanced deal on the Foreign Minister) began to unravel.

This part of the chapter concentrates on the two institutional issues which proved to be the most difficult for the IGC to resolve: the Commission, and even more importantly, the definition of Qualified Majority Voting.

The Commission[40]: making it efficient, but not yet

The call to stick with the Nice Treaty which had echoed throughout the last few weeks of the Convention was still resonating when the IGC began its work in October 2003. But Nice meant different things to different Member States. For Spain and Poland it signified first and foremost retaining the system of weighted votes in the Council. For many others, it referred rather to the composition of the Commission and (erroneously) to the permanent maintenance of one Commissioner per Member State.

The Convention text provided for a two-tier system of Commissioners. The fact that there was little to distinguish between these two tiers was the price to pay for acceptance of the system. A determined group of Member States within the Convention had been tenacious in eroding the differences between the two types of Commissioners. As a result, when the IGC began, it appeared almost inevitable that this process would be pushed to its logical conclusion and result in everyone having a full Commissioner with voting rights. In fact the opposite happened; the IGC decided to abandon the two-tier system and agreed that there should be a move to a system of rotation with nationals from only two-thirds of the Member States being present in any one Commission at a time. There are several reasons for this shift of position.

Firstly, the balance of argument between legitimacy (in the eyes of some) and efficiency began to swing clearly in the direction of the latter. The most vocal supporters of one Commissioner per Member State had always been the smaller Member States, and within this group, the new Member States in particular, who argued that the presence of a Commissioner helped give their citizens a greater sense of ownership of the Brussels structures and processes. However this group had never been totally cohesive. The Benelux countries in particular had argued from the beginning that the interests of the smaller Member States would be much more effectively defended by a reduced Commission. Others, even if not completely convinced, began to see that they had a point. This included the Irish, who were in a strong position, both as a smaller Member State and as holder of the Presidency during the second half of the IGC, to influence the final outcome.

Secondly, the possible pain of not having a Commissioner was lessened by further postponing the implementation of the new system. Whilst the arrangements foreseen in the Convention text were intended to come into effect on 1 November 2009, the IGC decided that the first Commission after the entry into force of the Constitution should continue to consist of one Commissioner per Member State, thereby effectively postponing the new system until 2014. If a week is a long time in politics, ten years is an eternity.

Thirdly, there was a gradual realisation that the clamour for a return to Nice was incompatible with a permanent system of one Commissioner per Member State. The Nice Treaty is unequivocal in providing for a reduced Commission when the Union consists of twenty-seven Member States. Those few at the end who were still arguing for one Commissioner per Member State were not seeking to maintain the status quo but actually go back on earlier treaty commitments. As a matter of principle, this became difficult for others to accept.

In the end, by way of compromise, the IGC plumped for a proportion of nationals within the Commission of two-thirds rather than the more obvious half. The pretext was that this would be more acceptable since it would reduce the length of time during which any one Member State was prevented from having one of its nationals in the Commission. Paradoxically, by limiting further the number of Member States excluded at any one time, it could enhance the sense of isolation (and so of frustration) amongst the group temporarily excluded from influence.

The key to the acceptance of any system of a reduced Commission is the built-in guarantees that it will operate on the basis of equal rotation between the Member States. The exact formula is taken over wholesale from the Nice Treaty, although the details of the system (specifically the order of rotation) will require a unanimous decision of the European Council. The fact that the IGC opted for two-thirds rather than half means that this decision will not be easy to draft (not least because it will have to allow for future adaptations to take account of further accessions to the Union), but it is clear that it cannot in any way undermine the principle of equal rotation which is completely watertight[41].

One further issue on the Commission was a novel provision introduced by the Convention requiring each Member State to provide a list of three candidates for the post of Commissioner, from which the President-elect would choose the person he or she considered to be the most suitable. This proved too innovative for the IGC; Member States were fearful of either losing control, or of instituting a process which would discourage serious candidates from applying, or even worse of allowing it to degenerate into a farce, with lists comprising one serious and two spoof candidates. They probably had a point. The result is that the selection process is destined to remain relatively predictable, and probably less interesting.

Double Majority[42]: the whole edifice under threat

The Convention had decided on a radically new approach to decision-making in the Council. In so doing, it came close to sounding the death-knell of the entire Constitution. No other issue in the IGC proved more contentious than the Convention's proposal to move to a system of double majority voting. On no other issue were so many delegations prepared to stake the future of the whole Constitution, although paradoxically, with one or two notable exceptions (e.g. Poland), the issue attracted little public attention.

The Convention had been confronted with a system of vote weighting which, although it had served the Union well for over forty years, had been called into disrepute for reasons set out in earlier chapters. Giscard d'Estaing decided to go back to the drawing board and so proposed a double majority system which set two thresholds: a majority of Member States (i.e. more than 50 percent) and more than 60 percent of total population, both of which would be required for a decision in the Council to be adopted by Qualified Majority Vote. It would enter into effect on 1 November 2009, along with the provisions governing the composition of the Commission. The system proposed by the Convention appeared to reflect the principle of the Union's double legitimacy, and its simplicity was seductive – the procedures for decision-making in the Council would at long last be understandable to Europe's citizens. Furthermore it had the advantage of being applicable automatically whatever the size of the Union, eliminating the need for negotiations on the occasion of each new accession.

But several Member States were less impressed by the arguments of simplicity and durability. Spain and Poland, who stood to lose out considerably by comparison with the Nice system, pushed their objections as far as they reasonably could in the Convention. Likewise a tenacious group of smaller Member States remained convinced to the very end that the double majority system in the form in which it had been agreed by the Convention treated them unfairly. In short there was never a real consensus within the Convention on this issue, although no one was ungracious enough at the time to allow this to undermine its wider achievements.

However, this meant that the IGC was quickly confronted with an apparently intractable problem: how to maintain the principle of the double majority system (which was a sine qua non for several delegations – in particular Germany) and yet accommodate within that system the sometimes very different demands of various delegations. The answer lay in a series of devices, each designed to meet one or more concern, but each in its turn creating further problems. The result was a multilayered system of political fixes which made it possible for the IGC to reach agreement on the double majority system, but which in doing so rendered the entire construction obscurantist. The search for simplicity, which was the main reason behind the double majority system, was crushed by political expediency.

A succession of fixes: keeping the edifice in one piece

The first fix was to satisfy the Spanish and Poles, who were in the vanguard of the opposition to the double majority system, and initially simply requested nothing less than a return to the Nice system. However it was clear from early on that for Spain (and later for Poland also – despite continuing rhetoric from Warsaw about 'Nice or die'), the double majority system would be acceptable if they could retain more or less the same blocking power as under the Nice system. This would mean raising the population threshold from 60 to around 70 percent, a figure which would have made decision-making generally in the Council more difficult, and which was therefore completely unacceptable to a number of other Member States.

The situation became slightly easier in April 2004 following the election of a socialist government in Madrid: the demand fell from 70 to 66 percent, and in the end the Spanish accepted the final compromise of 65 percent. Poland continued to insist on the same treatment as under Nice and only fell into line following further guarantees in the form of a Council decision (see below). The raising of the threshold looks simple enough in itself, but further arithmetic contortions were going to be needed if the 65 percent figure was to be acceptable to everyone.

For those (mainly smaller) Member States who made it clear that they would never accept a 70 percent population threshold, 65 percent was better. But not much. They still had to be given a sweetener in the form of a further fix. The problem with a population threshold of 65 percent was not just that it made decision-making generally more difficult, but that decisions could be blocked by just three of the largest Member States. Set against the background of continuing tension between the larger and smaller Member States, this was too much. Part of the solution came in the form of a clause which states that a blocking minority must include at least four Council members to be valid. This has the effect, where a measure is opposed by only the three largest Member States, of allowing such a measure to be adopted with the support of just 58 percent of the Union's population, considerably lower than under the Nice Treaty.

But this was still not sufficient for the smaller Member States. Their position had always been that, to be acceptable, the double majority system should be on the basis of parity of thresholds. This would at least have had the advantage of genuine simplicity. But the problem was that it would also have swung the balance of advantage strongly in favour of the smaller

Member States (particularly since the most recent enlargement) and was therefore unacceptable to the others.

Faced with the impossibility of achieving parity, the smaller Member States insisted instead that the gap between the two thresholds should at least be no larger than 5 percent. Yet the proposed fix for Spain actually widened the gap (50 percent Member State threshold against a 65 percent threshold for the population). The answer involved a further fix consisting of two elements. Firstly, it was agreed that the Member State threshold should, in line with the population threshold, be raised by 5 percent, taking it to 55 percent. Secondly, a further provision was inserted which states that the figure of 55 percent should comprise at least fifteen Member States.

This second element, which through considerable mathematical ingenuity juxtaposes percentages and absolute figures, allowed everyone to save face, although it constituted a further blow to simplicity. In the current Union of twenty-five Member States, the minimum of fifteen represents 60 percent of the total, thereby meeting the concerns of those seeking a minimum 5 percent gap in thresholds. In a Union of twenty-seven, the figure of fifteen will be equivalent to 55 percent of the total. Since the accession of Bulgaria and Romania is set to take the total number of Member States to twenty-seven in 2007, which is when the Constitution is likely to come into force, this particular provision will serve no substantive purpose beyond that of helping secure an overall agreement.

The Polish problem: papering over the last crack

The last remains of simplicity in the double majority system disappeared under a final gloss which took the form of a so-called safeguard clause. The Poles, who were under huge domestic pressure not to cede any of the considerable advantage which they had obtained under the Nice voting arrangements, proved to be more obdurate negotiators than the Spanish. A population threshold of 65 percent was better for them than 60, but still not enough to match the blocking power they had under the Nice treaty. But since a further rise was out of the question, the solution had to be found elsewhere. Inspiration came from the experience of the 'Ioannina compromise' which had enabled British Prime Minister John Major to exit from a full-blown political crisis in 1994.

The solution takes the form of a draft Council decision which is intended (as the preambular paragraphs state) to allow for a smooth transition from the Nice Treaty voting arrangements to the double majority system. In practice it allows for a Member State, in cases where the normal blocking minority has not been attained, to indicate its opposition to the act in question being adopted and request that it be referred back to the Council for further discussion. The Council then tries to meet the concerns of that Member State within the obligatory time limits laid down by Union law, after which the procedures follow their normal course.

This provision is not a formal derogation to the double majority rules but rather allows a Member State to buy time by requesting a sort of second reading. Equally the mechanism cannot be invoked indiscriminately. The draft decision is clear that it can only be triggered if there is opposition to the measure in question from a group of Member States representing at least three-quarters of the population, or at least three-quarters of the number of Member States, necessary to constitute a blocking minority. These figures (which de facto constitute a 'fall-back' blocking minority) were not chosen arbitrarily, but are rather exactly equivalent to the blocking capacity of Poland (and Spain) under the Nice system. Through this final manipulation honour was saved and the double majority system was agreed.

The mathematicians protest

Honour may have been saved, but an unlikely group remained dissatisfied. Just before the final round of negotiations in June 2004, the governments of the Member States found themselves being lobbied by a group calling themselves 'Scientists for a democratic Europe'[43]. They rounded on the double majority system and the Nice system on the basis that both violate the basic democratic principle that the vote of a citizen of one Member State ought to be worth as much as that of another from any other Member State. They argued instead that the clearest way of ensuring that this principle was fulfilled was to give each Member State a voting weight equivalent to the square root of its population.

A large amount of academic literature exists on the problems of voting in the Council. Much of this draws on the work of game theorists and focuses on the relationship between vote weighting and voting power. The subject was pioneered by the British mathematician Lionel Penrose, who in the late 1940s developed a voting power index (subsequently adapted by an American, after whom it is now better known as the 'Banzhaf' index), which led him to develop what became known as 'Penrose's Square Root Law'. The impeccable logic underpinning the fairness of this approach constituted the main argument behind the mathematicians' attempt (an historical first) to influence the outcome of an Intergovernmental Conference[44].

The square root system had been floated discreetly by Sweden during the negotiations leading up to the Nice Treaty. At that time, it made virtually no headway since it ran up immediately against the French insistence on retaining parity with Germany. The Convention had not considered any alternative to the double majority system, and the IGC showed no inclination to do so either. Instead the simplicity of the double majority system continued to be used as an argument in its favour long after the multiplication of fixes had complicated it almost beyond recognition. Ironically, the square root system, since its first appearance in the 2000 IGC, and despite the faultless reasoning on which it is based, has consistently been rejected on the grounds that it is too complicated and likely to be ridiculed.

Although any voting system which deprives some Member States of some of their existing influence in the Council (however excessive) would be difficult to negotiate, the logic of the square root system cannot be challenged. But the IGC chose not to go down the route of logic – the chance encounter between politics and mathematics was, on this occasion at least, brief and unproductive.

For all its complexity, the double majority system as agreed by the IGC will certainly function satisfactorily. The assessment in this chapter has focused on the relative influence of the Member States within the system. However, for some it was equally important to ensure that the new system at least maintained, and preferably improved, the overall decision-making capacity of the Council. Whilst comparisons between the two different systems are difficult, there is no doubt that the double majority system will make a small contribution in this direction. The other advantage of the double majority system remains its durability. It can serve a Union of twenty-seven or more without further adaptation. Whether Europe's leaders are ready to accept that this will also be the case upon Turkish accession remains to be seen. Perhaps the time of the mathematicians has yet to come.

*   *   *   *   *   *

Member States' governments within the IGC recognised for the most part that the drafting of an entire Constitution by the Convention had been a remarkable achievement. It had accomplished more than anyone could have ever hoped for from a classical IGC. For that reason all were prepared to exercise the self-discipline called for by the Italian Presidency when the IGC got underway. As a result, many provisions which would never have even been put on the table of an IGC without a preceding Convention went entirely unchallenged.

But an IGC is still an arena where national interests are defended. Even those who invoke a higher European cause are acting out of self-interest; the two simply happen to coincide. In some cases, the provisions in the Constitution, particularly in the area of institutions, were unacceptable, and in these cases, Member States were willing to risk losing the Constitution for the sake of real or perceived national interest. They would probably have done so with regret. They might in some cases have miscalculated their balance of interests. But there is little doubt that if pushed they would have done so. The fact that such huge efforts were made to try to bridge in some cases apparently unbridgeable gaps must mean that they considered the Constitution worth fighting for. The next chapter looks at why that was the case, and provides an assessment of the Constitution as a whole. Was it all in the end worthwhile? Should the Constitution be embraced, ignored, or rejected?

9. The Constitution: an overall assessment

The final compromise presented by the Irish Presidency late in the evening of 18 June 2004 was accepted with only one minor amendment. Shortly afterwards the successful conclusion of the Intergovernmental Conference was celebrated by Europe's leaders with congratulatory speeches and glasses of champagne. For some present there was an acute sense of déjà vu. Almost exactly a year before the Convention had toasted its own success in an similar manner. Previous chapters have set out what happened between these two events: how the draft Constitution had been subjected to close scrutiny by the IGC, how it was adapted, and in some cases improved, but also how in some cases pressure of national interest led to changes which did little overall to improve the text.

What were Europe's leaders celebrating on the evening of 18 June? Was it simply relief at delivering an agreement at all (this would be understandable given the difficult and at times uncertain period of confinement), or was there genuine satisfaction at the quality of the end product? At the time the outcome was generally welcomed by Europe's press and public opinion. But few took the trouble to look into the details. For many commentators, the fact that agreement had been reached at all was the story. Giscard d'Estaing had admitted that the Convention text was not perfect. Even after the IGC it remained imperfect, not least in the area of institutions. However such criticisms were limited, and largely outweighed by a strong sense that the overall outcome represented a considerable achievement.

The agreement on 18 June was still not the end of the process. In order to enter into force, the Constitution requires ratification by all twenty-five Member States. That means either approval by national parliaments or, in a number of cases, a referendum in which the citizens will be asked to give their judgement. Whatever the route of ratification required or chosen, there is no opportunity for any reopening of the text. Put simply, it is a choice of take it or leave it. That means that the process of ratification has to involve an assessment of the Constitution in its entirety. Detailed scrutiny of the text will certainly help identify both its strong and weak points, but the process has to provide a satisfactory response to the question: does the Constitution as a whole stand up or not? This chapter aims to provide just such a response. It attempts to do so by viewing the Constitution from a number of different viewpoints: certainty, durability, readability, adaptability, and novelty. On the basis of these key criteria, it concludes that overall there are good arguments for welcoming the Constitution. And provided there are serious and objective debates in the Member States, there seems little reason why the national ratification processes should not come to the same conclusion.

Certainty: finally bringing the debate to a close

The nature of the Union, its objectives and its end purpose, has since its inception been the subject of inexhaustible research amongst academics and specialists, as well as (more importantly) of endless disputes amongst politicians. In some countries in particular these political disputes have spilled over into a more general and widespread public debate about the benefits and legitimacy of European integration. Much of this debate has been poorly informed, and frequently characterised by prejudice. Like many such debates it has become polarised, often ending up more as a reflection of internal political division than a serious attempt to grapple with the real issues.

The debate on Europe can be caricatured as having been monopolised by the two more extreme ends of the spectrum of opinion. At one end there are the so-called 'federalists'. Marked by an almost evangelical zeal in some cases, the federalists regard any move towards greater integration as self-evidently of benefit to Europe as a whole. Perhaps more importantly, they consider that the European Community, and subsequently the European Union, are only steps in a process towards a fully-fledged federation which is both Europe's destiny and its ultimate destination.

At the other end of the spectrum are the 'sceptics'. They consider that European integration is not a given but has at every stage to be justified on the basis of concrete results. For them there is no question of relinquishing national control in favour of a European federation: the nation state, as it emerged from the Treaty of Westphalia and the upheavals of the nineteenth century, is sovereign and inviolable. They therefore have a strong preference for intergovernmental cooperation over supranational arrangements.

In between these two very contrasting approaches sit the 'realists' (as they might wish to describe themselves). The realists, although largely silent, probably constitute the majority of mainstream opinion. They accept that the European Union has delivered a variety of benefits for its citizens, and that it should continue to constitute the principal framework for cooperation between European nation states. They are ready to accept the sharing of sovereignty which this involves, although are watchful that this does not lead to unnecessary interference in every aspect of life, and that it respects the identity of individual Member States.

Even the most casual observer of European affairs will be struck by the fact that the polarisation of the debate between 'federalists' and 'sceptics' is not only artificial and fruitless, but has been largely overtaken by events. The European Union has for many years been conducting a number of key policy areas (for example, trade, certain aspects of competition policy and monetary policy) on a federal basis with most people not even noticing and most of those who have noticed not calling it into question. At the same time, whilst the federal model has been successfully applied to a number of areas, this has not necessarily led to its application across the entire range of policies. Indeed quite the reverse: there are a number of areas which require, and will continue to require, their own particular methods of functioning. The reasons for this are both practical and political. Practical because the 'one size fits all' approach is not necessarily the best way to deliver results. Political because the Member States are unwilling to give up some of their prerogatives in areas considered to be of vital national interest.

One of the merits of the Constitution is that it aims to bring to a close this debate (which has become rather sterile over time) by introducing a degree of certainty about the nature of the Union. It does not come down on either one or other side of the debate, but rather recognises explicitly for the first time that the Union is, and will remain, a hybrid model. Having accepted this basic tenet, it sets out a number of basic principles to guide the functioning of the Union in the future. Some of these principles have already been examined in detail in earlier chapters, and can be considered to fall within two categories.

On the one hand, the Constitution is clear that not only does the Union owe its existence to the Member States, but that they will continue to be central to its functioning. Firstly, the Union is explicitly recognised as deriving its legitimacy from both the Member States and the peoples of Europe. Secondly, the Constitution makes clear that the Union only has such powers as those which are delegated to it by the Member States: it cannot accumulate or multiply powers against their wishes.

Thirdly, the principle of subsidiarity (restated and reinforced in the Constitution) subordinates the powers of the Union to those of the Member States in those areas where powers are shared. That means in practice that whilst in most cases the need for action at the Union level is quite clear, the arguments cannot necessarily be taken as given. Taken together, these elements will have the effect of putting a brake on further integration where this is driven by ideology rather than objective need. The arguments of habit or jurisprudence will no longer suffice. These principles also serve to reinforce the notion that the Constitution remains essentially an international treaty agreed between sovereign nation states. In short, one of the purposes of the Constitution is to render unto the Member States that which belongs to them and to the Union what belongs to it.

Yet the Constitution is clear that the Union is 'sui generis' and more than just another international organisation. The legal personality of the Union is clarified and simplified, and the primacy of Union law, within the limits of the powers of the Union, is made explicit for the first time. Its unique institutional structure, although slightly modified, continues to serve to underline the supranational character of many aspects of the Union. Furthermore, the powers of the Union, as attributed to it by the Member States, and either shared with them or in some cases transferred exclusively to the Union, are set out clearly for the first time. Deliberately, and for good reasons, the Member States have given up in part the power to exclusive control over their own destiny. In doing so they have created a unique organisation. So the Constitution recognises the paradox that the Union is created by the Member States as a political entity in its own right, with its own powers, but that it is also of one being with the Member States, dependent on them for its continued existence.

Certainty provides the citizen and the practitioner with greater security. Gone is the notion that the treaties are merely the vehicles for reaching a destination as yet undefined. Banished as a result is the interminable quarrel over what the end product should be and how one should get there. Instead the Constitution defines the Union for the first time and sets out a number of fundamental principles. In doing so, it presents the reader with the description of a result rather than a process, of an organisation which owes its existence to the nation state, yet one which has extensive powers of its own and which is without parallel in history.

Durability: a Constitution for five years or fifty?

The greater certainty over the nature of the Union will be an important factor in prolonging the life of the Constitution, even if the claim by Giscard d'Estaing that it is set to last fifty years may appear exaggerated. The frequent calls in the past for treaty revision have been due in part to external factors such as the need to address the requirements created by the accession of new members as well as to develop the Union's capacity to meet emerging policy challenges. But these are not the only reasons. IGCs have repeatedly fallen short of meeting their objectives because Member States have consistently been unwilling or unable to distance themselves from a rather narrow definition of their national interests. As a consequence the results have frequently borne the mark of messy compromise solutions which complicate an already byzantine organisation, and in some cases do not even solve the issues they were supposed to address. Not that the Member States have been unaware of their own inadequacies: all too often a mediocre result in an IGC has been accompanied by a commitment to convene a further Conference with the objective of doing better next time. The result has been a Union constantly trying to catch up with itself, making do with inadequate tools and an outdated institutional framework.

The long term consequences are significant. The Union has with some justification been criticised for overly concentrating on issues related to its internal functioning (issues which appear arcane to the general public) at the expense of tackling real problems of most direct concern to its citizens. As a result, public support for the Union has reached an all-time low.

The Constitution offers the best chance of providing the stability which is essential if the Union is to recover much of the public sympathy which has been lost over the last twenty years or so. Even if the claim that the Constitution will last fifty years should not be taken literally, there are a number of reasons why it can be expected to survive significantly longer than many of the treaties which have emerged from recent IGCs.

Firstly, the use of the term 'Constitution', whatever its real legal significance (or lack of it), conveys the notion of political stability. Just as national constitutions are not meant to be altered on the slightest pretext, so the creation of a Constitution for the European Union implies the fixing of lasting rules governing the way it operates. The constant recourse to Intergovernmental Conferences to change the rules of the game should be a thing of the past.

Secondly, as has just been set out above, the objective of finally bringing to a close the debate over the Union's ultimate destination helps end the interminable arguments over the very nature of the Union. Those who might try to reopen this debate will have to demonstrate that the Convention, despite its credentials of transparency and legitimacy, got it wrong.

Thirdly, the dropping of the phrase 'ever-closer Union', combined with the European Council conclusions of June 2004 referring to the completion of the process of European integration, mean that with the adoption of the Constitution, a line has been drawn in the sand.

Fourthly, the Constitution contains a number of provisions designed to allow for some articles, in particular those related to specific policy areas, to be adapted and updated in the future whilst avoiding a comprehensive review of the text as a whole. This innovation, which is covered in more detail below, has the double advantage of preserving the fundamentals of the Constitution intact but at the same time giving the Union some capacity to respond flexibly to problems of direct concern to Europe's citizens. Flexibility is a guarantee of durability.

There is a further factor which will militate in favour of the Constitution's longevity, but which is unconnected with its content. The difficulties of renegotiating the European Union's rules amongst twenty-five Member States were only too obvious during the IGC which followed the Convention. Some of the implications of this will be looked at in detail in the final chapter, but it is almost certain that the Member States will not lightly enter into a further process of wholesale treaty revision for the foreseeable future. The risks of failure are simply too high. At the same time this does not entirely exclude that they might choose to negotiate very specific and limited changes to the Constitution, not least to the less satisfactory parts, in particular the institutional arrangements. Nevertheless, the flexibility built into the Constitution should help keep future treaty amendment to a minimum. As far as possible, Member States will prefer to live with the existing text.

Readability: the challenge of making the European Union understandable

One of the main criticisms of the existing treaty texts is that they are almost completely inaccessible to the ordinary reader (the decision by the Danish government to distribute copies of the Maastricht Treaty to every one of its citizens, only to see it rejected by them in a referendum, perhaps provides a lesson to politicians throughout the Union). The main reason for this is that the current treaties constitute a compilation of provisions superimposed by successive Intergovernmental Conferences. The result is a set of texts of bewildering complexity. Before the Convention, no serious attempt was made, other than by academics, to introduce greater order or clarity, such an exercise being regarded as too politically sensitive.

The approach adopted by the Convention was radical. It rejected the traditional incremental approach adopted by earlier Intergovernmental Conferences and decided instead to rewrite the treaties in their entirety. The result, as has already been seen, does not necessarily mean that the existing provisions were automatically rejected. Far from it. But it did mean a complete reorganisation of the texts with the main objective being precisely to improve their presentation and so render them more readable and intelligible to the average reader. This was done in three ways.

Firstly, the most important provisions concerning the objectives, organisation and functioning of the Union, as well as the provisions taken over from the Charter of Fundamental Rights, were grouped together as Parts I and II at the beginning of the text. In this way the main 'constitutional' elements were consolidated in a relatively concise and systematic manner.

Secondly, a serious attempt was made to keep the language of the Constitution, and particularly Part I, as clear, simple and accessible as possible to the average reader.

Thirdly, the remaining provisions, in particular those concerning the Union's policies and which constitute the largest part of the Constitution, were re-grouped and ordered more systematically than in the past. The decision to end the separate 'pillar' structure introduced by the Maastricht Treaty made this task significantly easier.

It would be churlish to deny that the combination of these three elements has resulted in a text which is a significant improvement in terms of readability compared with the current treaties. Of course, as with any legal text, it is possible to play the game of finding articles which remain obscure and impenetrable. That is not the point. For the first time, any reasonably well informed and educated person can pick up the text in his or her own language and easily read and understand the first few dozen pages which form the 'constitutional' basis for the European Union. He or she should as a result have a clear idea of what the Union is, and just as importantly, what it is not. This is important if support for the Union in the longer term is to be recovered. It will of course also play a role in helping secure endorsement of the Constitution, in particular in those countries which will use a referendum in the ratification process.

Of course, although the text overall is very much clearer, it has its shortcomings. Some of the provisions of the Constitution remain complex and difficult to understand. But there are good reasons for this. Firstly, the Constitution reflects directly the complex nature of the Union: it has to take into account twenty-five political realities, and structures which enable twenty-five Member States between them to work together. Secondly, unlike national constitutions, which can take as read the sovereign powers of the nation state, the European Constitution has to define both the content and extent of the powers which the Member States have delegated to the Union. Thirdly, the Constitution does not exist just to sell the Union to its citizens; it is also an international treaty and a legally-binding text which must provide security for its users. Legal clarity and public accessibility do not always sit comfortably together. Whilst any attempt to explain the Union in simple terms should be welcome, simplification has its limits. The Constitution should as far as possible be a simple text; it should not be a simplistic one.

Some of the reasons for the complexity of the Union's basic texts have been forgotten over recent years as increased public disenchantment with the Union has led to growing pressure to render the Union more understandable. The vacuous catchphrase 'bringing Europe closer to the citizen' is used all too often. What exactly does it mean?   Ensuring that the Constitution is as accessible as possible is a worthy objective, but ever more exaggerated attempts to popularise EU treaty language are unlikely to increase support for the Union. Too frequently Member States' governments have indulged in calls for simpler and clearer language in the Constitution out of popular appeal, yet are all too ready to sacrifice readability when serious national interests are at stake. The obvious example is the double majority voting system. The Convention endorsed this system largely on the grounds that it was easy to understand. The pressure in the IGC from some Member States, for political reasons, for amendments and additions left some aspects of it difficult to explain or justify (for example the apparently arbitrary Member State threshold of 55%), and ended up with a system which is in general more complicated than that which it replaces.

In general, the Constitution is more readable than the existing treaties, and as such should be welcomed. But the text can only be expected to deliver so much; public support for the Union will not be built solely on the basis of a legal document. Rebuilding confidence in the Union will rather require the governments of the Member States to take their own responsibilities in this area more seriously than they have done up to now. This aspect will be covered in more detail in the next chapter.

Adaptability: evolution rather than revolution

The Constitution provides the possibility of stability for the Union, offering a breathing space within which some public support might be recovered. Yet the public is sensitive also to the need for the Union to adapt to changing circumstances. How many would have predicted the need for the Union to look for much more effective ways to address the threat of terrorism post 9/11? If the Union cannot be allowed to change constantly, so neither can it remain frozen in time.

There are two sets of provisions built into the Constitution which allow it to evolve without overturning the entire system. The first permits the Member

States collectively to bypass the normal procedures for treaty revision by making use of a fast track for amending specific parts of the Constitution, subject to a number of conditions. The second gives smaller groups of Member States, by working together, the possibility of moving ahead in any given policy area under the arrangements known as enhanced cooperation.

The provision of lighter procedures for treaty revision offers an alternative to the traditional and relatively cumbersome procedures of an Intergovernmental Conference. Separate provisions govern the possibility of extending the scope of both Qualified Majority Voting and the legislative procedure, and of amending the detailed provisions of the policy articles in Part III.

The extension of QMV has always been a sensitive issue. It proved to be so both in the Convention and in the subsequent IGC. Although there was a critical mass in the Convention in support of a considerable extension of QMV, it was accepted that some sensitive areas would have to continue to be subject to unanimity. The final Convention text therefore represented a compromise between these two positions (although it was not sufficiently robust to withstand some adjustment in the IGC). A key element in this compromise was the inclusion of a simplified procedure giving the European Council, acting unanimously, the power to extend the scope of QMV. This procedure was not called into question by the IGC. It should provide reassurance that the Union will not be bound indefinitely by its current procedures.

Similar provisions are designed to extend democratic legitimacy through a greater involvement of the European Parliament in the decision-making process: like the provisions for extending QMV, the European Council can decide by unanimity to replace the special legislative procedure with the normal legislative procedure (i.e. co-decision with the European Parliament).

The simplified procedure for amending the policy articles in Part III was introduced by the IGC. It gives limited powers of treaty revision through a unanimous decision of the European Council, thereby avoiding the need for an Intergovernmental Conference. The procedure can be activated by a proposal from any Member State government, the European Parliament or the Commission. Although any such decision still has to be ratified by the Member States, removing the need for an Intergovernmental Conference will minimise the drama of treaty revision. This in turn should make it easier to agree limited changes to the text whilst reducing the pressure for a complete reopening of the Constitution. One important condition of this provision is that any changes to the policy articles may not increase the competences attributed to the Union in the Constitution.

Further possibilities for revision are also foreseen in the area of institutions. For example in the section on the Commission, which foresees a reduction in Commissioners to two-thirds of the total number of Member States from 2014, the Constitution retains the existing possibility for the European Council, acting unanimously, to change the number of Commissioners.

The Constitution also provides some flexibility in the provisions on the arrangements governing the Presidency of the Council. There is only a cursory reference to the issue in the text of the Constitution itself; the main pro-visions are set out in a draft decision which was agreed by the IGC and which has to be adopted by the European Council once the Constitution is in force. The precise arrangements for the future therefore depend on the content of the decision, which is not only to be adopted by qualified majority, but can also be amended in future by the same procedure. This opens up the possibility in future, should Member States consider it useful, of moving from a continuation of the rotating Presidency to a model which (for example) might be much closer to a genuine 'team' system.

For those who doubt whether there will be sufficient political will to make use of these procedures for adapting the Constitution (whether or not they require unanimity), enhanced cooperation offers an alternative way forward. It gives the option to a reduced number of Member States of strengthening cooperation amongst themselves in a particular policy area and so to move ahead of their partners.

The possibility of enhanced cooperation has existed since its introduction in the Treaty of Amsterdam in 1997, but has never been used as such. This is probably because the areas in which its application was most promising (monetary union and the Schengen arrangements on the free movement of people) already had their own specific 'built-in' arrangements. Equally the complex conditions for activating enhanced cooperation in the potentially large number of other policy areas tended to act as a discouragement.

By addressing some of the weaknesses of the existing provisions, the Constitution increases the viability of enhanced cooperation. Firstly it extends the potential use of enhanced cooperation to all areas (whilst CFSP had subsequently been included under the Nice Treaty, matters having military or defence implications were still excluded). Secondly, the Constitution anticipates the possible use of enhanced cooperation in some specific areas (defence policy and judicial cooperation in criminal matters), and even provides streamlined procedures to enable these to be put into effect. Thirdly, the new articles contain a provision allowing those participating Member States to decide by unanimity to introduce QMV in the area covered by enhanced cooperation (with the exception of CFSP), even where the Constitution stipulates that unanimity is required.

The combination of lighter procedures for revising the Constitution in specifically identified areas and under certain conditions, as well as the improved arrangements to facilitate the use of enhanced cooperation, constitutes a major innovation. Although apparently technical, the impact of these provisions should not be under-estimated. Taken together they provide the Union with the capacity to evolve within the framework of the basic principles of the Constitution, and without opening up on each occasion the Pandora's box of major treaty revision. The future stability of the Union depends on a Constitution which includes a core set of provisions robust enough to last. But robustness should not be confused with rigidity: the Constitution offers the possibility for the Union to adapt whilst avoiding the dangers of either seizing up or crashing down.

Novelty: Giving the Union greater capacity to act

Much of what has been covered so far in this chapter relates to the reorgan-isation and clarification of provisions which already exist in the treaties. Does this mean that there is nothing new in the Constitution? The claim that the Constitution provides for substantial transfers of sovereignty to the Union from the Member States is clearly exaggerated, as has already been shown in earlier chapters. Equally, the suggestion that it is merely a 'tidy-ing-up' exercise (a straightforward repackaging of the existing treaties) is somewhat disingenuous. The reality lies somewhere between the two. There are a limited number of new provisions which will give the Union a greater capacity to act, or at least give it the potential to do so. They fall into three categories: policies, institutions, and extension of Qualified Majority Voting.

The new provisions in the area of policies have already been covered in some detail. The conclusion is that the Constitution is not the revolution which some might claim. The majority of the existing articles governing the Union's powers to act in a wide range of fields remain unchanged. Likewise the political balance of the existing treaties has been carried over into the Constitution: the policy mix of liberal economics and social policy (the so-called 'social market economy' or 'European social model') is maintained.

It is no accident that the more important new policy provisions are in fields which were highly topical during the period of the Convention and remain so today. For the most part, they are designed to address the com-plex mesh of security issues which have become so much the focus of atten-tion since the US and Europe have become higher risk targets for terrorist attacks. They take the form of new powers to improve cooperation between law enforcement agencies and the judiciaries on criminal matters as well as an improved capacity to act collectively in the security field, specifically with military capabilities. They fill some of the gaps in the Union's capacity to act in areas where few would deny that collective action is not just desir-able but essential.

The main innovation in the area of external policy is the creation of the post of Foreign Minister and of an External Action Service. The Foreign Minister post is primarily an institutional change, and its effectiveness will depend very much on how Javier Solana, as the first incumbent, chooses to use the resources at his disposal. Even more difficult to forecast are the effects of the new full-time President of the European Council. This also will depend very much on the first person to be appointed to the post, which cannot happen until the Constitution is in force. Neither post entails a formal transfer of powers to the Union, and in both cases, retaining the con-fidence of the Member States will be crucial. However, subject to this latter proviso, each has the potential to enhance considerably the Union's capacity to act both internally and externally.

The extension of Qualified Majority Voting, whilst not giving new powers to the Union, will certainly help it operate more efficiently. It responds to the concerns of those who fear that relying on unanimity in a Union of twenty-five or more Member States is a recipe for inaction. Some might argue that since QMV has traditionally been a tool to reach consensus by obliging all Member States to enter into the negotiating process, its real effect may be marginal. There are two responses to this: firstly and simply, voting might continue to be used more frequently; secondly, the role of the Commission in the process might unwittingly have been enhanced. This is a consequence of the rule that when the Council decides by QMV on a proposal from the Commission, it can only amend that proposal by unanimity. Traditionally this has given the Commission, which can amend its proposal at any stage in the negotiations, an influential role in the whole process. With more Member States around the table, this role can only increase, and should make for greater efficiency.

In all these areas, the Constitution will provide the Union with additional tools which should allow it to deliver more effectively where it matters. The real effectiveness of some of these tools, not least in the area of institutions, will only be clear once they are up and running. But the novelties of substance are not gimmicks, nor are they the remnants of ideological battles. They rather represent a serious attempt, despite the very different interests of twenty-five Member States, to improve the Union's ability to make a difference when it is in the common interest to do so. Few would wish otherwise.

*   *   *   *   *   *

No one would seriously claim that the Constitution is without flaws. The small minority who are viscerally hostile towards the European Union will be tempted to use the flaws to condemn the Constitution as a whole. But their condemnation is not of the Constitution but of the Union itself. No text would have been able to address their prejudices. Yet theirs is ultimately a lost cause because the very existence of the Union is a response to the increase in interdependence between nation states which is part of the dynamic of recent history.

Probably the majority of Europe's citizens will approach the Constitution with an open mind. They may question the value of the exercise. Many will certainly require convincing that the Constitution is in their interests. But they should not be asking themselves how much better the Constitution could have been, but rather the extent to which it is an improvement on the current treaties. Politics is the art of the possible not just the desirable. The fact that negotiations have to be conducted between twenty-five Member States, each one with its own overall approach and its specific objectives, creates severe constraints on what is deliverable. That we have the text of a European Constitution at all is itself a remarkable achievement.

So how to judge whether it is an improvement? This chapter has carried out an assessment on the basis of those criteria which are likely to be foremost in the minds of those being asked to approve it. Europe's citizens expect the Constitution to provide some certainty. They want it to last and to be couched in terms which they can understand. They expect it to provide the Union with both the means to face today's challenges, and the flexibility to adapt to new situations without the constant drama of treaty change. Against these expectations, it is reasonable to conclude that overall the Constitution will help contribute positively to the stability of the continent and to the lives of the citizens of the European Union.

Overall the Constitution consolidates what has gone before. It builds on the extraordinary achievement of the European Union in securing and guaranteeing peace between the nations of Europe after so many centuries of conflict and destruction. Few would deny it the chance of ensuring that continues.

10. Beyond the Constitution

The Constitution, like the Union, can never be an end in itself. It sets the objectives and the ground rules. It decides on the Union's powers and determines the procedures for exercising them. But it does not decide on policies; these require decisions in their own right, and these decisions themselves need to be implemented. Implementation of policies often requires money, sometimes large amounts. The Constitution will only begin to make a difference to the lives of Europe's citizens if it is used, and used effectively.

In any case, the Constitution will lie dormant for as long as it has not been ratified by all twenty-five Member States. This is a process which is expected to take at least two years. If the negotiation of the Constitution was a collective exercise, its ratification is the opposite since the Constitution itself states that each Member State ratifies 'according to its own constitutional requirements'. Some Member States suggested in the Council that efforts should be made at least to coordinate the course of ratification across the Union, but this received little support. Ratification takes different forms; for some it means following a parliamentary process; for others it involves a referendum or at least the option of one. Furthermore, it is up to individual governments to decide how the arguments in support of the Constitution are presented in their country; each will adapt the message to its own particular requirements. In the meantime the institutions will be under an obligation to choose their words carefully.

The Constitution is due to enter into force on 1 November 2006, provided that all the instruments of ratification have been deposited. If not, it will happen on the first day of the second month following the deposit of the instrument of the last Member State to complete its ratification procedures. In the event of a failed ratification, the Union will have to deal with the fall-out, although the consequences will to some extent depend on where ratification has failed and for what reasons. In any case, the Constitution foresees that if, after two years of signature, four-fifths of Member States have ratified and one or more have encountered difficulties, the matter shall be referred to the European Council.

It is however not the intention of this book to analyse these considerations. This final chapter therefore assumes that the Constitution enters into force, and looks further ahead. It specifically examines four issues confronting the Union.

Firstly, it sets out what has to be done to ensure that the Union functions

properly in a Union of twenty-five or more. That means not just implementing the Constitution, but also changing the behaviour of the institutions.

Secondly, it looks at the future limits, both external and internal, of the
Union: how it will define itself in terms of both territory and policy depth.

Thirdly, it looks at the main policy challenges facing the Union over next
few years, and asks how effective the Union is likely to be in delivering an
adequate response. This is not simply a question of the efficiency of the institutions, but raises the issue of whether an increasingly diverse group of
Member States have sufficient political will to translate the common purpose manifested in the Constitution into action.

Finally, the chapter looks at the wider issue of governance at the
European level and the related problem of the lack of a sense of ownership
of the Union by the public. It examines what is needed both to improve governance and increase public support, and how the Constitution might help.

None of these four issues is addressed directly by the Constitution. Not
because the Constitution is inadequate, but simply because they are not constitutional questions. Although it constitutes a major step forward, the
Constitution will leave the Union with many challenges still to be
addressed. In short, the Constitution is a tool: necessary, but in itself not
enough.

Getting the Union to function: implementing the Constitution

There are a number of provisions in the Constitution, in particular in the
area of institutions, which will need to be fleshed out before they can be
properly implemented. The three main issues which will need to be
addressed are the full-time President of the European Council, the Foreign
Minister and the detailed arrangements for the Presidency of the Council.

The arrival of the first full-time President of the European Council will
require some preparation, although the formal decision of appointment
cannot take place until after the entry into force of the Constitution. Since
the text makes clear that the European Council will be supported by the
General Secretariat of the Council, there is no requirement for the establishment of self-standing elaborate new structures. However the President will
need not just a private office, but probably also a small group of policy advisors within the Secretariat to ensure a functional link with the Council
Presidency (still basically operating under the rotating model), as well as to
maintain a political link with the other institutions. The difficult negotiations in the Convention on the description of the President's tasks suggest
that further attempts to codify the job would, at this stage, run into the sand.
Instead, much of the success of the post will depend on the abilities of the
first incumbent to exploit the considerable influence which the job could
wield, and so gradually carve out a distinctive role which complements
rather than competes with that of the President of the Commission.

The Constitution is clearer about the role of the Foreign Minister, which in any case is made easier since it is already confirmed that the first incumbent will be Javier Solana. Key will be the handling of the preparations of the External Action Service, which will constitute the Foreign Minister's main (and considerable) asset. Again, a formal decision on the establishment of this service can only be taken once the Constitution is in force, but a declaration annexed to the final act of the IGC foresees preparatory work on the service beginning once the Constitution is signed. This work will be both technically complicated and politically sensitive, since it will have to ensure that the service is capable of delivering results and yet also reflect the delicate balance between the two 'hats' of the Foreign Minister. Furthermore the final decision requires the agreement of both the Member States and the Commission. For these reasons discussions may well take the best part of the two years of the ratification process.

The third element on which preparatory work will be required is the issue of the Council Presidency. The provisions on this in the Constitution are sketchy, but are developed further in a draft decision of the European Council which formed part of the package of texts approved at the same time as the Constitution. As described in an earlier chapter, the IGC essentially agreed to continue the current rotating Presidency system, although the draft decision foresees this being organised in such a way as to provide for pre-established groups of three Member States to work together as a team. The list of future Presidencies, presented in successive groups of three, is set out in an implementing decision which was given political approval by the Council in December 2004[45]. The details of the functioning of the European Council President, Foreign Minister and the Council Presidency together constitute the main work required to get the Constitution up and running.

However the Constitution, even when fully up and running, will not in itself be a panacea for the functioning of the Union's institutions. To operate effectively, the institutions of a Union of twenty-five Member States have to change not just their rules, but also their behaviour.

Getting the Union to function: changing behaviour

The three institutions will be increasingly confronted by what Giscard d'Estaing described as the *effet nombre*: the simple fact that the larger the number of people, the more difficult it is to reach agreement. The European Parliament is the least affected, since its overall size will increase only marginally (to 750 from 732), and it is in any case divided into a limited number of relatively homogeneous political groups. In addition, negotiations are prepared initially within specialised committees, and are facilitated by the recourse to the traditional parliamentary practice of slicing up dossiers and voting on individual amendments rather than trying to reach a consensus on the whole. The main difficulty which the Parliament has had to confront over the years is the adaptation of its two buildings to accommodate the increased number of MEPs. This time the work has been limited to installing additional interpreting booths.

The Commission is not completely spared the effects of enlargement since it will have to continue to work with one Commissioner from each Member State until 2014. The College seeks as far as possible to work through consensus, but votes (by simple majority) when necessary. In practice this happens rarely. Individual Commissioners are responsible for submitting to the College draft proposals within their own area of responsibility, but usually only do so after first ironing out any problems with their colleagues. The mechanism for doing this is the normal day-to-day coordination between the relevant Commission services, and the use of working groups consisting of Commissioners with related responsibilities.

The Prodi Commission, which endorsed the approach of one Commissioner from each Member State, tried to take coordination a step further by suggesting early on in the IGC that the working groups of Commissioners (which it proposed calling 'clusters') should be given delegated power to take all but the most important decisions on behalf of the College. This proposal was viewed with suspicion by some of the smaller Member States who, notwithstanding the principle of the independence of the Commission, were nervous that this approach would lead to their exclusion from influence in important policy areas. As a result the Commission will continue with the same (perhaps slightly reinforced) informal coordinating mechanisms. At worst, some Commissioners will find themselves with time on their hands, and the increased numbers could dilute the sense of collegiality. History shows that the effectiveness of the Commission as a whole depends more on the skills of its President than on innovative procedures.

The Council is the institution which is the most affected by enlargement. No other institution has found it so difficult to change its habits. Its diplomatic roots have invested it with a strong culture of intergovernmentalism. At the same time, it continues to be hybrid in nature (with an important policy-making as well as legislative function). Its problems are only partly addressed by the Constitution, which is not a criticism, simply a reflection that the problems are less about rules than about the way in which Member States behave.

The Council has still not entirely broken away from its origins as a diplomatic conference. Yet in order to adapt to a Union of twenty-five Member States or more, it has on the one hand as a legislature to adjust its working habits so that they more closely resemble those of a parliament, and on the other hand ensure that when it is exercising its policy-making function it is able to operate efficiently and so give proper political direction.

The legislative function of the Council is now largely exercised together with the Parliament under the co-decision procedure. In so doing the Council is increasingly seen as fulfilling the role of a second chamber. Furthermore the larger numbers around the table serve to underline further this more parliamentary character. The fundamental problem is that it has not adjusted its working methods accordingly.

Even when legislating, the Council has always tended to seek consensus. In the early years of the Community, it virtually never voted because every attempt was made to reach a compromise which could be supported by all delegations. With six around the table, that worked much of the time. With fifteen, it worked sometimes, With twenty-five or more, it is no longer a serious option.

Furthermore some of the advantages of the parliamentary system are not available to the Council. For example the groups of officials which prepare the work of the Council have the same number of members as the Council itself. So reaching agreement on particularly intractable issues is no easier in a preparatory group than in the Council (indeed it is more difficult given that officials usually have less scope for compromise than politicians). In addition, the difficulties of negotiating in a larger Council have increased the tendency to concentrate overly on procedural aspects or to produce lengthy but vacuous declarations instead of delivering policy. All too often process triumphs over substance.

These problems also apply to the Council when operating in its policy-making function. In some ways even more so, because the procedural framework is less well defined, and decisions are more frequently taken by unanimity. The recourse to declarations for their own sake is a particular problem for the Council when exercising its policy-making function (especially in the area of CFSP). However not only does the end-product sometimes fall short of expectations, but the process itself is frequently cumbersome, with lengthy table rounds and interventions that are often repetitive or simply unnecessary.

How can the Council be weaned away from these habits? The Constitution itself, although not offering a direct response, is bound to act as a catalyst for change, not least by providing for the first time a clear distinction between the two principal functions of the Council: legislative (which it exercises jointly with the European Parliament) and policy-making.

The Constitution takes an important step towards recognising the increasingly parliamentary nature of the Council by providing for it to meet in public when it is acting in its legislative function. Together with the effect of increased numbers round the table, this is likely to have an effect on voting culture. The search for consensus, even when Qualified Majority Voting is available, will become more of a luxury. The Council is likely to vote earlier and more frequently. The extension of QMV provided for in the Constitution will help push the Council in this direction. The opening up of the Council to the public is also likely to have an effect on Member States' behaviour, although it is difficult to predict how. Ministers will always be tempted individually to play to the gallery, but will at the same time have a collective interest in giving the impression of the Council as an efficient business-like institution. At the very least greater transparency should help ensure that ministers are present throughout Council meetings.

The problems of those Council formations which have more of a policy-making than a legislative function are more difficult to overcome. Although the Constitution does not offer a direct solution to these problems, here also it is likely to encourage change. The separation of the General Affairs and

External Relations Council into its two component parts is particularly significant.

For the first time the General Affairs Council (GAC) is given an overall coordinating role, including preparing and following up meetings of the European Council. This means that the full-time President of the European Council will need to take a particular interest in the work of the GAC, and through it play a role in encouraging better coordination between the different Council formations. For historical reasons, the GAC, as the primus inter pares of the Council configurations, has been in the hands of Foreign Ministers. They have proved unwilling to relinquish control of it, but equally unwilling to devote the necessary time to tackling the issues on its agenda. The Constitution therefore presents an opportunity for Member States to review both their internal coordinating mechanisms and their representation in the Council. In an ideal world, Member States would be represented in the GAC by a senior cabinet rank minister with overall responsibility for the coordination of national policy on Europe. However it is of course for each Member State to decide how it is represented in the Council and how it organises itself internally.

The decline of serious negotiation in the Council generally will put greater onus on the Presidency, together with the Council Secretariat, to give momentum to the Council's work. That means more activity outside the Council meeting itself: the Presidency will in particular need to devote more time to exploring the possibilities for compromises with individual delegations. It will also have to use successive Council meetings to test revised proposals, not in the expectation that much headway can be made in the meeting itself, but to enable subsequently revised texts to be drawn up which each time more closely reflect a broad consensus. The concept of the team Presidency as set out in the Constitution could assist by helping spread the additional burden of work that this will inevitably entail.

It is likely that, in order to help overcome blockage in the Council, small numbers of delegations, representing groups of like-minded Member States, will increasingly work together to try to clear the ground on particularly difficult issues. Although such a process would have to remain informal, it could be used in a more systematic and agreed manner, thereby rendering it more transparent. The presence of the Presidency and Council Secretariat would in particular provide the necessary reassurances to some of the smaller Member States who are wary of even the faintest hint (however spurious) of having their hands forced.

Finally, the Presidency will also have some responsibility for helping change the culture of the Council. Attempts have been made to introduce some greater discipline, not least through the adoption of a code of conduct, but this is only exhortatory and so has had little effect.

But however effective the Presidency, improving behaviour in the Council is first and foremost an issue for the Member States. That means putting their own houses in order. Even with greater recourse to voting, it is impossible for a Council meeting to make progress if the 25 delegations round the table have no flexibility to negotiate. Delegations must have sufficient room for manoeuvre from their capitals to make compromises and cut deals. They have to approach each meeting focussed on achieving an outcome rather than on simply protecting their position. But this will only happen if there is proper arbitration within capitals. Too few Member States have effective bureaucratic mechanisms for coordinating EU policy. As a result they come to meetings unprepared to negotiate seriously because they have no strategy. One of the consequences of this is that different Council formations occasionally adopt different positions on exactly the same subject.

Old habits die hard. But if the old habits remain, the Council risks running into the sand. Much can be done to improve the functioning of the Council; the Constitution will help. But it is largely up to the Member States to deliver. Whilst the Council is legally more than the sum of its parts, its practical aspects depend almost entirely on the behaviour of the Member States. They cannot with integrity make grand claims for the Constitution, and yet not address the continuing daily problems which hinder the ability of the Council to function effectively.

Defining limits: the external boundaries of the Union

The need for more effective working methods must become more pressing as the Union enlarges further. Twenty-five today, set to increase to twenty-seven in 2007, and with the prospect of Turkey, Croatia, and in due course other Balkan countries joining, the Union will increasingly resemble a united nations of Europe. The Constitution says nothing about whether or where this process should stop. Paradoxically, given the apparently unfailing ability of the Union to attract newcomers, the only provision with any direct bearing on the future size of the Union in the Constitution is a new article which formalises for the first time the right of a Member State to leave.

The increased stability, security and prosperity offered by the Union have generated a logic of constant extension: every enlargement creates new neighbours and with it potential insecurities. These can best be addressed by bringing the next ring of countries into the fold; and so on. Yet some current members are uneasy. They worry that a continuous process of enlargement risks putting a stop to further integration – the old dialectic between deepening and widening. Furthermore the Union is now old enough to have created its own sense of nostalgia; there is a temptation to look back on a golden age when the founding six Member States worked in perfect harmony. Mere dreams. The risk of such a mix of introversion and nostalgia is that it gives the impression that the Union is an end in itself.

Yet even the most ardent supporters of enlargement would accept that the Union is beginning to reach its geographical limits. To the south the Mediterranean constitutes a natural frontier to the Union. The border with Russia will determine the Union's eastern limits (the accession of Russia being unrealistic on the simple grounds of size). Apart from the few countries which have taken a conscious decision not to join (Switzerland,

Norway and Iceland), what is left in between is a patchwork consisting of acceding or candidate countries (Bulgaria, Romania, Turkey, Croatia), potential candidates (the remaining Balkan countries) and those countries running up to the frontier with Russia. It is difficult to imagine these few remaining countries not being considered for inclusion (however far in the future that might be) provided they meet the established political and economic criteria. It is equally difficult to imagine throwing the net any wider than the natural frontiers to the south and east. Enlargement will remain a sensitive issue, both for public opinion within the Union and in terms of the expectations of potential newcomers. Handling it will in part depend on the ability of the Union to distinguish clearly between the issue of the principle of accession and the timing. In the end the size of the Union will be determined by a mixture of geography and common sense.

Defining limits: the internal boundaries of the Union

Enlargement raises questions about the very nature of the Union. Not simply about its capacity to function, which has already been touched upon, but also about the ability of such a diverse set of countries to continue to define a set of collective interests and to sustain a commitment to developing common policies. For this reason, some remain nervous that the enlargement process will undermine future integration. Yet enlargement has developed its own momentum, and in its wake, the deepening versus widening debate has been largely set to one side. But not completely. Everyone agrees that if there are some Member States who wish to push ahead more quickly than the rest, they should not be prevented from doing so. The enhanced cooperation provisions in the Constitution provide them with the means.

The main proponents of enhanced cooperation come from the founding six, some of whom clearly regard it as a tool not just for pursuing a single policy initiative, but more widely for establishing a core of countries wishing to take the lead by furthering deeper integration across a range of sectors. Many other Member States, whilst happy to include enhanced cooperation in the Constitution, remain to be convinced of its usefulness. They point out that the existing provisions introduced in 1997 have never been used. Moreover they say that many of those championing enhanced cooperation have been able to offer precious few concrete examples of where it might be applied, perhaps reflecting more profound differences in policy between them than they might wish to acknowledge.

Alternatives to using the formal treaty provisions on enhanced cooperation would be for a group of Member States to take the initiative either to cooperate in an area outside the EU framework, or to develop a single and indivisible approach to a particular policy area enabling them to operate as a caucus within the Council. Neither option is formally excluded by the existing treaties or the Constitution, but the first is likely to run into difficulties in relation to EU treaty obligations. The second would depend on two or more Member States (perhaps Franco-German cooperation constitutes an embryonic model?) being able to agree on a complete and permanent identification of shared interests going much further then the temporary and selective alliances which are already a feature of negotiating in the Council.

Even if the doubters are ready to accept that enhanced cooperation constitutes a solution, few of them are certain that there is really a problem. Integration may appear to have begun to run up against its natural limits, at least for the time being, but it is far from certain that this is solely, or even largely, the result of enlargement. Since enhanced cooperation, if used at all, is likely to make only limited progress in a small number of areas, it is probably ultimately a futile diversion from the real challenge of engaging within a Union of twenty-five or more. That requires a commitment from all Member States to find the necessary political will to deliver on policies, to respect commitments at a European level, and to be ready not just to take the credit when the Union delivers but also to shoulder the blame when things go wrong. In the current climate, this is a tall order, as the remainder of the chapter will show.

Delivering policies: putting the Constitution to work

The ratification of the Constitution means endorsing a structure. Certainly it is a structure with aims and objectives: these are set out at the beginning of the Constitution. In addition, the swathes of articles in Part III contain the legal bases for policies which attribute powers to the Union and give some indication of the areas in which the Union will legislate and act. But beyond that, it is unclear from reading the Constitution how in practice it is likely to affect the daily lives of Europe's citizens.

There is a simple explanation for this. The Constitution does not prejudge how the institutions will use the powers which are conferred on them. Some have criticised the Constitution for being economically too liberal, others for veering too much towards a social agenda. Both criticisms are wrong. Insofar as the Constitution contains the basis for pursuing both objectives, the direction in which the Union chooses to go in the future will be much less about the provisions of the Constitution, and more about the policy choices which are made at the time.

Nor does the Constitution take effect in a vacuum. The final provisions are clear that the entire corpus of legislation, agreements and decisions already in effect (traditionally known by the French term 'acquis') remain in force. It is up to the institutions to build on the acquis in the way they see fit, and in the light of the circumstances at the time. As already highlighted with regard to the Common Agriculture Policy, political will is likely to be much more of a block on progress than outdated treaty provisions.

Where are the policy challenges for the immediate future? One of the most important is the 'Lisbon Strategy'. Conceived under the Portuguese Presidency in 2000, it was designed to attain the strategic goal of making the

Union 'the most competitive and dynamic knowledge-based economy in the world capable of sustainable economic growth with more and better jobs and greater social cohesion'. Originally built around two basic axes, economic and social, to which the environment was subsequently added, it touches on almost every aspect of the Union's internal policies.

Very many of the issues covered by the Lisbon Strategy are practical and ought to strike a chord with Europe's citizens: facilitating the establishment of small businesses, cutting red tape, investing in infrastructure, increasing the numbers of computers in schools, improving training for young people, reducing the tax burden on the low-paid. To name but a few.

The Strategy is so wide-ranging that it touches on many areas which do not strictly fall within the competences of the Union. This meant that some creativity was required from the outset. The main innovation was a new approach known as the 'open method of coordination'. This is a system which enables pressure to be brought on Member States to deliver on commitments to which they have signed up at a Union level but which relate to areas in which the Union has no direct power to intervene. Its basic concept is one of peer review (or, to put it in the vernacular 'naming and shaming') through the use of fixed objectives, timetables and benchmarks for monitoring progress. The task of keeping the scoreboard falls to the Commission. Much time was spent in the Convention debating whether the 'open method' should be included in the Constitution. Purists felt it would undermine the existing legal-based system; others considered that its inclusion would help give it more credibility. In the end it stayed out.

The economic arm of the Lisbon process is directly linked to the proper functioning of Economic and Monetary Union. The lengthy debates in the Convention working group on economic governance left open the question as to whether the Stability and Growth Pact, the principal mechanism for ensuring budgetary discipline, which has been used as a political football, should be strengthened or loosened. The only point on which everyone seems to be in agreement is that it needs to be modified in some form, so long as the basic disciplines of the Pact remain in place. The prospect over the next few years of the new Member States joining the Eurozone (they have all signed up to do so once they meet the necessary conditions – only Denmark and the UK have opt-outs) places greater urgency on getting economic policy coordination right.

Equally important as the Lisbon Strategy is the web of issues related to the Union's own security, both internal and external. In both cases, the clear advances in the Constitution should make it easier to formulate, agree and implement policy in these areas. The new sense of insecurity brought about by the increased threat of terrorism has acted as a catalyst for the Union to take more serious collective action against internal threats. At the same time, a more robust United States foreign policy has stimulated the search for a distinctive European approach to the rest of the world based on international cooperation and multilateral action. That means combining the traditional use of 'softer' instruments such as development assistance, with the development of military capabilities for use in peace-keeping and crisis management situations. In general, Union action falling under the two broad areas of internal and external security finds ready support from the European public, sometimes even more than from their governments.

There is a wide range of Union policies – such as the structural funds designed to reduce economic and social disparities between regions of the Union, agriculture, research and development cooperation – which require large sums of money. One of the greatest challenges facing the Union in the shorter term will be to agree on the overall expenditure ceilings for the Union for the period 2007 to 2013. Serious sums are involved; well over €100 billion annually for the seven year period has been proposed by the Commission. Not surprisingly the net contributors to the budget find themselves as usual ranged against the net recipients. However the recent round of enlargement has introduced a new dynamic to the negotiations as the traditional recipients fight their corner in the face of the huge requirements of the new Member States. Nothing gets Member States digging their heels in more than money.

The entry into force of the Constitution will not lead to a reversal of policies, nor is it itself likely to lead to extensive new policy initiatives. The principal challenges facing the Union will remain those set out above. Delivering these policies will continue to depend very little on either the Constitution or the legendary 'eurocrats' of Brussels, but almost entirely on the willingness of the Member States.

Delivering policies: the need for political will

The complexity of the Union's structures means that it is all too easy to blame someone else when the Union fails to deliver. The institutions blame each other; individual Member States blame each other, and Member States collectively blame the institutions. In fact delivery failure can almost always be laid at the feet of the Member States themselves.

One of the most manifest examples of delivery failure is the backlog of national transposition of EU legislation. When the Union legislates, it does so normally on the basis of a Commission proposal. The objective of the Council is to reach a satisfactory result, even if this means substantially modifying the Commission proposal. The implementation of legislation, once adopted, is the responsibility of individual Member States. In the case of directives, Member State governments have a responsibility to transpose Community legislation into national law (the same will apply under the Constitution with European framework laws). Even when legislation is directly applicable, responsibility for its enforcement is primarily for the Member States. Despite a succession of calls by EU Heads of State and Government, the figures for transposition reveal a serious backlog. In July 2004 the Commission reported that (excluding the ten new Member States) only five countries reached the agreed transposition target, and a number were seriously behind. The worst offender had failed to transpose 62 directives, and overall 134 Internal Market directives still had to be transposed into national law by at least one Member State.

In November 2004, former Dutch Prime Minister Wim Kok delivered a report as part of the preparation of the mid-term review of the Lisbon Strategy. It recognised that the results so far have fallen short of expectations: 'Progress to date has been inadequate, largely due to a lack of commitment and political will. More political ownership is the pre-condition for success'. His report called for a simplified system of benchmarking, and a more overt culture of 'naming and shaming'. There is also a recognition in the report that national parliaments and citizens need to be more closely associated with the process. This would lessen the chances of Member States slipping out of commitments to which, if they had been made at the national level, they would have been more clearly accountable.

If large parts of the Lisbon process depend on living up to political commitments, there is also an aspect which is rules-based. The Union is after all essentially a legal construct, and respect for the rules is crucial to the overall integrity of the system. When in 2003 some Member States began to play fast and loose with the procedures for determining excessive budget deficits under the Stability and Growth Pact, the effect was to call into question the long-term sustainability of the Pact. Paradoxically Member State solidarity worked against the immediate interests of the Union: those facing censure for excessive deficits were able to rely on those who had reason to think they would be next in the firing line. The Commission sought to protect the integrity of the procedures by referring the matter to the European Court of Justice, but recognised at the same time the need to reflect a new political reality by proposing that the Pact be amended in substance. For a short time the Pact became a battleground between a rules-based approach and political expediency. The whole episode served to lift the corner of the veil on the potential fragility of governance in today's Union.

Less obvious delivery failure relates to the substantial role played by the Member States in the management of the Union's finances. About 80% of the Union's budget (in particular its two largest elements, agriculture and structural funds) is channelled through national governmental or non-governmental agencies. Effective spending and budget discipline is therefore also an area within which the Member States cannot escape their responsibility. A combination of an unwillingness on the part of the institutions to admit the limits to their own powers of oversight, and an obvious reluctance of the Member States to highlight their own shortcomings, means that problems in this whole area issue go largely unaddressed. Shared control means that accountability frequently falls between two stools. Although highlighted in successive reports from the Court of Auditors, the problem remains (in the words of Alain Lamassoure) one of the last remaining taboos.

The adoption of the Constitution, although skilfully negotiated, was only made possible through political will. The Member States rightly take ownership of the Constitution as the set of rules which will govern the Union in the future. But they also have to take responsibility for decisions which they take collectively in the Council on the basis of the Constitution.

Governance: a problem of ownership

Failure to take responsibility means failure to govern. This problem of governance lies at the heart of many of the deficiencies of today's Union. For as long as Member States' governments fail to address this issue, the Union will continue to be confronted with its most fundamental problem: lack of basic support and sense of ownership from its 450 million citizens in whose interests and on whose behalf it acts.

Not that the problem of public support goes unrecognised. Indeed it is now the subject of regular and collective soul-searching sessions by ministers and heads of government alike. The result has been a steady stream of suggested solutions. But because they consider lack of public support as a problem rather than a symptom, most miss the point.

Take for example the steady demand for increased transparency and openness. This is almost certainly in itself a worthy objective, but does virtually nothing to increase the overall level of support for the Union. The institutions are now as transparent as the most open-minded Member States. The vast majority of documents produced by the Union are now accessible to the public. That is helpful to lobbyists and interest groups wishing to access information in their own area of expertise. It does little to assist the average citizen to understand the Union, let alone come to love it.

Understanding the Union is also important. The Constitution itself takes this message on board by setting out in plain language the Union's objectives, values, powers, institutions and methods of functioning. In so doing it offers for the first time a reasonably straightforward guide to what is an immensely complex organisation. But it cannot in itself guarantee public support. The comparison with individual Member States is instructive. Relatively few people have read or are familiar with their national constitutions; even fewer understand in detail their national legislative and governmental systems. Yet that does not call into question the legitimacy of the whole system, nor (beyond normal daily grumbles about politicians) does it undermine or displace the functioning of government. As at the national level, the average citizen is perfectly capable of understanding the basics of the Union, but for the most part is neither interested nor sees any need to know.

If openness and understanding cannot deliver public support, the solution must lie elsewhere. One answer has been to see the problem in terms of democratic legitimacy. Insiders call this addressing the 'democratic deficit'. All this means is giving Europe's citizens a greater say in who governs them at the European level.

The only direct say available at the moment is through the elections to the European Parliament. One means of enhancing direct legitimacy at the European level would therefore be through a strengthening of the

Parliament. In fact this has already happened both in the legislative field and through a steady increase (partly acquired by stealth) in its capacity to exercise control over the Commission. It has however signally failed to excite any interest amongst the European electorate. The figures for participation in European elections not only remain pitifully low, but are going in the wrong direction: in the 2004 elections the turnout was the lowest in the history of the EU, below 40% in some Member States. Furthermore, the campaigns for the European Parliament are fought almost entirely over domestic issues, with little evidence of the emergence of a single European political constituency.

Apart from the Parliament, another option for enhancing legitimacy would be to give Europe's citizens the possibility of electing the Commission. A suggestion along these lines was floated in the Convention but never taken seriously. The more radical alternative of giving Europe's citizens a complete say in who governs them at the European level is not a viable option for as long as there is no single 'government'. Going down this path would require the transformation of the European Union into a complete federal institutional structure. For the large majority of Member States, and much of public opinion, this is out of the question, at least for the moment.

In short, the key to democratic accountability of government – choice through the ballot box – is not available at the European level, and is unlikely to be for the foreseeable future, if ever. So an alternative has to be found if citizens are to have a stake in the Union and ownership of the decisions which are taken on their behalf. This is first and foremost the responsibility of the Member States, who have to appropriate the Union for themselves instead of all too often seeking scapegoats for decisions they do not like. The Union is after all the creation of the Member States. They have created it, but all too often forget that paternity carries responsibilities.

Governance: taking the Union seriously

Governance of course means exercising leadership, although this is itself difficult in a Union in which there is no single political authority and which depends on a relationship of constructive tension between the different institutions. But governance is also more than leadership. Governance is the exercise of authority within a framework of standards and principles which constrain that authority from being exercised in an unfettered manner.

At the national level, political authority earns its legitimacy through respect for this framework, which is part of every nation's shared culture, and through its ability to deliver policies which the people want. These two elements are reflected in the decisions taken by the electorate through the ballot box.

The Union also has its framework in the form of the treaties (or the Constitution). This framework includes a number of core values (democracy, respect for human rights, the rule of law etc) which are similarly part of modern Europe's shared values. These values constitute a broad frame of reference for all action undertaken by the Union as well as an important set of benchmarks for those wishing to join it.

But the framework goes wider than simply core values. The Union is a rules-based system. It cannot work otherwise. The nexus of rules are set out in both the treaties (or Constitution) and in the body of Union laws, decisions and regulations. Together these commitments constitute a vital part of the framework within which governance has to be exercised in the Union. But as the examples set out above show, Member States are too ready to show scant respect for obligations which they have imposed on themselves by either disclaiming responsibility for them or dispensing themselves from them entirely.

Such disregard for agreed commitments at the national level would not go down well with the electorate. In the Union it is different. Any government can get away with disregarding its obligations by pushing responsibility upwards to the Union level, and specifically to the institutions. They can do this because many political commitments (as opposed to the core values on which the Union is founded) do not have the legitimacy offered by a shared culture and are not therefore taken seriously as constraints on the collective action of governments within the Council. As a result the public do not hold their government to account, and of course the alternative option of the ballot box at the European level is not available. The result is unwitting collusion between public and government.

It is perhaps easier to see the similarities between the national and European level in terms of policy delivery. In both cases, political authority is earned by responding to the demands of the public. The difference is that at the national level, whilst a particular policy choice might be questioned, the principle that a government has the right to intervene is usually taken as read. At the European level, every action has to be justified. Europe's citizens will not be won over by institutional issues but by policies which have a direct bearing on their lives. So the energy and vision which has gone into founding and building up the institutions of the European Union over the years (most recently in the drawing up of the Constitution) now has to focus on policy delivery. But this point goes hand in hand with the previous one. Policies need to be effective in themselves, delivering real benefits to Europe's citizens, but also owned in their entirety by national governments. If this happens, it will begin the slow process of enabling individual national electorates to coalesce, and so perhaps lay the foundation for a broader European political constituency.

*   *   *   *   *   *

By its very nature, the Constitution should offer a opportunity for the Union to cease its endless and apparently constant process of reorganisation. It is vital that this opportunity should be used to bring the level of public support back up to the level of ambition of the Union itself. As set out above, this is essentially a task for national governments.

The Constitution will certainly make a substantial contribution to communicating better to Europe's citizens the purpose of the European Union and how it can respond to their concerns and deliver benefits for them. This is not a guarantee of public support, but it is a start.

The Constitution will also help the Union to do more (where this is necessary) and do it better. It should reassure Europe's citizens that the Union will only get involved where there is a clear benefit in its doing so.

In many ways the entry into force of the Constitution will be a defining moment for the Union. In one sense it will have arrived at its destination. Yet at the same time the Constitution equips it to face up to the very many challenges of the future. Not only is there no realistic alternative, but there are good reasons to be optimistic.

Footnotes

[1] For further information on the history of European integration, see: Denis de Rougemont, *Vingt-huit siècles d'Europe*, Paris, 1961; *Securitas et tranquillitas europae*, Ministero per i Beni culturali, Roma 1996; E. Chrystos, P.M. Kitromilides *The idea of European Community in History*, 2 vol. Proceedings of the International conference held in Athens in March 2003, National University of Athens; B. Geremek, *Common roots of Europe*, Cambridge Policy Press, 1996; N. Davies, *Europe: A history*, Oxford University Press, Oxford, 1996.

[2] For further information on the contemporary history of European integration, see: W. Lipgens (ed.), *Documents on the history of European integration*, 4 vol. New York: De Gruyter, 1985-1991: *Continental plans for European union 1939-1945 ; Plans for European Union in Great Britain and in exile 1939-1945 ; The struggle for European Union by political parties and pressure groups in Western European countries 1945-1950 ; Transnational organizations of political parties and pressure groups in the struggle for European Union 1945-1950*; A.J. Zurcher, *The struggle to unite Europe, 1940-1958; an historical account of the development of the contemporary European movement from its origin in the Pan-European Union to the drafting of the treaties for Euratom and the European Common Market*. New York: New York University Press, 1958, Westport: Greenwood Press, 1975

[3] Lord Lothian, *Pacifism is not enough nor patriotism either*, www.federalunion.org.uk/archives/pacifism.shtml

[4] E. Jünger, *La Paix*, Editions de la Table Ronde, Paris, 1992

[5] Laeken Declaration on the future of the European Union, Presidency conclusions, Laeken European Council, 14 - 15 December 2001, www.consilium.eu.int
For further information about the European Council in Laeken, see P. Ludlow, *The Laeken European Council* (Brussels 2000)

[6] For further details on the negotiation of the Treaty of Amsterdam, see Bobby McDonagh, *Original sin in a brave new world, an account of the negotiation of the Treaty of Amsterdam*, Institute of European Affairs, 1998

[7] For further information about the European Council in Santa Maria da Feira see P. Ludlow, *The European Council at Feira. A view from Brussels*; No 8 July 2000, (CEPS Brussels)

[8] For further details on the Nice Intergovernmental Conference and its results, see: D. Galloway, *The Treaty of Nice and Beyond, Realities and Illusions of Power in the EU*, Sheffield Academic Press, 2000

[9] *Reorganisation of the European Treaties, Final Report*, European University Institute, Robert Schuman Centre for Advanced Studies, Florence, May 2000

[10] Declaration on the future of the European Union annexed to the Nice Treaty, www.consilium.eu.int

[11] An account of the European Convention can be found in the following publications: *Valéry Giscard d'Estaing présente la Constitution pour l'Europe*, Albin Michel/Fondation Robert Schuman, 2003; Alain Dauvergne, *L'Europe en otage ? Histoire secrète de la Convention*, Saint-Simon, 2004; Alain Lamassoure, *L'histoire*

secrète de la Convention, Albin Michel/Fondation Robert Schuman, 2004; Peter Norman, *An accidental Constitution,* Eurocomments, 2003; Etienne de Poncins, *Vers une Constitution européenne,* 10/18 documents, 2003,

[12] Opening speech by the President of the European Convention, 28 February 2002, www.european-convention.eu.int/speeches

[13] For the composition of the European Convention, see: www.european-convention.eu.int/composition

[14] A description of the cooperation between the smaller Member States can be found in: *Die Kooperation der Klein und Mittelstaaten im EU-Konvent,* Herausgeber: Hannes Farnleitner, Media Med Consulting GmbH, Wien, 2004 (in German and English)

[15] See J.-C. Piris, *Does the European Union have a Constitution?,* European Law Review, vol. 24, nr 6, December 1999.

[16] See doc. 10679/04 REV 2 at www.consilium.eu.int

[17] See Article I-11

[18] See Articles I-12 to I-17

[19] See Article I-7

[20] See Title V, Articles I-33 to I-39

[21] See Article I-54

[22] See Article I-55

[23] See Article I-44

[24] See Article I-40

[25] See Article I-42

[26] See doc. CONV 459/02 at www.european-convention.eu.int

[27] See Article I-28

[28] See working group's final report: doc. CONV 461/02 at www.european-convention.eu.int

[29] See Article I-41

[30] See working group's final report: doc. CONV 426/02 at www.european-convention.eu.int

[31] See working group's final report: doc. CONV 357/02 at www.european-convention.eu.int

[32] See working group's final report: doc. CONV 516/1/03 at www.european-convention.eu.int

[33] Interview of Jean-Louis Bourlanges by Baudouin Bollaert, *Le Figaro,* 15 October 2003

[34] See Article I-20

[35] The text of the Article as proposed by Giscard read as follows: *The Congress of the Peoples of Europe shall provide a forum for contact and consultation in European political life. It shall meet at least once a year. Its meetings shall be public. The President of the European Parliament shall convene and chair them. The Congress shall not intervene in the Council's legislative procedure. The President of the European Council shall report on the state of the Union. The President of the Commission shall present the annual legislative programme. One third of the Congress shall be members of the European Parliament: two thirds shall be representatives of national Parliaments. The total shall not exceed seven hundred.*

[36] See Article I-5(1)

[37] See Article I-24
[38] See Article I-20
[39] See Article I-27
[40] See Article I-26
[41] Article I-26 of the Constitution states that "each successive Commission shall be so composed as to reflect satisfactorily the demographic and geographical range of all the Member States". Before this provision can be put into effect, a list will have to be drawn up reflecting these criteria and setting out the order in which Member States are present in the Commission. A similar list of the order in which Member States (in teams of three) will hold the office of Presidency of the Council was approved by the Council in December 2004 (see Annex II). Since this second list has to reflect exactly the same criteria as those governing presence in the Commission, it would in principle be possible to draw up the sequencing in the Commission in such a way as to ensure that no Member State holding the Presidency could at the same time have a national in the Commission, so maintaining an overall balance between Member States in the allocation of key responsibilities within the Union.
[42] See Article I-25
[43] http://silly.if.uj.edu.pl/~karol/pdf/OpenLetter.pdf
[44] The mathematicians' approach, which draws on game theory, is based on the principle that when there is a vote in the Council the ballot of every citizen of the Union, whatever his or her country of origin, should carry equal weight. In order to achieve this, two conditions must be respected: 1) the attribution of votes to each Member State should be proportional to the square root of its population (Penrose's law), and 2) the voting power of each Member State should be as close as possible to its theoretical maximum capacity to constitute effective coalitions. This second condition is reached by applying a qualified majority threshold of between 60% and 65% of the total number of weighted votes.
[45] See Annex II

ANNEX I

TREATY ESTABLISHING A
CONSTITUTION FOR EUROPE

PREAMBLE

HIS MAJESTY THE KING OF THE BELGIANS, THE PRESIDENT OF THE CZECH REPUBLIC, HER MAJESTY THE QUEEN OF DENMARK, THE PRESIDENT OF THE FEDERAL REPUBLIC OF GERMANY, THE PRESIDENT OF THE REPUBLIC OF ESTONIA, THE PRESIDENT OF THE HELLENIC REPUBLIC, HIS MAJESTY THE KING OF SPAIN, THE PRESIDENT OF THE FRENCH REPUBLIC, THE PRESIDENT OF IRELAND, THE PRESIDENT OF THE ITALIAN REPUBLIC, THE PRESIDENT OF THE REPUBLIC OF CYPRUS, THE PRESIDENT OF THE REPUBLIC OF LATVIA, THE PRESIDENT OF THE REPUBLIC OF LITHUANIA, HIS ROYAL HIGHNESS THE GRAND DUKE OF LUXEMBOURG, THE PRESIDENT OF THE REPUBLIC OF HUNGARY, THE PRESIDENT OF MALTA, HER MAJESTY THE QUEEN OF THE NETHERLANDS, THE FEDERAL PRESIDENT OF THE REPUBLIC OF AUSTRIA, THE PRESIDENT OF THE REPUBLIC OF POLAND, THE PRESIDENT OF THE PORTUGUESE REPUBLIC, THE PRESIDENT OF THE REPUBLIC OF SLOVENIA, THE PRESIDENT OF THE SLOVAK REPUBLIC, THE PRESIDENT OF THE REPUBLIC OF FINLAND, THE GOVERNMENT OF THE KINGDOM OF SWEDEN, HER MAJESTY THE QUEEN OF THE UNITED KINGDOM OF GREAT BRITAIN AND NORTHERN IRELAND,
DRAWING INSPIRATION from the cultural, religious and humanist inheritance of Europe, from which have developed the universal values of the inviolable and inalienable rights of the human person, freedom, democracy, equality and the rule of law,
BELIEVING that Europe, reunited after bitter experiences, intends to continue along the path of civilisation, progress and prosperity, for the good of all its inhabitants, including the weakest and most deprived; that it wishes to remain a continent open to culture, learning and social progress; and that it wishes to deepen the democratic and transparent nature of its public life, and to strive for peace, justice and solidarity throughout the world,
CONVINCED that, while remaining proud of their own national identities and history, the peoples of Europe are determined to transcend their former divisions and, united ever more closely, to forge a common destiny,
CONVINCED that, thus "United in diversity", Europe offers them the best chance of pursuing, with due regard for the rights of each individual and in awareness of their responsibilities towards future generations and the Earth, the great venture which makes of it a special area of human hope,
DETERMINED to continue the work accomplished within the framework of the Treaties establishing the European Communities and the Treaty on European Union, by ensuring the continuity of the Community acquis,
GRATEFUL to the members of the European Convention for having prepared the draft of this Constitution on behalf of the citizens and States of Europe,
HAVE DESIGNATED AS THEIR PLENIPOTENTIARIES:

[...]

WHO, having exchanged their full powers, found in good and due form, have agreed as follows:

PART I

TITLE I

DEFINITION AND OBJECTIVES OF THE UNION

ARTICLE I-1
Establishment of the Union

1. Reflecting the will of the citizens and States of Europe to build a common future, this Constitution establishes the European Union, on which the Member States confer competences to attain objectives they have in common. The Union shall coordinate the policies by which the Member States aim to achieve these objectives, and shall exercise on a Community basis the competences they confer on it.
2. The Union shall be open to all European States which respect its values and are committed to promoting them together.

ARTICLE I-2
The Union's values

The Union is founded on the values of respect for human dignity, freedom, democracy, equality, the rule of law and respect for human rights, including the rights of persons belonging to minorities. These values are common to the Member States in a society in which pluralism, non-discrimination, tolerance, justice, solidarity and equality between women and men prevail.

ARTICLE I-3
The Union's objectives

1. The Union's aim is to promote peace, its values and the well-being of its peoples.
2. The Union shall offer its citizens an area of freedom, security and justice without internal frontiers, and an internal market where competition is free and undistorted.
3. The Union shall work for the sustainable development of Europe based on balanced economic growth and price stability, a highly competitive social market economy, aiming at full employment and social progress, and a high level of protection and improvement of the quality of the environment. It shall promote scientific and technological advance.

   It shall combat social exclusion and discrimination, and shall promote social justice and protection, equality between women and men, solidarity between generations and protection of the rights of the child.

   It shall promote economic, social and territorial cohesion, and solidarity among Member States.

   It shall respect its rich cultural and linguistic diversity, and shall ensure that Europe's cultural heritage is safeguarded and enhanced.

4.   In its relations with the wider world, the Union shall uphold and promote its values and interests. It shall contribute to peace, security, the sustainable development of the Earth, solidarity and mutual respect among peoples, free and fair trade, eradication of poverty and the protection of human rights, in particular the rights of the child, as well as to the strict observance and the development of international law, including respect for the principles of the United Nations Charter.

5.   The Union shall pursue its objectives by appropriate means commensurate with the competences which are conferred upon it in the Constitution.

ARTICLE I-4

Fundamental freedoms and non-discrimination

1.   The free movement of persons, services, goods and capital, and freedom of establishment shall be guaranteed within and by the Union, in accordance with the Constitution.

2.   Within the scope of the Constitution, and without prejudice to any of its specific provisions, any discrimination on grounds of nationality shall be prohibited.

ARTICLE I-5

Relations between the Union and the Member States

1.   The Union shall respect the equality of Member States before the Constitution as well as their national identities, inherent in their fundamental structures, political and constitutional, inclusive of regional and local self-government. It shall respect their essential State functions, including ensuring the territorial integrity of the State, maintaining law and order and safeguarding national security.

2.   Pursuant to the principle of sincere cooperation, the Union and the Member States shall, in full mutual respect, assist each other in carrying out tasks which flow from the Constitution.

     The Member States shall take any appropriate measure, general or particular, to ensure fulfilment of the obligations arising out of the Constitution or resulting from the acts of the institutions of the Union.

     The Member States shall facilitate the achievement of the Union's tasks and refrain from any measure which could jeopardise the attainment of the Union's objectives.

ARTICLE I-6

Union law

The Constitution and law adopted by the institutions of the Union in exercising competences conferred on it shall have primacy over the law of the Member States.

ARTICLE I-7

Legal personality

The Union shall have legal personality.

ARTICLE I-8

The symbols of the Union

The flag of the Union shall be a circle of twelve golden stars on a blue background.

The anthem of the Union shall be based on the "Ode to Joy" from the Ninth Symphony by Ludwig van Beethoven.

The motto of the Union shall be: "United in diversity".

The currency of the Union shall be the euro.

Europe day shall be celebrated on 9 May throughout the Union.

TITLE II

FUNDAMENTAL RIGHTS AND CITIZENSHIP OF THE UNION

ARTICLE I-9

Fundamental rights

1. The Union shall recognise the rights, freedoms and principles set out in the Charter of Fundamental Rights which constitutes Part II.
2. The Union shall accede to the European Convention for the Protection of Human Rights and Fundamental Freedoms. Such accession shall not affect the Union's competences as defined in the Constitution.
3. Fundamental rights, as guaranteed by the European Convention for the Protection of Human Rights and Fundamental Freedoms and as they result from the constitutional traditions common to the Member States, shall constitute general principles of the Union's law.

ARTICLE I-10

Citizenship of the Union

1. Every national of a Member State shall be a citizen of the Union. Citizenship of the Union shall be additional to national citizenship and shall not replace it.
2. Citizens of the Union shall enjoy the rights and be subject to the duties provided for in the Constitution. They shall have:
(a) the right to move and reside freely within the territory of the Member States;
(b) the right to vote and to stand as candidates in elections to the European Parliament and in municipal elections in their Member State of residence, under the same conditions as nationals of that State;
(c) the right to enjoy, in the territory of a third country in which the Member State of which they are nationals is not represented, the protection of the diplomatic and consular authorities of any Member State on the same conditions as the nationals of that State;
(d) the right to petition the European Parliament, to apply to the European Ombudsman, and to address the institutions and advisory bodies of the Union in any of the Constitution's languages and to obtain a reply in the same language.

These rights shall be exercised in accordance with the conditions and limits defined by the Constitution and by the measures adopted thereunder.

TITLE III

UNION COMPETENCES

ARTICLE I-11
Fundamental principles

1. The limits of Union competences are governed by the principle of conferral. The use of Union competences is governed by the principles of subsidiarity and proportionality.
2. Under the principle of conferral, the Union shall act within the limits of the competences conferred upon it by the Member States in the Constitution to attain the objectives set out in the Constitution. Competences not conferred upon the Union in the Constitution remain with the Member States.
3. Under the principle of subsidiarity, in areas which do not fall within its exclusive competence, the Union shall act only if and insofar as the objectives of the proposed action cannot be sufficiently achieved by the Member States, either at central level or at regional and local level, but can rather, by reason of the scale or effects of the proposed action, be better achieved at Union level.

   The institutions of the Union shall apply the principle of subsidiarity as laid down in the Protocol on the application of the principles of subsidiarity and proportionality. National Parliaments shall ensure compliance with that principle in accordance with the procedure set out in that Protocol.
4. Under the principle of proportionality, the content and form of Union action shall not exceed what is necessary to achieve the objectives of the Constitution. The institutions of the Union shall apply the principle of proportionality as laid down in the Protocol on the application of the principles of subsidiarity and proportionality.

ARTICLE I-12
Categories of competence

1. When the Constitution confers on the Union exclusive competence in a specific area, only the Union may legislate and adopt legally binding acts, the Member States being able to do so themselves only if so empowered by the Union or for the implementation of Union acts.
2. When the Constitution confers on the Union a competence shared with the Member States in a specific area, the Union and the Member States may legislate and adopt legally binding acts in that area. The Member States shall exercise their competence to the extent that the Union has not exercised, or has decided to cease exercising, its competence.
3. The Member States shall coordinate their economic and employment policies within arrangements as determined by Part III, which the Union shall have competence to provide.
4. The Union shall have competence to define and implement a common foreign

and security policy, including the progressive framing of a common defence policy.

5. In certain areas and under the conditions laid down in the Constitution, the Union shall have competence to carry out actions to support, coordinate or supplement the actions of the Member States, without thereby superseding their competence in these areas.

  Legally binding acts of the Union adopted on the basis of the provisions in Part III relating to these areas shall not entail harmonisation of Member States' laws or regulations.

6. The scope of and arrangements for exercising the Union's competences shall be determined by the provisions relating to each area in Part III.

ARTICLE I-13

Areas of exclusive competence

1. The Union shall have exclusive competence in the following areas:
(a) customs union;
(b) the establishing of the competition rules necessary for the functioning of the internal market;
(c) monetary policy for the Member States whose currency is the euro;
(d) the conservation of marine biological resources under the common fisheries policy;
(e) common commercial policy.

2. The Union shall also have exclusive competence for the conclusion of an international agreement when its conclusion is provided for in a legislative act of the Union or is necessary to enable the Union to exercise its internal competence, or insofar as its conclusion may affect common rules or alter their scope.

ARTICLE I-14

Areas of shared competence

1. The Union shall share competence with the Member States where the Constitution confers on it a competence which does not relate to the areas referred to in Articles I-13 and I-17.

2. Shared competence between the Union and the Member States applies in the following principal areas:
(a) internal market;
(b) social policy, for the aspects defined in Part III;
(c) economic, social and territorial cohesion;
(d) agriculture and fisheries, excluding the conservation of marine biological resources;
(e) environment;
(f) consumer protection;
(g) transport;
(h) trans-European networks;
(i) energy;
(j) area of freedom, security and justice;
(k) common safety concerns in public health matters, for the aspects defined in Part III.

3. In the areas of research, technological development and space, the Union shall

have competence to carry out activities, in particular to define and implement programmes; however, the exercise of that competence shall not result in Member States being prevented from exercising theirs.

4.   In the areas of development cooperation and humanitarian aid, the Union shall have competence to carry out activities and conduct a common policy; however, the exercise of that competence shall not result in Member States being prevented from exercising theirs.

ARTICLE I-15

The coordination of economic and employment policies

1.   The Member States shall coordinate their economic policies within the Union. To this end, the Council of Ministers shall adopt measures, in particular broad guidelines for these policies.

Specific provisions shall apply to those Member States whose currency is the euro.

2.   The Union shall take measures to ensure coordination of the employment policies of the Member States, in particular by defining guidelines for these policies.

3.   The Union may take initiatives to ensure coordination of Member States' social policies.

ARTICLE I-16

The common foreign and security policy

1.   The Union's competence in matters of common foreign and security policy shall cover all areas of foreign policy and all questions relating to the Union's security, including the progressive framing of a common defence policy that might lead to a common defence.

2.   Member States shall actively and unreservedly support the Union's common foreign and security policy in a spirit of loyalty and mutual solidarity and shall comply with the Union's action in this area. They shall refrain from action contrary to the Union's interests or likely to impair its effectiveness.

ARTICLE I-17

Areas of supporting, coordinating or complementary action

The Union shall have competence to carry out supporting, coordinating or complementary action. The areas of such action shall, at European level, be:

(a)   protection and improvement of human health;
(b)   industry;
(c)   culture;
(d)   tourism;
(e)   education, youth, sport and vocational training;
(f)   civil protection;
(g)   administrative cooperation.

ARTICLE I-18

Flexibility clause

1.   If action by the Union should prove necessary, within the framework of the poli-

cies defined in Part III, to attain one of the objectives set out in the Constitution, and the Constitution has not provided the necessary powers, the Council of Ministers, acting unanimously on a proposal from the European Commission and after obtaining the consent of the European Parliament, shall adopt the appropriate measures.

2. Using the procedure for monitoring the subsidiarity principle referred to in Article I-11(3), the European Commission shall draw national Parliaments' attention to proposals based on this Article.

3. Measures based on this Article shall not entail harmonisation of Member States' laws or regulations in cases where the Constitution excludes such harmonisation.

TITLE IV

THE UNION'S INSTITUTIONS AND BODIES

CHAPTER I

THE INSTITUTIONAL FRAMEWORK

ARTICLE I-19

The Union's institutions

1. The Union shall have an institutional framework which shall aim to:
– promote its values,
– advance its objectives,
– serve its interests, those of its citizens and those of the Member States,
– ensure the consistency, effectiveness and continuity of its policies and actions.
   This institutional framework comprises:
– The European Parliament,
– The European Council,
– The Council of Ministers (hereinafter referred to as the "Council"),
– The European Commission (hereinafter referred to as the "Commission"),
– The Court of Justice of the European Union.

2. Each institution shall act within the limits of the powers conferred on it in the Constitution, and in conformity with the procedures and conditions set out in it. The institutions shall practise mutual sincere cooperation.

ARTICLE I-20

The European Parliament

1. The European Parliament shall, jointly with the Council, exercise legislative and budgetary functions. It shall exercise functions of political control and consultation as laid down in the Constitution. It shall elect the President of the Commission.

2. The European Parliament shall be composed of representatives of the Union's citizens. They shall not exceed seven hundred and fifty in number.

Representation of citizens shall be degressively proportional, with a minimum threshold of six members per Member State. No Member State shall be allocated more than ninety-six seats.

The European Council shall adopt by unanimity, on the initiative of the European Parliament and with its consent, a European decision establishing the composition of the European Parliament, respecting the principles referred to in the first subparagraph.

3. The members of the European Parliament shall be elected for a term of five years by direct universal suffrage in a free and secret ballot.

4. The European Parliament shall elect its President and its officers from among its members.

ARTICLE I-21

The European Council

1. The European Council shall provide the Union with the necessary impetus for its development and shall define the general political directions and priorities thereof. It shall not exercise legislative functions.

2. The European Council shall consist of the Heads of State or Government of the Member States, together with its President and the President of the Commission. The Union Minister for Foreign Affairs shall take part in its work.

3. The European Council shall meet quarterly, convened by its President. When the agenda so requires, the members of the European Council may decide each to be assisted by a minister and, in the case of the President of the Commission, by a member of the Commission. When the situation so requires, the President shall convene a special meeting of the European Council.

4. Except where the Constitution provides otherwise, decisions of the European Council shall be taken by consensus.

ARTICLE I-22

The European Council President

1. The European Council shall elect its President, by a qualified majority, for a term of two and a half years, renewable once. In the event of an impediment or serious misconduct, the European Council can end his or her term of office in accordance with the same procedure.

2. The President of the European Council:

(a) shall chair it and drive forward its work;

(b) shall ensure the preparation and continuity of the work of the European Council in cooperation with the President of the Commission, and on the basis of the work of the General Affairs Council;

(c) shall endeavour to facilitate cohesion and consensus within the European Council;

(d) shall present a report to the European Parliament after each of the meetings of the European Council.

The President of the European Council shall, at his or her level and in that capacity, ensure the external representation of the Union on issues concerning its common foreign and security policy, without prejudice to the powers of the Union Minister for Foreign Affairs.

3. The President of the European Council shall not hold a national office.

ARTICLE I-23

The Council of Ministers

1. The Council shall, jointly with the European Parliament, exercise legislative and budgetary functions. It shall carry out policy-making and coordinating functions as laid down in the Constitution.
2. The Council shall consist of a representative of each Member State at ministerial level, who may commit the government of the Member State in question and cast its vote.
3. The Council shall act by a qualified majority except where the Constitution provides otherwise.

ARTICLE I-24

Configurations of the Council of Ministers

1. The Council shall meet in different configurations.
2. The General Affairs Council shall ensure consistency in the work of the different Council configurations.

    It shall prepare and ensure the follow-up to meetings of the European Council, in liaison with the President of the European Council and the Commission.
3. The Foreign Affairs Council shall elaborate the Union's external action on the basis of strategic guidelines laid down by the European Council and ensure that the Union's action is consistent.
4. The European Council shall adopt by a qualified majority a European decision establishing the list of other Council configurations.
5. A Committee of Permanent Representatives of the Governments of the Member States shall be responsible for preparing the work of the Council.
6. The Council shall meet in public when it deliberates and votes on a draft legislative act. To this end, each Council meeting shall be divided into two parts, dealing respectively with deliberations on Union legislative acts and non-legislative activities.
7. The Presidency of Council configurations, other than that of Foreign Affairs, shall be held by Member State representatives in the Council on the basis of equal rotation, in accordance with the conditions established by a European decision of the European Council. The European Council shall act by a qualified majority.

ARTICLE I-25

Definition of qualified majority within the European Council and the Council

1. A qualified majority shall be defined as at least 55% of the members of the Council, comprising at least fifteen of them and representing Member States comprising at least 65% of the population of the Union.

    A blocking minority must include at least four Council members, failing which the qualified majority shall be deemed attained.
2. By way of derogation from paragraph 1, when the Council does not act on a proposal from the Commission or from the Union Minister for Foreign Affairs, the qualified majority shall be defined as at least 72% of the members of the Council,

representing Member States comprising at least 65% of the population of the Union.

3.   Paragraphs 1 and 2 shall apply to the European Council when it is acting by a qualified majority.

4.   Within the European Council, its President and the President of the Commission shall not take part in the vote.

ARTICLE I-26

The European Commission

1.   The Commission shall promote the general interest of the Union and take appropriate initiatives to that end. It shall ensure the application of the Constitution, and measures adopted by the institutions pursuant to the Constitution. It shall oversee the application of Union law under the control of the Court of Justice of the European Union. It shall execute the budget and manage programmes. It shall exercise coordinating, executive and management functions, as laid down in the Constitution. With the exception of the common foreign and security policy, and other cases provided for in the Constitution, it shall ensure the Union's external representation. It shall initiate the Union's annual and multiannual programming with a view to achieving interinstitutional agreements.

2.   Union legislative acts may be adopted only on the basis of a Commission proposal, except where the Constitution provides otherwise. Other acts shall be adopted on the basis of a Commission proposal where the Constitution so provides.

3.   The Commission's term of office shall be five years.

4.   The members of the Commission shall be chosen on the ground of their general competence and European commitment from persons whose independence is beyond doubt.

5.   The first Commission appointed under the provisions of the Constitution shall consist of one national of each Member State, including its President and the Union Minister for Foreign Affairs who shall be one of its Vice-Presidents.

6.   As from the end of the term of office of the Commission referred to in paragraph 5, the Commission shall consist of a number of members, including its President and the Union Minister for Foreign Affairs, corresponding to two thirds of the number of Member States, unless the European Council, acting unanimously, decides to alter this number.

The members of the Commission shall be selected from among the nationals of the Member States on the basis of a system of equal rotation between the Member States. This system shall be established by a European decision adopted unanimously by the European Council and on the basis of the following principles:

(a) Member States shall be treated on a strictly equal footing as regards determination of the sequence of, and the time spent by, their nationals as members of the Commission; consequently, the difference between the total number of terms of office held by nationals of any given pair of Member States may never be more than one;

(b) subject to point (a), each successive Commission shall be so composed as to reflect satisfactorily the demographic and geographical range of all the Member States.

7. In carrying out its responsibilities, the Commission shall be completely inde-
    pendent. Without prejudice to Article I-28(2), the members of the Commission
    shall neither seek nor take instructions from any government or other institu-
    tion, body, office or entity. They shall refrain from any action incompatible with
    their duties or the performance of their tasks.
8. The Commission, as a body, shall be responsible to the European Parliament. In
    accordance with Article III-340, the European Parliament may vote on a censure
    motion on the Commission. If such a motion is carried, the members of the
    Commission shall resign as a body and the Union Minister for Foreign Affairs
    shall resign from the duties that he or she carries out in the Commission.

ARTICLE I-27

The President of the European Commission

1. Taking into account the elections to the European Parliament and after having
    held the appropriate consultations, the European Council, acting by a qualified
    majority, shall propose to the European Parliament a candidate for President of
    the Commission. This candidate shall be elected by the European Parliament by
    a majority of its component members. If he or she does not obtain the required
    majority, the European Council, acting by a qualified majority, shall within one
    month propose a new candidate who shall be elected by the European
    Parliament following the same procedure.
2. The Council, by common accord with the President-elect, shall adopt the list of
    the other persons whom it proposes for appointment as members of the
    Commission. They shall be selected, on the basis of the suggestions made by
    Member States, in accordance with the criteria set out in Article I-26(4) and (6),
    second subparagraph.
        The President, the Union Minister for Foreign Affairs and the other mem-
    bers of the Commission shall be subject as a body to a vote of consent by the
    European Parliament. On the basis of this consent the Commission shall be
    appointed by the European Council, acting by a qualified majority.
3. The President of the Commission shall:
(a) lay down guidelines within which the Commission is to work;
(b) decide on the internal organisation of the Commission, ensuring that it acts con-
    sistently, efficiently and as a collegiate body;
(c) appoint Vice-Presidents, other than the Union Minister for Foreign Affairs, from
    among the members of the Commission.
    A member of the Commission shall resign if the President so requests. The
    Union Minister for Foreign Affairs shall resign, in accordance with the pro-
    cedure set out in Article I-28(1), if the President so requests.

ARTICLE I-28

The Union Minister for Foreign Affairs

1. The European Council, acting by a qualified majority, with the agreement of the
    President of the Commission, shall appoint the Union Minister for Foreign
    Affairs. The European Council may end his or her term of office by the same
    procedure.
2. The Union Minister for Foreign Affairs shall conduct the Union's common
    foreign and security policy. He or she shall contribute by his or her proposals

to the development of that policy, which he or she shall carry out as mandated by the Council. The same shall apply to the common security and defence policy.

3. The Union Minister for Foreign Affairs shall preside over the Foreign Affairs Council.

4. The Union Minister for Foreign Affairs shall be one of the Vice-Presidents of the Commission. He or she shall ensure the consistency of the Union's external action. He or she shall be responsible within the Commission for responsibilities incumbent on it in external relations and for coordinating other aspects of the Union's external action. In exercising these responsibilities within the Commission, and only for these responsibilities, the Union Minister for Foreign Affairs shall be bound by Commission procedures to the extent that this is consistent with paragraphs 2 and 3.

ARTICLE I-29

The Court of Justice of the European Union

1. The Court of Justice of the European Union shall include the Court of Justice, the General Court and specialised courts. It shall ensure that in the interpretation and application of the Constitution the law is observed.

    Member States shall provide remedies sufficient to ensure effective legal protection in the fields covered by Union law.

2. The Court of Justice shall consist of one judge from each Member State. It shall be assisted by Advocates-General.

    The General Court shall include at least one judge per Member State.

    The judges and the Advocates-General of the Court of Justice and the judges of the General Court shall be chosen from persons whose independence is beyond doubt and who satisfy the conditions set out in Articles III-355 and III-356. They shall be appointed by common accord of the governments of the Member States for six years. Retiring judges and Advocates-General may be reappointed.

3. The Court of Justice of the European Union shall in accordance with Part III:

(a) rule on actions brought by a Member State, an institution or a natural or legal person;

(b) give preliminary rulings, at the request of courts or tribunals of the Member States, on the interpretation of Union law or the validity of acts adopted by the institutions;

(c) rule in other cases provided for in the Constitution.

CHAPTER II

THE OTHER UNION INSTITUTIONS AND ADVISORY BODIES

ARTICLE I-30

The European Central Bank

1. The European Central Bank, together with the national central banks, shall constitute the European System of Central Banks. The European Central Bank, together with the national central banks of the Member States whose currency

is the euro, which constitute the Eurosystem, shall conduct the monetary policy of the Union.

2. The European System of Central Banks shall be governed by the decision-making bodies of the European Central Bank. The primary objective of the European System of Central Banks shall be to maintain price stability. Without prejudice to that objective, it shall support the general economic policies in the Union in order to contribute to the achievement of the latter's objectives. It shall conduct other Central Bank tasks in accordance with Part III and the Statute of the European System of Central Banks and of the European Central Bank.

3. The European Central Bank is an institution. It shall have legal personality. It alone may authorise the issue of the euro. It shall be independent in the exercise of its powers and in the management of its finances. Union institutions, bodies, offices and agencies and the governments of the Member States shall respect that independence.

4. The European Central Bank shall adopt such measures as are necessary to carry out its tasks in accordance with Articles III-185 to III-191 and Article III-196, and with the conditions laid down in the Statute of the European System of Central Banks and of the European Central Bank. In accordance with these same Articles, those Member States whose currency is not the euro, and their central banks, shall retain their powers in monetary matters.

5. Within the areas falling within its responsibilities, the European Central Bank shall be consulted on all proposed Union acts, and all proposals for regulation at national level, and may give an opinion.

6. The decision-making organs of the European Central Bank, their composition and operating methods are set out in Articles III-382 and III-383, as well as in the Statute of the European System of Central Banks and of the European Central Bank.

ARTICLE I-31

The Court of Auditors

1. The Court of Auditors is an institution. It shall carry out the Union's audit.
2. It shall examine the accounts of all Union revenue and expenditure, and shall ensure good financial management.
3. It shall consist of one national of each Member State. Its members shall be completely independent in the performance of their duties, in the Union's general interest.

ARTICLE I-32

The Union's advisory bodies

1. The European Parliament, the Council and the Commission shall be assisted by a Committee of the Regions and an Economic and Social Committee, exercising advisory functions.
2. The Committee of the Regions shall consist of representatives of regional and local bodies who either hold a regional or local authority electoral mandate or are politically accountable to an elected assembly.
3. The Economic and Social Committee shall consist of representatives of organisations of employers, of the employed, and of other parties representative of civil society, notably in socio-economic, civic, professional and cultural areas.

4. The members of the Committee of the Regions and the Economic and Social Committee shall not be bound by any mandatory instructions. They shall be completely independent in the performance of their duties, in the Union's general interest.
5. Rules governing the composition of these Committees, the designation of their members, their powers and their operations are set out in Articles III-386 to III-392.

    The rules referred to in paragraphs 2 and 3 governing the nature of their composition shall be reviewed at regular intervals by the Council to take account of economic, social and demographic developments within the Union. The Council, on a proposal from the Commission, shall adopt European decisions to that end.

TITLE V

EXERCISE OF UNION COMPETENCE

CHAPTER I

COMMON PROVISIONS

ARTICLE I-33

The legal acts of the Union

1. To exercise the Union's competences the institutions shall use as legal instruments, in accordance with Part III, European laws, European framework laws, European regulations, European decisions, recommendations and opinions.

    A European law shall be a legislative act of general application. It shall be binding in its entirety and directly applicable in all Member States.

    A European framework law shall be a legislative act binding, as to the result to be achieved, upon each Member State to which it is addressed, but shall leave to the national authorities the choice of form and methods.

    A European regulation shall be a non-legislative act of general application for the implementation of legislative acts and of certain provisions of the Constitution. It may either be binding in its entirety and directly applicable in all Member States, or be binding, as to the result to be achieved, upon each Member State to which it is addressed, but shall leave to the national authorities the choice of form and methods.

    A European decision shall be a non-legislative act, binding in its entirety. A decision which specifies those to whom it is addressed shall be binding only on them.

    Recommendations and opinions shall have no binding force.
2. When considering draft legislative acts, the European Parliament and the Council shall refrain from adopting acts not provided for by the relevant legislative procedure in the area in question.

ARTICLE I-34

Legislative acts

1. European laws and framework laws shall be adopted, on the basis of proposals from the Commission, jointly by the European Parliament and the Council under the ordinary legislative procedure as set out in Article III-396. If the two institutions cannot reach agreement on an act, it shall not be adopted.
2. In the specific cases provided for in the Constitution, European laws and framework laws shall be adopted by the European Parliament with the participation of the Council, or by the latter with the participation of the European Parliament, in accordance with special legislative procedures.
3. In the specific cases provided for in the Constitution, European laws and framework laws may be adopted at the initiative of a group of Member States or of the European Parliament, on a recommendation from the European Central Bank or at the request of the Court of Justice or the European Investment Bank.

ARTICLE I-35

Non-legislative acts

1. The European Council shall adopt European decisions in the cases provided for in the Constitution.
2. The Council and the Commission, in particular in the cases referred to in Articles I-36 and I-37, and the European Central Bank in the specific cases provided for in the Constitution, shall adopt European regulations and decisions.
3. The Council shall adopt recommendations. It shall act on a proposal from the Commission in all cases where the Constitution provides that it shall adopt acts on a proposal from the Commission. It shall act unanimously in those areas in which unanimity is required for the adoption of a Union act. The Commission, and the European Central Bank in the specific cases provided for in the Constitution, shall adopt recommendations.

ARTICLE I-36

Delegated European regulations

1. European laws and framework laws may delegate to the Commission the power to adopt delegated European regulations to supplement or amend certain non-essential elements of the law or framework law.

    The objectives, content, scope and duration of the delegation of power shall be explicitly defined in the European laws and framework laws. The essential elements of an area shall be reserved for the European law or framework law and accordingly shall not be the subject of a delegation of power.
2. European laws and framework laws shall explicitly lay down the conditions to which the delegation is subject; these conditions may be as follows:
(a) the European Parliament or the Council may decide to revoke the delegation;
(b) the delegated European regulation may enter into force only if no objection has been expressed by the European Parliament or the Council within a period set by the European law or framework law.

    For the purposes of (a) and (b), the European Parliament shall act by a majority of its component members, and the Council by a qualified majority.

ARTICLE I-37

Implementing acts

1. Member States shall adopt all measures of national law necessary to implement legally binding Union acts.
2. Where uniform conditions for implementing legally binding Union acts are needed, those acts shall confer implementing powers on the Commission, or, in duly justified specific cases and in the cases provided for in Article I-40, on the Council.
3. For the purposes of paragraph 2, European laws shall lay down in advance the rules and general principles concerning mechanisms for control by Member States of the Commission's exercise of implementing powers.
4. Union implementing acts shall take the form of European implementing regulations or European implementing decisions.

ARTICLE I-38

Principles common to the Union's legal acts

1. Where the Constitution does not specify the type of act to be adopted, the institutions shall select it on a case-by-case basis, in compliance with the applicable procedures and with the principle of proportionality referred to in Article I-11.
2. Legal acts shall state the reasons on which they are based and shall refer to any proposals, initiatives, recommendations, requests or opinions required by the Constitution.

ARTICLE I-39

Publication and entry into force

1. European laws and framework laws adopted under the ordinary legislative procedure shall be signed by the President of the European Parliament and by the President of the Council.

    In other cases they shall be signed by the President of the institution which adopted them.

    European laws and framework laws shall be published in the Official Journal of the European Union and shall enter into force on the date specified in them or, in the absence thereof, on the twentieth day following their publication.
2. European regulations, and European decisions which do not specify to whom they are addressed, shall be signed by the President of the institution which adopted them.

    European regulations, and European decisions when the latter do not specify to whom they are addressed, shall be published in the Official Journal of the European Union and shall enter into force on the date specified in them or, in the absence thereof, on the twentieth day following that of their publication.
3. European decisions other than those referred to in paragraph 2 shall be notified to those to whom they are addressed and shall take effect upon such notification.

CHAPTER II

SPECIFIC PROVISIONS

ARTICLE I-40

Specific provisions relating to the common foreign and security policy

1. The European Union shall conduct a common foreign and security policy, based on the development of mutual political solidarity among Member States, the identification of questions of general interest and the achievement of an ever-increasing degree of convergence of Member States' actions.
2. The European Council shall identify the Union's strategic interests and determine the objectives of its common foreign and security policy. The Council shall frame this policy within the framework of the strategic guidelines established by the European Council and in accordance with Part III.
3. The European Council and the Council shall adopt the necessary European decisions.
4. The common foreign and security policy shall be put into effect by the Union Minister for Foreign Affairs and by the Member States, using national and Union resources.
5. Member States shall consult one another within the European Council and the Council on any foreign and security policy issue which is of general interest in order to determine a common approach. Before undertaking any action on the international scene or any commitment which could affect the Union's interests, each Member State shall consult the others within the European Council or the Council. Member States shall ensure, through the convergence of their actions, that the Union is able to assert its interests and values on the international scene. Member States shall show mutual solidarity.
6. European decisions relating to the common foreign and security policy shall be adopted by the European Council and the Council unanimously, except in the cases referred to in Part III. The European Council and the Council shall act on an initiative from a Member State, on a proposal from the Union Minister for Foreign Affairs or on a proposal from that Minister with the Commission's support. European laws and framework laws shall be excluded.
7. The European Council may, unanimously, adopt a European decision authorising the Council to act by a qualified majority in cases other than those referred to in Part III.
8. The European Parliament shall be regularly consulted on the main aspects and basic choices of the common foreign and security policy. It shall be kept informed of how it evolves.

ARTICLE I-41

Specific provisions relating to the common security and defence policy

1. The common security and defence policy shall be an integral part of the common foreign and security policy. It shall provide the Union with an operational capacity drawing on civil and military assets. The Union may use them on missions outside the Union for peace-keeping, conflict prevention and strengthening international security in accordance with the principles of the

United Nations Charter. The performance of these tasks shall be undertaken using capabilities provided by the Member States.

2. The common security and defence policy shall include the progressive framing of a common Union defence policy. This will lead to a common defence, when the European Council, acting unanimously, so decides. It shall in that case recommend to the Member States the adoption of such a decision in accordance with their respective constitutional requirements.

    The policy of the Union in accordance with this Article shall not prejudice the specific character of the security and defence policy of certain Member States, it shall respect the obligations of certain Member States, which see their common defence realised in the North Atlantic Treaty Organisation, under the North Atlantic Treaty, and be compatible with the common security and defence policy established within that framework.

3. Member States shall make civilian and military capabilities available to the Union for the implementation of the common security and defence policy, to contribute to the objectives defined by the Council. Those Member States which together establish multinational forces may also make them available to the common security and defence policy.

    Member States shall undertake progressively to improve their military capabilities.

    An Agency in the field of defence capabilities development, research, acquisition and armaments (European Defence Agency) shall be established to identify operational requirements, to promote measures to satisfy those requirements, to contribute to identifying and, where appropriate, implementing any measure needed to strengthen the industrial and technological base of the defence sector, to participate in defining a European capabilities and armaments policy, and to assist the Council in evaluating the improvement of military capabilities.

4. European decisions relating to the common security and defence policy, including those initiating a mission as referred to in this Article, shall be adopted by the Council acting unanimously on a proposal from the Union Minister for Foreign Affairs or an initiative from a Member State. The Union Minister for Foreign Affairs may propose the use of both national resources and Union instruments, together with the Commission where appropriate.

5. The Council may entrust the execution of a task, within the Union framework, to a group of Member States in order to protect the Union's values and serve its interests. The execution of such a task shall be governed by Article III-310.

6. Those Member States whose military capabilities fulfil higher criteria and which have made more binding commitments to one another in this area with a view to the most demanding missions shall establish permanent structured cooperation within the Union framework. Such cooperation shall be governed by Article III-312. It shall not affect the provisions of Article III-309.

7. If a Member State is the victim of armed aggression on its territory, the other Member States shall have towards it an obligation of aid and assistance by all the means in their power, in accordance with Article 51 of the United Nations Charter. This shall not prejudice the specific character of the security and defence policy of certain Member States.

    Commitments and cooperation in this area shall be consistent with commitments under the North Atlantic Treaty Organisation, which, for those States which are members of it, remains the foundation of their collective defence and the forum for its implementation.

8. The European Parliament shall be regularly consulted on the main aspects and basic choices of the common security and defence policy. It shall be kept informed of how it evolves.

ARTICLE I-42

Specific provisions relating to the area of freedom, security and justice

1. The Union shall constitute an area of freedom, security and justice:
(a) by adopting European laws and framework laws intended, where necessary, to approximate laws and regulations of the Member States in the areas referred to in Part III;
(b) by promoting mutual confidence between the competent authorities of the Member States, in particular on the basis of mutual recognition of judicial and extrajudicial decisions;
(c) by operational cooperation between the competent authorities of the Member States, including the police, customs and other services specialising in the prevention and detection of criminal offences.
2. National Parliaments may, within the framework of the area of freedom, security and justice, participate in the evaluation mechanisms provided for in Article III-260. They shall be involved in the political monitoring of Europol and the evaluation of Eurojust's activities in accordance with Articles III-276 and III-273.
3. Member States shall have a right of initiative in the field of police and judicial cooperation in criminal matters, in accordance with Article III-264.

ARTICLE I-43

Solidarity clause

1. The Union and its Member States shall act jointly in a spirit of solidarity if a Member State is the object of a terrorist attack or the victim of a natural or man-made disaster. The Union shall mobilise all the instruments at its disposal, including the military resources made available by the Member States, to:
(a) -   prevent the terrorist threat in the territory of the Member States;
    -   protect democratic institutions and the civilian population from any terrorist attack;
    -   assist a Member State in its territory, at the request of its political authorities, in the event of a terrorist attack;
(b) assist a Member State in its territory, at the request of its political authorities, in the event of a natural or man-made disaster.
2. The detailed arrangements for implementing this Article are set out in Article III-329.

CHAPTER III

ENHANCED COOPERATION

ARTICLE I-44

Enhanced cooperation

1. Member States which wish to establish enhanced cooperation between them-
    selves within the framework of the Union's non-exclusive competences may
    make use of its institutions and exercise those competences by applying the rel-
    evant provisions of the Constitution, subject to the limits and in accordance with
    the procedures laid down in this Article and in Articles III-416 to III-423.

    Enhanced cooperation shall aim to further the objectives of the Union, pro-
    tect its interests and reinforce its integration process. Such cooperation shall be
    open at any time to all Member States, in accordance with Article III-418.

2. The European decision authorising enhanced cooperation shall be adopted by
    the Council as a last resort, when it has established that the objectives of such
    cooperation cannot be attained within a reasonable period by the Union as a
    whole, and provided that at least one third of the Member States participate in
    it. The Council shall act in accordance with the procedure laid down in Article
    III-419.

3. All members of the Council may participate in its deliberations, but only mem-
    bers of the Council representing the Member States participating in enhanced
    cooperation shall take part in the vote.

    Unanimity shall be constituted by the votes of the representatives of the
    participating Member States only.

    A qualified majority shall be defined as at least 55% of the members of the
    Council representing the participating Member States, comprising at least 65%
    of the population of these States.

    A blocking minority must include at least the minimum number of Council
    members representing more than 35% of the population of the participating
    Member States, plus one member, failing which the qualified majority shall be
    deemed attained.

    By way of derogation from the third and fourth subparagraphs, where the
    Council does not act on a proposal from the Commission or from the Union
    Minister for Foreign Affairs, the required qualified majority shall be defined as
    at least 72% of the members of the Council representing the participating
    Member States, comprising at least 65% of the population of these States.

4. Acts adopted in the framework of enhanced cooperation shall bind only partic-
    ipating Member States. They shall not be regarded as part of the acquis which
    has to be accepted by candidate States for accession to the Union.

TITLE VI

THE DEMOCRATIC LIFE OF THE UNION

ARTICLE I-45

The principle of democratic equality

In all its activities, the Union shall observe the principle of the equality of its citizens, who shall receive equal attention from its institutions, bodies, offices and agencies.

ARTICLE I-46

The principle of representative democracy

1. The functioning of the Union shall be founded on representative democracy.
2. Citizens are directly represented at Union level in the European Parliament. Member States are represented in the European Council by their Heads of State or Government and in the Council by their governments, themselves democratically accountable either to their national Parliaments, or to their citizens.
3. Every citizen shall have the right to participate in the democratic life of the Union. Decisions shall be taken as openly and as closely as possible to the citizen.
4. Political parties at European level contribute to forming European political awareness and to expressing the will of citizens of the Union.

ARTICLE I-47

The principle of participatory democracy

1. The institutions shall, by appropriate means, give citizens and representative associations the opportunity to make known and publicly exchange their views in all areas of Union action.
2. The institutions shall maintain an open, transparent and regular dialogue with representative associations and civil society.
3. The Commission shall carry out broad consultations with parties concerned in order to ensure that the Union's actions are coherent and transparent.
4. Not less than one million citizens who are nationals of a significant number of Member States may take the initiative of inviting the Commission, within the framework of its powers, to submit any appropriate proposal on matters where citizens consider that a legal act of the Union is required for the purpose of implementing the Constitution. European laws shall determine the provisions for the procedures and conditions required for such a citizens' initiative, including the minimum number of Member States from which such citizens must come.

ARTICLE I-48

The social partners and autonomous social dialogue

The Union recognises and promotes the role of the social partners at its level, taking into account the diversity of national systems. It shall facilitate dialogue between the social partners, respecting their autonomy.

The Tripartite Social Summit for Growth and Employment shall contribute to social dialogue.

ARTICLE I-49

The European Ombudsman

A European Ombudsman elected by the European Parliament shall receive, examine and report on complaints about maladministration in the activities of the Union institutions, bodies, offices or agencies, under the conditions laid down in the Constitution. The European Ombudsman shall be completely independent in the performance of his or her duties.

ARTICLE I-50

Transparency of the proceedings of Union institutions, bodies, offices and agencies

1. In order to promote good governance and ensure the participation of civil society, the Union institutions, bodies, offices and agencies shall conduct their work as openly as possible.
2. The European Parliament shall meet in public, as shall the Council when considering and voting on a draft legislative act.
3. Any citizen of the Union, and any natural or legal person residing or having its registered office in a Member State shall have, under the conditions laid down in Part III, a right of access to documents of the Union institutions, bodies, offices and agencies, whatever their medium.

   European laws shall lay down the general principles and limits which, on grounds of public or private interest, govern the right of access to such documents.
4. Each institution, body, office or agency shall determine in its own rules of procedure specific provisions regarding access to its documents, in accordance with the European laws referred to in paragraph 3.

ARTICLE I-51

Protection of personal data

1. Everyone has the right to the protection of personal data concerning him or her.
2. European laws or framework laws shall lay down the rules relating to the protection of individuals with regard to the processing of personal data by Union institutions, bodies, offices and agencies, and by the Member States when carrying out activities which fall within the scope of Union law, and the rules relating to the free movement of such data. Compliance with these rules shall be subject to the control of independent authorities.

ARTICLE I-52

Status of churches and non-confessional organisations

1. The Union respects and does not prejudice the status under national law of churches and religious associations or communities in the Member States.

2. The Union equally respects the status under national law of philosophical and non-confessional organisations.
3. Recognising their identity and their specific contribution, the Union shall maintain an open, transparent and regular dialogue with these churches and organisations.

TITLE VII

THE UNION'S FINANCES

ARTICLE I-53

Budgetary and financial principles

1. All items of Union revenue and expenditure shall be included in estimates drawn up for each financial year and shall be shown in the Union's budget, in accordance with Part III.
2. The revenue and expenditure shown in the budget shall be in balance.
3. The expenditure shown in the budget shall be authorised for the annual budgetary period in accordance with the European law referred to in Article III-412.
4. The implementation of expenditure shown in the budget shall require the prior adoption of a legally binding Union act providing a legal basis for its action and for the implementation of the corresponding expenditure in accordance with the European law referred to in Article III-412, except in cases for which that law provides.
5. With a view to maintaining budgetary discipline, the Union shall not adopt any act which is likely to have appreciable implications for the budget without providing an assurance that the expenditure arising from such an act is capable of being financed within the limit of the Union's own resources and in compliance with the multiannual financial framework referred to in Article I-55.
6. The budget shall be implemented in accordance with the principle of sound financial management. Member States shall cooperate with the Union to ensure that the appropriations entered in the budget are used in accordance with this principle.
7. The Union and the Member States, in accordance with Article III-415, shall counter fraud and any other illegal activities affecting the financial interests of the Union.

ARTICLE I-54

The Union's own resources

1. The Union shall provide itself with the means necessary to attain its objectives and carry through its policies.
2. Without prejudice to other revenue, the Union's budget shall be financed wholly from its own resources.
3. A European law of the Council shall lay down the provisions relating to the system of own resources of the Union. In this context it may establish new categories of own resources or abolish an existing category. The Council shall act unanimously after consulting the European Parliament. That law shall not enter

into force until it is approved by the Member States in accordance with their respective constitutional requirements.

4. A European law of the Council shall lay down implementing measures of the Union's own resources system insofar as this is provided for in the European law adopted on the basis of paragraph 3. The Council shall act after obtaining the consent of the European Parliament.

ARTICLE I-55

The multiannual financial framework

1. The multiannual financial framework shall ensure that Union expenditure develops in an orderly manner and within the limits of its own resources. It shall determine the amounts of the annual ceilings of appropriations for commitments by category of expenditure in accordance with Article III-402.
2. A European law of the Council shall lay down the multiannual financial framework. The Council shall act unanimously after obtaining the consent of the European Parliament, which shall be given by a majority of its component members.
3. The annual budget of the Union shall comply with the multiannual financial framework.
4. The European Council may, unanimously, adopt a European decision authorising the Council to act by a qualified majority when adopting the European law of the Council referred to in paragraph 2.

ARTICLE I-56

The Union's budget

A European law shall establish the Union's annual budget in accordance with Article III-404.

TITLE VIII

THE UNION AND ITS NEIGHBOURS

ARTICLE I-57

The Union and its neighbours

1. The Union shall develop a special relationship with neighbouring countries, aiming to establish an area of prosperity and good neighbourliness, founded on the values of the Union and characterised by close and peaceful relations based on cooperation.
2. For the purposes of paragraph 1, the Union may conclude specific agreements with the countries concerned. These agreements may contain reciprocal rights and obligations as well as the possibility of undertaking activities jointly. Their implementation shall be the subject of periodic consultation.

TITLE IX

UNION MEMBERSHIP

ARTICLE I-58

Conditions of eligibility and procedure for accession to the Union

1. The Union shall be open to all European States which respect the values referred to in Article I-2, and are committed to promoting them together.
2. Any European State which wishes to become a member of the Union shall address its application to the Council. The European Parliament and national Parliaments shall be notified of this application. The Council shall act unanimously after consulting the Commission and after obtaining the consent of the European Parliament, which shall act by a majority of its component members. The conditions and arrangements for admission shall be the subject of an agreement between the Member States and the candidate State. That agreement shall be subject to ratification by each contracting State, in accordance with its respective constitutional requirements.

ARTICLE I-59

Suspension of certain rights resulting from Union membership

1. On the reasoned initiative of one third of the Member States or the reasoned initiative of the European Parliament or on a proposal from the Commission, the Council may adopt a European decision determining that there is a clear risk of a serious breach by a Member State of the values referred to in Article I-2. The Council shall act by a majority of four fifths of its members after obtaining the consent of the European Parliament.

    Before making such a determination, the Council shall hear the Member State in question and, acting in accordance with the same procedure, may address recommendations to that State.

    The Council shall regularly verify that the grounds on which such a determination was made continue to apply.
2. The European Council, on the initiative of one third of the Member States or on a proposal from the Commission, may adopt a European decision determining the existence of a serious and persistent breach by a Member State of the values mentioned in Article I-2, after inviting the Member State in question to submit its observations. The European Council shall act unanimously after obtaining the consent of the European Parliament.
3. Where a determination under paragraph 2 has been made, the Council, acting by a qualified majority, may adopt a European decision suspending certain of the rights deriving from the application of the Constitution to the Member State in question, including the voting rights of the member of the Council representing that State. The Council shall take into account the possible consequences of such a suspension for the rights and obligations of natural and legal persons.

    In any case, that State shall continue to be bound by its obligations under the Constitution.
4. The Council, acting by a qualified majority, may adopt a European decision

varying or revoking measures adopted under paragraph 3 in response to changes in the situation which led to their being imposed.

5. For the purposes of this Article, the member of the European Council or of the Council representing the Member State in question shall not take part in the vote and the Member State in question shall not be counted in the calculation of the one third or four fifths of Member States referred to in paragraphs 1 and 2. Abstentions by members present in person or represented shall not prevent the adoption of European decisions referred to in paragraph 2.

    For the adoption of the European decisions referred to in paragraphs 3 and 4, a qualified majority shall be defined as at least 72% of the members of the Council, representing the participating Member States, comprising at least 65% of the population of these States.

    Where, following a decision to suspend voting rights adopted pursuant to paragraph 3, the Council acts by a qualified majority on the basis of a provision of the Constitution, that qualified majority shall be defined as in the second sub-paragraph, or, where the Council acts on a proposal from the Commission or from the Union Minister for Foreign Affairs, as at least 55% of the members of the Council representing the participating Member States, comprising at least 65% of the population of these States. In the latter case, a blocking minority must include at least the minimum number of Council members representing more than 35% of the population of the participating Member States, plus one member, failing which the qualified majority shall be deemed attained.

6. For the purposes of this Article, the European Parliament shall act by a two-thirds majority of the votes cast, representing the majority of its component members.

ARTICLE I-60

Voluntary withdrawal from the Union

1. Any Member State may decide to withdraw from the Union in accordance with its own constitutional requirements.

2. A Member State which decides to withdraw shall notify the European Council of its intention. In the light of the guidelines provided by the European Council, the Union shall negotiate and conclude an agreement with that State, setting out the arrangements for its withdrawal, taking account of the framework for its future relationship with the Union. That agreement shall be negotiated in accordance with Article III-325(3). It shall be concluded by the Council, acting by a qualified majority, after obtaining the consent of the European Parliament.

3. The Constitution shall cease to apply to the State in question from the date of entry into force of the withdrawal agreement or, failing that, two years after the notification referred to in paragraph 2, unless the European Council, in agreement with the Member State concerned, unanimously decides to extend this period.

4. For the purposes of paragraphs 2 and 3, the member of the European Council or of the Council representing the withdrawing Member State shall not participate in the discussions of the European Council or Council or in European decisions concerning it.

    A qualified majority shall be defined as at least 72% of the members of the Council, representing the participating Member States, comprising at least 65% of the population of these States.

5. If a State which has withdrawn from the Union asks to rejoin, its request shall
    be subject to the procedure referred to in Article I-58.

4. **Declaration on Article I-24(7) concerning the European Council
    decision on the exercise of the Presidency of the Council**

    The Conference declares that the Council should begin preparing the
European decision establishing the measures for applying the European
decision of the European Council on the exercise of the Presidency of the
Council as soon as the Treaty establishing a Constitution for Europe is signed
and should give its political approval within six months. A draft European
decision of the European Council, which will be adopted on the date of entry
into force of the said Treaty, is set out below:

*Draft European decision of the European Council on the exercise of the
Presidency of the Council*

ARTICLE 1
1. The Presidency of the Council, with the exception of the Foreign Affairs config-
    uration, shall be held by pre-established groups of three Member States for a
    period of 18 months. The groups shall be made up on a basis of equal rotation
    among the Member States, taking into account their diversity and geographical
    balance within the Union.
2. Each member of the group shall in turn chair for a six-month period all con-
    figurations of the Council, with the exception of the Foreign Affairs configura-
    tion. The other members of the group shall assist the Chair in all its
    responsibilities on the basis of a common programme. Members of the team
    may decide alternative arrangements among themselves.

ARTICLE 2
The Committee of Permanent Representatives of the Governments of the
Member States shall be chaired by a representative of the Member State chairing the General Affairs Council.
    The Chair of the Political and Security Committee shall be held by a repre-
sentative of the Union Minister for Foreign Affairs.
    The chair of the preparatory bodies of the various Council configurations,
with the exception of the Foreign Affairs configuration, shall fall to the member
of the group chairing the relevant configuration, unless decided otherwise in
accordance with Article 4.

ARTICLE 3
The General Affairs Council shall ensure consistency and continuity in the work
of the different Council configurations in the framework of multiannual programmes in cooperation with the Commission. The Member States holding the
Presidency shall take all necessary measures for the organisation and smooth
operation of the Council's work, with the assistance of the General Secretariat of
the Council.

ARTICLE 4

The Council shall adopt a European decision establishing the measures for the implementation of this decision.

5. Declaration on Article I-25

The Conference declares that the European decision relating to the implementation of Article I-25 will be adopted by the Council on the day the Treaty establishing a Constitution for Europe enters into force. The draft decision is set out below:

Draft European decision of the Council relating to the implementation of Article I-25

THE COUNCIL OF THE EUROPEAN UNION,

Whereas:
(1) Provisions should be adopted allowing for a smooth transition from the system for decision-making in the Council by a qualified majority as defined in the Treaty of Nice and set out in Article 2(2) of the Protocol on the transitional provisions relating to the institutions and bodies of the Union annexed to the Constitution, which will continue to apply until 31 October 2009, to the voting system provided for in Article I-25 of the Constitution, which will apply with effect from 1 November 2009.
(2) It is recalled that it is the practice of the Council to devote every effort to strengthening the democratic legitimacy of decisions taken by a qualified majority.
(3) It is judged appropriate to maintain this decision as long as is necessary to ensure smooth transition to the new voting system provided for in the Constitution,

HAS DECIDED AS FOLLOWS:

ARTICLE 1

If members of the Council, representing:
(a) at least three quarters of the population, or
(b) at least three quarters of the number of Member States
     necessary to constitute a blocking minority resulting from the application of Article I-25(1), first subparagraph, or Article I-25(2), indicate their opposition to the Council adopting an act by a qualified majority, the Council shall discuss the issue.

ARTICLE 2

The Council shall, in the course of these discussions, do all in its power to reach, within a reasonable time and without prejudicing obligatory time limits laid down by Union law, a satisfactory solution to address concerns raised by the members of the Council referred to in Article 1.

ARTICLE 3

To this end, the President of the Council, with the assistance of the Commission and in compliance with the Rules of Procedure of the Council, shall undertake any initiative necessary to facilitate a wider basis of agreement in the Council. The members of the Council shall lend him or her their assistance.

ARTICLE 4

This decision shall take effect on 1 November 2009. It shall remain in force at least until 2014. Thereafter the Council may adopt a European decision repealing it.

ANNEX II

Draft Decision of the Council on the exercise of the Council Presidency*

Germany	January-June	2007
Portugal	July-December	
Slovenia	January-June	2008
France	July-December	
Czech Republic	January-June	2009
Sweden	July-December	
Spain	January-June	2010
Belgium	July-December	
Hungary	January-June	2011
Poland	July-December	
Denmark	January-June	2012
Cyprus	July-December	
Ireland	January-June	2013
Lithuania	July-December	
Greece	January-June	2014
Italy	July-December	
Latvia	January-June	2015
Luxembourg	July-December	
Netherlands	January-June	2016
Slovakia	July-December	
Malta	January-June	2017
United Kingdom	July-December	
Estonia	January-June	2018
Bulgaria	July-December	
Austria	January-June	2019
Romania	July-December	
Finland	January-June	2020

* with the exception of the Foreign Affairs Council

ANNEX III

THE COMPARISON OF WEIGHT OF MEMBER STATES' VOTES ACCORDING TO DIFFERENT SYSTEMS *

Member State	Population rounded up (in millions)	Treaty of Nice	Treaty establishing Constitution for Europe**	Mathematic Approach**
Germany	82.5	29	59	33
France	60	29	43	28
United Kingdom	59.5	29	42	28
Italy	57.8	29	41	28
Spain	42.2	27	30	24
Poland	38.2	27	27	22
Romania	21.7	14	15	17
Netherlands	16.2	13	12	15
Greece	11	12	8	12
Portugal	10.5	12	7	12
Belgium	10.4	12	7	12
Czech Republic	10.2	12	7	12
Hungary	10.1	12	7	12
Sweden	8.9	10	6	11
Austria	8.1	10	6	10
Bulgaria	7.8	10	6	10
Denmark	5.4	7	4	8
Slovakia	5.4	7	4	8
Finland	5.2	7	4	8
Ireland	4	7	3	7
Lithuania	3.4	7	2	7
Latvia	2.3	4	2	6
Slovenia	1.9	4	1	5
Estonia	1.3	4	1	4
Cyprus	0.7	4	0.5	3
Luxembourg	0.4	4	0.3	2
Malta	0.4	3	0.3	2
Total	485.5	345	345	345

*   Each of the systems includes in addition a requirement for a minimum number of Member States in order to reach a qualified majority. The real impact of each Member State's voting weight depends on taking into account both the existence and level of this requirement.

**   In order to compare the three systems. the figures have been extrapolated in each case on the basis of a total number of 345 votes (current figure under the Nice treaty).